Contents

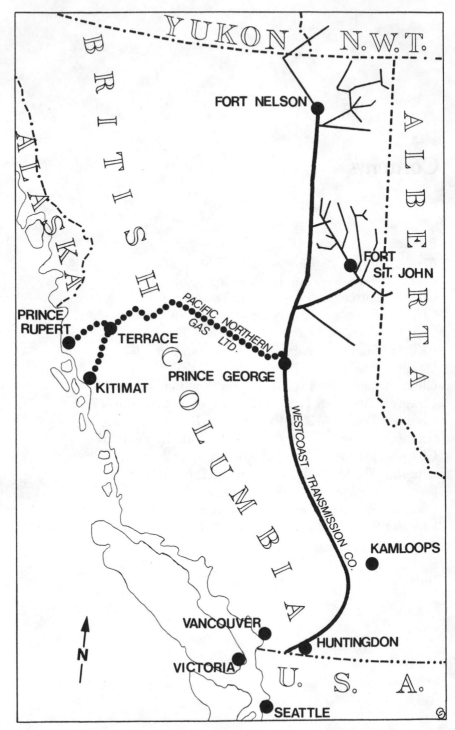

Westcoast Transmission pipeline, Canada's first major natural gas pipeline system.

Preface

One of Canada's pioneer oil companies went out of business in 1979. Pacific Petroleums Ltd had been purchased by Canada's national oil company, Petro-Canada, for a record $1.5 billion.

Pacific was young for a pioneer firm, only four decades old. But most of Canada's oil and gas producing industry was even younger, born in the wake of Alberta's Leduc oil field discovery of 1947. The history of Pacific Petroleums was closely linked with another enterprise which it had sponsored, Westcoast Transmission Company Limited. The histories of Pacific and Westcoast were, in turn, both closely linked with Frank McMahon, the founder of both companies.

Construction in 1957 of Westcoast Transmission, Canada's first major natural gas pipeline, was the culmination of a quarter of a century of tenacious struggle by McMahon and his associates, a defiance of insurmountable odds. It was made possible only by the earlier success of Pacific in the oil fields of Alberta. The interwoven story of Pacific Petroleums and Westcoast Transmission is an important chapter in the industrial development of Canada, particularly western Canada. But more than that, it is an epic story of daring gambles and audacious promotions.

It was to capture this history that this book was commissioned by Petro-Canada and Westcoast Transmission. It could not have been undertaken without their financial support. I am most grateful to Bill Hopper, chairman and chief executive officer of Petro-Canada, and to Ed Phillips, chairman and chief executive officer of Westcoast, for proposing this project to me, and for sponsoring it.

7

The manuscript, however, was left entirely to my discretion, including content, approach, conclusions, interpretation, opinions, and other matters. The sponsors reviewed the manuscript for factual accuracy only (a review which I welcomed), but otherwise left me with a completely free reign.

Any opinions expressed are thus entirely mine, and any errors that may appear are also entirely my responsibility.

Earle Gray
Woodville, Ontario

CHAPTER ONE

The Man from Moyie

Francis Murray Patrick McMahon was born with the mantle of a fortune seeker destined to spend his days in quest of a mother-lode. He was driven by the unassailable conviction of wildcatters that pay dirt lies just a few feet in front of the drill bit, and all that is required to find it is determination and faith.

It was a quest that would ultimately lead to the formation of two remarkable firms, Pacific Petroleums Ltd and Westcoast Transmission Company Limited. Together they were to play a crucial role in the development of the oil and natural gas resources that stimulated the entire economy of Canada.

The quest involved a series of escalating gambles, and true to the tradition of wildcatters the first results were a string of spectacular failures. The mark of the true wildcatter is a faith that remains unshaken by a seemingly endless series of holes that have missed pay dirt. He is a man convinced of ultimate success beyond all prudent reason and one able to convince others with money that the next hole is bound to be the strike. "When a man is exploring for oil, the only reality is the next wildcat, the one that will come in," Ruth Sheldon Knowles wrote in a history of US wildcatters, *The Greatest Gamblers*. "He lives so completely in his undiscovered wealth that the struggle to pay his bills is what seems like a dream."

In the mining camps of British Columbia at the turn of the century, thousands of men lived in dreams of wealth not from oil, but from hardrock minerals – gold, silver, copper, lead, zinc. It was at the small Kootenay mining town of Moyie, fifteen miles north of Idaho in southeastern British Columbia, that Frank McMahon was born, the first of three sons of Francis Joseph

9

McMahon and the former Stella Maud Soper. The ore deposit near Moyie, on Yahk mountain, had been discovered nine years before, and the St Eugene mine was already the largest silver and lead producer in Canada. The bustling town on the shore of Lake Moyie boasted a population of 500, and six hotels, one of them owned by Frank McMahon, senior, and his older brother, Pat.

For countless ages, men have been subject to afflictions of mineral fever, accompanied by vivid hallucinations of wealth. The future founder of Pacific Petroleums and Westcoast Transmission probably was born with these afflictions, for his father was a roaming fortune seeker and the fever pervaded the air in the mining boom towns that had been splattered on the narrow valleys and steep slopes of British Columbia's endless chains of mountains.

"Whether north or south of the line, in British Columbia, Idaho or Montana, men talked of mines, struggled for mines, and founded their laws and industries on mines," an early historian of the region reported. "Other forms of industry were subsidiary to mining."

It was with just such visions of wealth that, five decades earlier, a gold rush had brought the first large invasion of Europeans into what became British Columbia and triggered much of the rapid development that had taken place. Prior to 1858 there were no roads, no railways, and no towns, other than the village of Victoria with a population of less than 500. There were no outlying settlements, other than a few fur trading posts and Indian villages, and no industries, other than the fur trade and a few small lumber mills at the edge of the ocean. The area was larger than all of Great Britain, Spain, and West Germany; the potential was enormous.

The precursor was the California gold rush in 1849. Eight years later, in late 1857, news trickled out that a few nuggets had been found along the Fraser and Thompson rivers. The following spring, the Hudson's Bay Company steamer *Otter* pulled into San Francisco with a consignment of gold for the US mint, and the blast of its whistle signalled the start of another gold rush. Prospectors heading north had first to obtain a permit in Victoria, where the mineral rights throughout this vast domain of the Hudson's Bay Company had been reserved in the name of the Crown. In April, 1858, the US steamer *Commodore* landed in Victoria with 450 miners, and the population of the seaport doubled. Before the end of that summer, 25,000 prospectors had passed through Victoria on their way to the newest gold fields.

Along the West Coast of the United States, shipping was disrupted as sailors jumped ship, sawmills were closed as loggers abandoned the woods, all of them bound for the gold fields. "None too poor and none too rich to go; none too young and none too old to go, even the decrepit go," correspondent Donald Fraser reported in the *London Times*.

From the Fraser and Thompson rivers, the searchers spread farther north through the wide and rolling valley of the Cariboo country and up the fast flowing mountain streams, culminating in a site where a brawling Welsh seaman, Billy Barker, and six English associates formed the Billy Barker Company to work a group of claims that other prospectors derided as worthless. Judge Matthew Begbie, known as the hanging judge and later Chief Justice of British Columbia, reportedly loaned Barker and his associates $700 to help them get out of the country. Instead, they spent the money to sink a fifty-foot shaft that eventually produced more than $600,000 worth of gold. The town of Barkerville sprang up overnight, claiming to be the largest settlement "west of Chicago and north of San Francisco." Barker spent his fortune even faster than he had made it, found work as a cook in a road construction camp, and thirty years later died penniless in the Old Man's Home in Victoria.

Steamers brought prospectors up the Fraser River to Yale, and from there it was a journey of five or six weeks overland to the Cariboo gold camps and Barkerville. The cost of moving supplies and equipment to the town was $1,000 a ton. By 1865, the Cariboo wagon road had been built as far as Barkerville under the direction of the Royal Engineers, part of it blasted out of the sheer rock walls of the Fraser Canyon, and part of it suspended precariously on trestles. It was the first real road in British Columbia, and along it stage coaches and wagons were pulled by horses, mules, steam tractors, and camels, hauling out gold at rates up to $4.5 million a year.

Production of gold washed from gravel at BC's placer mines reached its peak in 1867, but four years later it had fallen off by two-thirds. By the time the Canadian Pacific Railway was completed in 1886, these mines were nearly all exhausted. The Cariboo placer gold mines were no sooner depleted than farther north, in the Yukon, the even more spectacular Klondike gold

11

rush was on in 1898. An estimated 300,000 people set out on the epic trek to the Klondike. Some 50,000 actually got there. "They're all millionaires in their minds," wrote Robert Service of the travellers on the trail of '98.

Although the first lush pickings from British Columbia were soon exhausted, the fortune seekers had paved the way for permanent settlement, leaving in their wake roads, bridges, towns, farms, sawmills, and other enterprises. Some who came in search of instant wealth stayed to pursue more permanent, if less spectacular endeavours.

Of far greater and more enduring importance than the gold fields were the base metal mines that followed, centred chiefly in the Kootenay region, a 10,000-square-mile area of remote mountains and lakes. Over a ten-year period starting in 1883, a rash of ore discoveries dotted the region, and production of copper, lead, zinc, and silver made British Columbia Canada's largest mineral producing province by the turn of the century. Instant mining towns sprang up: Rossland, Trail, Nelson, Kaslo, Kimberley, Moyie, and a host of others. More roads, bridges, and hundreds of miles of railway branch lines were built, and smelters were erected. A typical Kootenay mining town at the turn of the century featured "prize fights in theatres, keno tables in gaming houses; boa-feathered dance-hall girls; bars; and orchestras and bands which play round the clock," according to BC historian Margaret Ormsby in *British Columbia, A History*.

Among those who had come to find their fortunes in the glittering mining camps of the west were two lean and hardy Irish brothers from York County, Ontario, Frank and Pat McMahon. They joined the Klondikers on the trail of 1898 to Dawson City, where Frank sought his fortune in the gold fields, while brother Pat looked for his at the card tables. Neither one yielded any great fortunes, but the two brothers appear to have left the Klondike with some savings and were soon looking for fresh opportunities in the new mining towns of the Kootenays. The start of the twentieth century found them as owners of the small Moyie hotel.

At Moyie, Frank's fancy was captured by a petite young music teacher, and in 1901 he married eighteen-year-old Stella Maud Soper. Work on the railway branch lines being built to haul the ores and metals from the new mines had brought the Sopers to the Kootenays, and the family appears to have been as adventurous as the McMahons.

In the 1890s, US railways were making strong bids to capture the business of hauling ore from the Kootenay mines. The Northern Pacific Railway, the Great Northern Railway, and others were already moving the ore from mines in Montana, Idaho, and Washington, the "Inland Empire" immediately south across the border from the Kootenay country. Only short extensions would be required to haul the Kootenay ores to the smelters already operating in the Inland Empire, principally at Spokane. To head the US railways off at the pass, as it were, the CPR had purchased the largest smelter in the Kootenays, built at Trail in 1895 by US copper magnate Frederick Augustus Heinze. A pair of mines at nearby Rossland and the St Eugene mine at Moyie were contracted to provide ore for the Trail smelter. With the ores and smelter under its control, starting in 1898 the CPR was then able to build its Crowsnest branch line from Lethbridge, Alberta, to Kootenay Lake. One of the contractors engaged by the CPR to build bridges was Major Soper.

The younger Frank McMahon was born in Moyie on October 2, 1902; the second son, George, in 1904; and the third son, John, in 1905. Much later, Frank McMahon recalled his early childhood days at Moyie in an interview:

> Then as now, I suppose, small children didn't spend too much time worrying about whether their families were rich or poor as long as they could get outdoors and play games and get enough to eat; and I think that was the case with me. I have the feeling we made a decent living, at least until the St Eugene mine played out. Probably the best way of putting it is that I never had the feeling as a small boy that we were absolutely poor, but looking back I suppose we weren't absolutely affluent, either.

The three young McMahon boys were, in any event, left with few childhood memories of their father. The third son, John, was only a few months old when the elder Frank McMahon set off once again in search of fresher fields. Seven decades later the younger Frank McMahon spoke about his father:

> I guess you could say that both my father and his brother, Pat, were members of a breed that has long since vanished; self-

13

taught prospectors who would get together a grubstake and then go out on their own or for anyone who would employ them for a few months or a season and roam the countryside looking for a big strike. Much more often than not, of course, they didn't hit it, but if and when they ever did they would settle down for a few months or a few years until the wanderlust hit them again, and then they'd move along. We think of them as drifters or boomers, and that's exactly what they were; but it's probably fair to say in the process they did a lot towards opening up the country and making it possible for a lot of other people to earn a pretty fair living. . . . I honestly don't believe there was any deep bitterness involved in my father and mother going their separate ways. It was simply that my father felt he had to follow the mining booms wherever they took him, and he liked the atmosphere of the boom towns.

Frank McMahon soon lost touch with his former wife and young family as he wandered across the west. He and Pat were in San Francisco at the time of the 1906 earthquake and fire that destroyed much of the city. The next year the brothers were back in the hotel business, with two small-town hotels in Oregon. Frank then turned up in the Peace River country where, with backing from German financial interests, he was involved in a land development project. That fell through with the outbreak of the First World War. In the 1920s, Frank owned a wooden-framed, three-storey, flat-roofed hotel in the booming BC coal mining town of Coalmont. The hotel, a splendour in its day, had been built in 1911, but it fell on hard times after one of the original owners had been shot and killed in a hotel poker game. Nestled in the narrow valley of the Tulameen River beside the CPR's Kettle Valley railway line, Coalmont called itself the "City of Destiny," but after an underground explosion in the Blakeburn mine killed forty-five workers in 1930, the extraction industry soon petered out. By 1981 Coalmont was largely a ghost town, but the hotel still stood, a living museum of the past, with a beer parlour operating in a tiny corner of the ground floor.

The Depression years of the 1930s brought higher prices for at least one commodity, gold, and a revival of the old gold camps, including historic Barkerville. It and a few other sites were the only boom towns left, tiny islands of relative prosperity in the ocean of Depression. Here the elder Frank McMahon spent his declining years, a white-thatched, courtly gentleman with black bow-tie and polished black dress shoes, in a two-storey, false-front, clapboard building that contained living quarters and a confectionery shop called "The Red Front Cigar Store." He sold milkshakes in the front and whisky in the back.

The senior Frank McMahon had left Moyie just before the big St Eugene mine had suddenly and unexpectedly run out of ore. In 1906, the CPR had merged the smelting operations at Trail with its main ore suppliers, the War Eagle and Centre Star mines at Rossland and the St Eugene at Moyie, to form Consolidated Mining and Smelting Company, now Cominco Limited, in which the CPR still holds a majority interest. The merger had hardly been completed before Consolidated Mining was left looking for a new supply of ore to keep its smelter busy. It turned to nearby Kimberley, where it eventually developed the largest lead and zinc mine in the world.

In 1892, two groups of claims had been staked by prospectors on either side of a turbulent mountain stream called Mark Creek. To the north were claims with such names as North Star, Full House, Queen of the Hills, and Good Luck, while to the south were the claims staked by a red-headed Irish adventurer, Pat Sullivan, and two partners. The North Star mine was brought into production by the Canadian railway contractors William Mackenzie and Donald Mann, and the Sullivan mine was developed by Spokane interests. The Spokane investors, dreaming of rewards as rich as the fabled diamond mines in South Africa, called the new town Kimberley.

Kimberley sprang up like a typical, instant Kootenay mining town: a ramshackle collection of tents, cabins, bunkhouses, a few houses and false-fronted business buildings, board sidewalks, and mud streets. "Since the branch railway to Kimberley is practically assured, the camp is experiencing considerable activity in real estate and mining," the *Kimberley Prospector* reported in 1899. Another edition of the *Prospector* that year carried this advertisement: "Wanted – white laundry. Support of citizens guaranteed. Object being to get rid of Chinese."

Major Soper appears to have been involved in the construction of the CPR's branch line from Cranbrook to Kimberley, and in the early 1900s his widow, Mary Soper, purchased one of the town's first buildings, the three-storey North Star Hotel, boasting the town's only elevator. With Moyie sliding into oblivion, prospects seemed much better at Kimberley, and in 1907 Stella McMahon and her three young sons moved there and took up residence with Mary Soper. A local history of the area, *Mountain Treasures*, reported that the town at that time "consisted of the railway station, the North Star Hotel, and a very few small stores and houses."

Despite initial optimism, the early fortunes of the Kimberley mines were erratic. Most of the North Star was mined out by 1905, and production dwindled until it was finally shut down in 1910. The Sullivan Mining Company, meanwhile, was having trouble with its much larger ore body. The original smelter was unable to extract the zinc satisfactorily, a problem that was to take Consolidated Mining and Smelting, after it had purchased the Sullivan mine in 1910, a decade of intensive research to resolve fully.

Kimberley was no longer a booming mining town when the McMahons arrived in 1907. The town's first school had opened in 1900 with twelve students, but by 1908 it was shut down for lack of pupils. "A few children were given instruction by a teacher who came to Kimberley [from Cranbrook] and taught lessons in the North Star Hotel," according to *Mountain Treasures*. "A one-room school was re-opened in 1911 [when the McMahon boys were aged nine, seven, and six years], but in order to maintain the minimum eight pupils required by the Department of Education, the attendance records were padded by having a couple of under-aged children warm the desk seats for a few hours each day."

The McMahon brothers grew up in Kimberley under the watchful eye of a strong-willed mother filled with great ambitions for her sons. Life in a frontier mining town offered young boys ample scope for adventure and outdoor activities. Young Frank developed a special pal, a pet bear that had been given to him as a very young cub by a prospector. Frank fed the infant with a bottle until it learned to eat solid food, and for nearly a year the growing bear roamed the hotel like a shaggy dog. Out-of-town visitors would drop over from the railway station to see the town's pet bear, but as it grew it became more difficult to keep. Frank had a special affection for his half-tamed, cage-crashing pet, perhaps because they were kindred spirits, both consumed by restless energy, determination, and a yearning to roam free.

Frank completed his first eight grades of school at Kimberley, attended Western Canada College in Calgary for one year, completed high school at Whitworth College, a Roman Catholic institution in Spokane, and then attended Gonzaga University in the same city. One of Frank's younger classmates earned pocket money by singing at smokers, boxing matches, and private parties. He became a life-long friend: Bing Crosby.

Summer months during the university years Frank spent at Kimberley, working at whatever jobs were available and playing baseball every opportunity he could find. "He used to hitch rides on the freight train into Cranbrook to play in ball games," recalls a contemporary of the Kimberley days, Grennie Musser. "It was illegal . . ., so Frank would hop off at the edge of town." He played shortstop and catcher, and was good enough that at Whitworth he was scouted by professional teams and briefly envisioned a career as a professional ballplayer.

During his third year at university, as restless as his caged bear in Kimberley, Frank dropped out of school for a short-lived career as a salesman, selling gasoline coupon books door-to-door for Standard Oil of California, before finding his first real vocation, as a hardrock driller.

It was a job fit for the McMahon spirit: hard work, danger, good pay, travel to the remote and wild places of the west, and the excitement of the mining towns, tamer now than in the earlier boom years but with something of the old atmosphere still prevailing. He started out in Kimberley working as a helper for the Mitchell Diamond Drilling Company of Spokane on a three-man crew and was soon a diamond setter, working in the mines out of Sandon. Once known as the "Capital of the Silvery Slocan," Sandon in 1898 had boasted a population of 5,000, with 24 hotels, 23 saloons, stores, mining brokers' offices, and newspapers. When the silver mines shut down, Sandon became a ghost town. But in the 1920s new mining and metallurgical processes made the recovery of lower-grade ore attractive, and Sandon experienced a second mini-boom, with a population this time of only several hundred. The miners worked eight hours a day, seven days a week, for $4 to $5 a day. At a reunion of Sandon miners held in Vancouver in 1980, James Wallace recalled

17

that in the 1920s the town had "four or five stores, two schools, a hospital, four or five hotels, but no saloons. The coming of Prohibition a few years earlier had put them out of business. But in spite of Prohibition there was no serious drought. Some of those fancy ladies of the old days stayed on and now . . . they survived by dispensing liquor to thirsty miners."

In 1926, McMahon moved to Vancouver, joined his mother and two brothers, and opened an office for the Mitchell Diamond Drilling Company. John and George McMahon were both in the investment business in the city, selling insurance, municipal bonds, and stocks. In 1922, his mother married again, this time to Owen C. Thompson, a Kimberley mining engineer. Thompson had taken a lease on the abandoned North Star mine in 1918, and for two years he had successfully shipped ore from the tailings dump and shallow surface diggings. In 1926, the Thompsons moved to Vancouver, where Owen would soon become associated with one of Frank McMahon's early oil ventures.

McMahon became a drilling contractor in 1927. On the strength of a contract from British Metals Corporation, then exploring on Vancouver Island, he bought a small diamond-core rig, powered by a Ford automobile engine, from the Mitchell Company. In an interview in 1981, McMahon recalled that working for the Mitchell company he had been making,

> more than most people were making, seven or eight dollars a day, sometimes a little more than that. I could save money because it didn't cost me any more to live than any ordinary driller. So I came up with a few thousand dollars, and when I went into the diamond drilling business I was able to make a few payments and then I borrowed the rest of it, and paid for the equipment as I did some drilling.

McMahon soon had three drilling rigs, and he worked with his crews on contract jobs along the West Coast, from California to Alaska.

There were slack times, however, when the rigs were idle, and between contracts McMahon tried his hand at whatever would turn a dollar. In 1928, he returned to Vancouver from California where he had been drilling on the twenty-five-mile tunnel in the Coast Mountain range through which San Francisco receives its water supply from the Hetch Hetchy Reservoir, 167 miles away. The rigs were stacked in Vancouver, and for several months

McMahon knocked on doors selling oil furnaces. Basically a shy person, the man who would later make multi-million dollar deals with some of the largest financial institutions did not find it easy selling door-to-door. He would walk several times around a block before knocking.

When Frank returned to Vancouver from the job in California, his brother George was dating an attractive young lady, Jessie Grant. Frank met Jessie's sister, Isobel, a stunningly attractive blonde, and promptly announced to George, "I'm going to marry that girl."

They were two of four daughters – and one son – of John Grant, who had retired to Vancouver in middle-class affluence after operating a coal mine on Vancouver Island near Nanaimo. Isobel had dropped out of her third year at the University of British Columbia to take a secretarial course, much to her father's chagrin. By the time she met Frank, Isobel was working as a private secretary, had a second job at the Vancouver Stock Exchange in the evenings, was successfully dabbling in the commodities market with another secretary, had saved enough money to buy a car, and had no intention of getting married.

Frank courted Isobel with the same earnest determination that he threw into every job he tackled. Virtually every day he called on her at the office for lunch, and again in the evening for dinner. As husky and lean as a stevedore, he sported a stylish straw boater bought in California that did not entirely shade his intense and serious face, but the infectious, broad Irish grin was not yet as frequent as it was to become. The hard-working driller from the mining camps of the Kootenays had had little opportunity and less time to participate in the type of social activities enjoyed by young people from middle-class Vancouver families in the Roaring Twenties. But he was an apt student and carefully studied the manners and diversions of his new circle of friends. He was determined to be in the swim of things, even if he could not swim. At a beach party, he amazed Isobel and her friends by boldly walking into the ocean wearing a pair of water wings.

Frank was persistent, and he and Isobel were married in the Grant house at 2547 Spruce Street on September 17, 1928. Jessie Grant was bridesmaid, and John McMahon was best man. The wandering senior McMahon was not present, and if anyone knew where he was, no one admitted it. A brief account of the wedding in the *Vancouver Sun* identified the groom as the "son of Mrs O.C. Thompson of this city and the late Mr McMahon."

The winning of Isobel had not been easy, for he had not only to convince Isobel but also her father.

"How do you intend to look after her?" John Grant had asked.

"Oh, I intend to look after her very well," McMahon had replied. "I am going to be a millionaire."

Spoken with the true faith of a wildcatter.

CHAPTER TWO

The Birth of a Dream

Between Vancouver and the US border, twenty-five miles southeast, lies a pocket-sized potential petroleum province beneath the flat farmlands of the Fraser River Delta where sediments swept down by the river have accumulated over millions of years. The possibility that oil and gas might be found in this sedimentary basin had long been known. A number of shallow holes had been drilled, starting as early as 1891, a few small shows of natural gas had been encountered, but nothing large enough to develop.

It was here that Frank McMahon began his career as a wildcatter looking for natural gas. It was a good place to look, on the doorstep of a ready market. The BC Electric Company had been distributing manufactured gas in Vancouver for decades, but natural gas would be much cheaper, especially such a close supply. And the even larger Seattle market was not that far away.

During 1928 and 1929, McMahon's diamond-drilling rigs had been working at scattered sites on Vancouver Island for subsidiaries of the British Metals Corporation. Isobel was pregnant with their first child, and Frank's mother, concerned about Isobel's condition, had taken her to a medical specialist in Seattle. The child she was carrying had an RH negative blood factor, and Isobel was immediately admitted to hospital. Frank was advised by telegram, rushed to Victoria, and chartered an aircraft to Seattle. Their child, Frank Grant, was born in the Seattle hospital on May 16, 1929.

It was a precarious time to begin a family. The Great Depression was ushered in seven months later with the stock market crash of October, 1929, and Frank's drilling work was to last

21

only a few more months. Don Lamont, then a jobless stock-broker, recalls working on McMahon's last hardrock drilling contract. He was on a crew of ten men who worked two shifts drilling for Quatsino Copper and Gold Company on Quatsino Sound at the northwest tip of Vancouver Island. Supplies were brought in by ship to Port Hardy, by truck to the site of Coast Copper Mines, then back-packed up the side of a mountain to the drilling rig. Lamont recalls that if the supplies were not too heavy, he could manage to carry in two loads in a day.

By early 1930, all the McMahon rigs were stacked, except for the one at Quatsino Sound, and drilling there would soon be finished. It looked as though it would be back to selling oil furnaces, or whatever else might earn a dollar. One prospect that seemed to offer a glimmer of hope was a leasing play in the Fraser Delta. The lack of success at earlier holes in this basin had cooled the fever of the wildcatters, and with the Depression already well underway, money for drilling was very hard to find. But leases could be had for very little money, if any, plus a royalty arrangement with those farmers in the delta who owned the oil and gas rights beneath their land. When McMahon heard that others were starting to pick up leases in this old play, he decided to join the action. All that was required was to call on the farmers and persuade them to sign a piece of paper. In the Depression years it was not that difficult to persuade a farmer to sign in return for the prospect that the paper might some day produce some money. There were not that many possibilities around. Thus, Frank McMahon negotiated a few deals and acquired his first oil and gas leases.

Among others who were acquiring leases in the delta at that time were Charles Stewart Shippey and Victor J. Freeman. Shippey was from Neodesha, Kansas, where he had made some money drilling shallow gas wells. He had been one of the original promoters of the Missouri Kansas Pipeline Company which had built a gas line from Kansas City to Detroit in the early 1920s. Shippey saw in the small Fraser River Delta basin a possibility of finding the type of shallow gas production that he had developed in Kansas. Freeman, according to a 1931 item in the *Vancouver Sun*, was "well known locally as an outstanding oil man," who had started in the oil fields of West Virginia, Ohio, and Pennsylvania and had "devoted his whole life to association with the oil and gas industry." He had reportedly been "instrumental in locating and drilling upon some of the most valuable oil lands in Wyoming and his wide experience extends through every great oil producing area in the United States."

It was Shippey who contacted McMahon, suggesting that they pool their leases and use one of McMahon's stacked diamond-core rigs to drill.

International Pipe Lines Limited, incorporated under the British Columbia Companies Act on July 28, 1930, was the vehicle organized by Shippey, Freeman, and McMahon to drill for gas in the delta. The very name reflected the grand undertaking that Charles Shippey had in mind: the discovery and development of a supply of natural gas and the construction of a pipeline system to supply consumers in British Columbia's lower mainland and the adjacent Puget Sound area of the United States. It was Shippey who created the same vision in the mind of Frank McMahon, a vision that he was to pursue during more than a quarter of a century. Eventually, the potential source of gas for this grand scheme would shift more than 700 miles to the Peace River country, but the basic idea was still the same.

For a venture with such big plans, International Pipe Lines Limited was a modest enough start. The company issued 600,000 treasury shares to Shippey, Freeman, McMahon, and their associates in return for the assignment of 25,000 acres of leases and offered a skeptical public the opportunity to purchase 50,000 shares at $1 each. The shares issued for the leases included 150,000 each to Shippey and the Victor J. Freeman syndicate, and 100,000 personally to Freeman, Samuel Orloff, and Ephriam Robinson Sugarman. McMahon received an allotment of the shares issued to Shippey in return for his leases. The company's prospectus listed the directors as Shippey, who was identified as a "capitalist," Freeman, identified as a "field manager," Orloff, "agent," Sugarman, "solicitor," and Eugene Metz of Kansas City, a "manager."

McMahon, with a contract from International Pipe Lines, began drilling at Stevenston on Lulu Island near the site of an earlier well that had found some gas. There was not that much money for drilling. A directors' report filed with the British Columbia Registrar of Companies, showed that by the fall of 1930 International Pipe Lines had raised, and largely spent, the grand total of $32,663.75. The public offering of shares raised $12,500, and the balance was advanced by the directors, primarily

Shippey. The first hole was a failure. The major shareholders surrendered more than half the 600,000 shares they had acquired in order to help raise more money, and drilling resumed.

By fall of 1931, four holes had been drilled to a maximum depth of 900 feet, and International Pipe Lines had one producing well, supplying a mixture of sand, salt water, and some gas. McMahon rigged up a plug valve at the foot of a perforated pipe. The valve shut off the sand, and the perforations allowed the water and gas to flow to a steel box at the surface which had been constructed as a separator. The water flowed out of the bottom of the box, and the gas flowed out through a valve at the top. The drilling at Lulu Island brought only limited success as well as a tragedy. John Grant, Isobel's father, visited the drilling site from time to time and often lent a helping hand. On one visit he was struck and killed by a length of drill pipe.

This single gas well was not about to supply the city of Vancouver. It had been drilled on the farm of Henry Fentiman under a lease that Shippey had negotiated. There was just enough gas for McMahon to rig up a line to service the Fentiman house, where it fueled the kitchen stove, the hot water heater, a fireplace in the den, and heaters in the dining room and hall. According to Fentiman's daughter-in-law, Mrs George Fentiman, the gas supply lasted twelve years before the line silted up and the well was capped.

International Pipe Lines died as soon as the gas well had been drilled, but the grand idea lived on in the mind of Frank McMahon.

CHAPTER THREE

Saga of the Flathead

Dad was comfortably well off but he was a practical man. He and our neighbour, Frank McMahon, used to walk to town from 49th and Angus to beat the seven-cent trolley fare. . . . My Dad told me, keep your pants pressed and your shoes shined, and on the coldest day of the year you can sit in any hotel lobby in town.

> Public relations man Bill Clancey, talking
> about Vancouver in the 1930s, quoted by
> Denny Boyd in the *Vancouver Sun*, May, 1981.

For a drilling contractor without any drilling contracts, a promoter with nothing to promote but himself, two things were essential for survival in the Depression years of the early 1930s in Vancouver: watching the pennies and keeping up appearances. Only the rich could afford to look poor. So Frank McMahon wore his best suit, kept his shoes shined, and walked downtown in search of work. There was little work to be had, and the bills piled up. Returning home one evening from a rare night out at the movies, Frank and Isobel found a service man from BC Electric shutting off the line that brought manufactured gas into their house. Frank let out a roar and chased the man down the block. The man who had wanted to provide a supply of natural gas for all of Vancouver – and later would – could not afford gas for his own house.

Without a pressed suit and polished shoes, McMahon may never have landed the contract that would put one of his stacked rigs back to work and re-launch his career as a petroleum promoter. The event was reported in a tiny item buried in the back pages of Vancouver's *Financial News* for October 15, 1931:

Diamond drilling equipment for the Crow's Nest – Glacier Oil Company left Vancouver last weekend for the Flathead Valley and was to be transported directly to the wells by truck. Roads were reported in good condition. V.J. Freeman, now in charge of operations, anticipated that the diamond drill will show results at No 1 well within the first month.

The Flathead Valley is in the extreme southeast corner of British Columbia, some seventy miles southeast of Kimberley. It lies on the western slope of the towering first range of the Rocky Mountains, within a dozen miles of the Continental Divide that marks the border between British Columbia and Alberta. A few miles farther west, the next range of mountains rises almost as high. The Flathead River begins in these mountains and runs southeast 100 miles through the valley floor, across the corner of British Columbia and through Montana to Flathead Lake. Hemmed in by mountain walls, it was one of the most inaccessible areas of the province.

A number of mountain streams feed the Flathead River. One of these is Sage Creek, fifteen miles north of Montana and about the same distance west of Alberta. At Sage Creek, seepages of oil and gas bubbled up in springs, and visions of wealth bubbled up in the minds of men. These seepages had attracted widespread attention and intermittent efforts to develop commercial oil production over a period of forty years, and McMahon was to help keep the quest alive for a further twenty years. It was the contract to deepen a well that had already been drilling off and on for more than a dozen years that first brought McMahon to Sage Creek. It was the most prominent of a number of oil seepages in the Flathead Valley.

It seemed like one of the least likely places to search for oil and gas. The sedimentary rocks in which oil and gas are found normally lie deposited – over the last several hundred million years – on the original earth's crust, the much older Precambrian rocks. No one has yet found an oil or gas field in rocks of Precambrian age. In the Flathead, the Precambrian rocks lie at or very near the surface. Yet, here were these seepages of oil and gas, percolating like coffee through springs of water at Sage Creek.

What had happened is clear enough. Eons ago, where the Rocky Mountains now stand, there had been a great trench. When stupendous subterranean forces thrust what are now the

26

Rockies up through this trough, the adjacent land and layers of rock were set in a great upheaveal and jumble by this intrusion of enormous mass. Layers of Precambrian rock were thrust over layers of much younger sedimentary rocks. In geologist's terms, the potential oil and gas bearing sedimentary rocks in the valley were covered by an over-thrust, in this case, a prominent feature known ·as the Lewis over-thrust. Fissures in the Precambrian cover allowed the oil and gas to migrate to the surface.

It was not difficult for hopeful prospectors before McMahon's time to imagine that if they could penetrate this Precambrian cap, below it they might find trapped enormous accumulations of oil and gas. There were problems, however. Precambrian rocks are very hard and very tough to drill. No one knew how many hundreds or thousands of feet of this over-thrust would have to be drilled before reaching the softer rocks where the oil and gas might be found. As well, there was always the possibility that most of whatever oil and gas may have been in these underlying rocks had already migrated through the fissures in the Precambrian cap and escaped at the surface in seepages like those at Sage Creek. But that is not the type of thing that a wildcatter with true faith would ever imagine.

Reports of oil seepages in the Flathead, and on the other side of the mountains in what is now Waterton National Park in Alberta, had been brought to the attention of fur traders and early settlers. Dr Alfred R.C. Selwyn, director of the Geological Survey of Canada, investigated the seepages in the summer of 1891. Some of the oil at Sage Creek, Selwyn reported, "was of a light lemon yellow colour, but most of it nearly the colour of pale brandy, and with a powerful petroleum odour." He suggested that some shallow shafts might be made to further investigate the nature of the oil occurrences. Dr George Dawson, who succeeded Selwyn as director of the Geological Survey, also visited Sage Creek a few years later and was the first to advance the over-thrust theory to explain this "anomalous occurrence of petroleum." Dawson concluded that, "The indications certainly seem sufficiently promising to warrant some outlay in development work."

It was not long after this that prospectors were seeking oil rights in the Flathead. "In October of 1901, Mr R.G. Leckie, Mining Engineer, of Vancouver, together with Mr Hugh Baker . . . reported having made a number of oil locations and brought

27

with them samples of the oil found there," according to the 1902 annual report of the British Columbia Minister of Mines. "From twenty to twenty-five square miles of land, supposed to cover oil-bearing rocks, have been staked by Mr Leckie and friends, and applications for record, which are as yet under consideration, have been made." The applications covered seepages on three tributaries of the Flathead, the Starvation, Kishinena, and Sage creeks. Although no new discoveries had been made, the BC report concluded that, "The locations mentioned indicate an attempt to actually turn these oil occurrences to use."

The attempt, however, was delayed by litigation and politics. When the CPR built its branch line to the Kootenay mines through the Crowsnest Pass, it was, in the fashion of railway building, given a large land grant as a subsidy. The CPR chose the Flathead Valley, covering both coal deposits and the oil seepages, for part of its grant, but the BC government had different ideas. Despite a widely publicized law suit, the government refused to include the Flathead Valley among the lands finally given to the CPR in 1902. The government seems to have had thoughts of developing the hoped-for oil fields itself, and the matter became an issue in the provincial election of 1903. When the new Conservative Government of Richard McBride at last opened the area for leasing, there had been so much publicity that the valley was covered with the stakes of many applicants claiming the same plots of ground. The result was years of litigation before most of the contenders agreed to pool their interests into a new firm, Amalgamated Oil Company, which in late 1911 obtained title to most of the oil rights in the Flathead.

Amalgamated, controlled largely by Vancouver investors, had some 15,000 acres of Crown-granted oil rights in the Flathead, some of which it held for more than forty years. A string of companies was organized to drill on the lands: Akamina Valley Oil Company Limited, Majestic Oil Company, BC Oil & Development Company Limited, Crow's Nest Oil Company, and Glacier Oil Company. The latter two subsequently merged to form Crow's Nest-Glacier Oil Company. Amalgamated was to receive lease rental payments and royalties on any production that might result. By 1930, half a dozen holes had been punched down to varying depths on the BC side of the Flathead Valley, with a couple more across the border in Montana. Colonel Guy H. Kirkpatrick, president of Amalgamated Oil Company, estimated that drilling expenditures during a period of some two decades on the British Columbia side of the valley amounted to "not less than $600,000, and probably considerably more."

None of the Flathead wells had managed to get deep enough to penetrate the hard Precambrian rocks and reach the younger formations that were expected to yield prolific flows of oil and gas. But the drilling did produce gushers of publicity.

"I would look to the Sage Creek district as being one of the most promising areas in the Dominion as an oil field," a "mineralogist" with the BC Department of Mines stated in a report in 1910. A California consulting engineer, Allen G. Nichols, reported in 1914 that, "The oil to be produced from this section is extremely high grade, rich in paraffin, in gasoline and lubricating stock." The following year, an eminent American geologist, Ralph Arnold, in a report for Guy Kirkpatrick of Amalgamated, noted that one hole had been drilled to a depth of 130 feet. He observed that it could produce oil at a rate of "possibly a few gallons daily, as it is so shallow." Arnold predicted that at a depth of 2,500 feet a well would be able to produce oil at a rate of fifty barrels a day, "or possibly more." By January, 1927, the *Western Oil Examiner* in Calgary reported that both the BC Oil & Development Company and the Glacier Oil Company were drilling and had encouraging shows of oil.

"Buy Amalgamated Oil," General Sales Service Ltd advertised in the *Vancouver Sun* in May, 1928, "200,000 treasury shares offered at 25¢." By September, 1929, the *Western Oil Examiner* was reporting that oil men in Vancouver "are confident that . . . the Crow's Nest-Glacier No 1 well will be a splendid well. . . . If the well is as big as some geologists have claimed it should be, British Columbia will far outdistance Turner Valley in grade and quantity of production." The following month, officials of Crow's Nest-Glacier were reported to be planning construction of a refinery in the Flathead and a pipeline to Vancouver. Nearly a year later, in September, 1930, the *Financial News* reported that the company's "officials place great faith in the predictions of O.T. Major, who is the inventor of an oil-locating instrument. . . . It is impossible to say whether his predictions are of any value either way, but he has made an estimate of a production from this well of at least 5,000 barrels a day."

Out in the field, however, things at the well were not really that good. Drilling had started in 1918, and when it was not

29

stopped for lack of money it seemed to be stopped while the crew went fishing for tools lost down the hole. By July, 1927, a total of 3,265 feet of hole had been drilled, but the steep-dipping rocks of the Precambrian cap had deviated the pounding bit of the cable-tool rig, with the result that the hole was actually drilled at an angle. No one knew what the angle was, so no one knew how far the bit had penetrated vertically below the surface.

Five hundred quarts of nitro-glycerine had been exploded at the bottom of the hole, fracturing the rocks enough to release a flow of gas and indications of oil. The blast also caused part of the hole to cave in, or bridge, cutting off the flow of gas and trapping a string of drilling tools. It took two years to clean out the hole, only to have it bridged once more. The hole was cleaned out again, and then yet another string of tools was lost in it. This, in the late summer of 1931, meant that drilling would have to be resumed several hundred feet above the depth of 3,265 feet that had been reached four years earlier. It was at this point that Victor Freeman was hired by the Crow's Nest-Glacier Oil Company to take charge of drilling operations. Through Freeman, McMahon convinced Crow's Nest-Glacier that there was a better way. Instead of using cable tools where the bit is pounded up and down to smash through the rock, McMahon argued that his diamond-coring equipment could handle the job better by actually cutting through the rock.

McMahon's equipment was shipped by rail from Vancouver to Columbia Falls, Montana, from where it was to be trucked over seventy miles of narrow forestry road to Sage Creek. By this time, winter had set in, and the Flathead Valley was filled with snow. It was not until the following year that the equipment could be trucked to the well site and drilling resumed.

In the spring of 1932, the McMahons moved to the collection of shacks and cabins that constituted the drilling camp at Sage Creek. The group included Frank and Isobel, their two boys, then aged two and three years; Isobel's cousin, Bain Grant; and George McMahon, who had had a job selling bonds in Vancouver but not much income, because no one was buying bonds in 1932. There was a crew of about twenty-five, a good part of which was kept busy cutting firewood to fuel the boiler at the heavy-timbered derrick. At times enough oil was baled from the well or from the nearby spring to run a small electrical generating plant. Sage Creek was a good refuge from the Depression, at least it provided accommodation and food. Frank ran the rig, George looked after the administration and worked as camp cook for awhile, Bain Grant kept the machinery in running order, and Isobel became an expert fly fisherman. The area teemed with wildlife, and fish and venison were a staple part of the camp fare. The camp offered everything, except money. The Crow's Nest-Glacier Oil Company was on the verge of bankruptcy and was not always able to meet the payroll. When that happened, company shares were issued for wages. George and Isobel wrote letters to the several thousand shareholders of the company, asking for donations of at least one dollar each to keep the drilling going, and with it some hope for a return on sunk investments. From then on, George was associated with all of Frank's oil ventures.

Drilling for an outfit that could not meet its payroll was no way to become a millionaire, nor did it afford a proper chance to develop the large oil reserves that everyone was convinced were still waiting to be found, if only someone could drill deep enough. The answer, McMahon decided, would be to promote a new venture to undertake the task.

That summer, Frank arranged for Dr George Hume of the Geological Survey of Canada to visit the area and prepare a report on its geology and oil prospects. His step-father, Owen Thompson, an experienced mining engineer, also inspected the properties, as did Victor Dolmage of Vancouver, consulting geologist for the Crow's Nest-Glacier Company.

Hume was impressed by the diamond-coring operation and by the oil escaping at rates up to one and a half gallons a day which, he said, provided "evidence of large volumes from which the seepages are derived." In his report for the Geological Survey, Hume commented that drilling through the Precambrian rocks at Sage Creek with standard cable tools had presented "much difficulty," with "several wells lost . . . due to tools lost in the hole, and excessive drilling costs have resulted for small amounts of footage drilled." He noted that the diamond-drilling equipment at the Sage Creek well "was not in good condition," but "its effectiveness for drilling the highly metamorphosed rocks was amply demonstrated."

When the drilling season ended in the fall of 1932, the hole had been re-drilled to its previous depth of 3,265 feet. The bit was unable to go any farther because of shattered rock conditions created by the earlier blast of nitro-glycerine, and Crow's Nest-Glacier was unable to go any further because it had run out of money. But by the time he returned to Vancouver, McMahon was ready to promote yet one more drilling venture in the Flathead, the graveyard of hope for so many earlier promoters. By agreements dated October 22, 1932, McMahon obtained, for the sum of $10, options to lease 1,601 acres of oil lands from Crow's Nest-Glacier and Amalgamated Oil. The options could be exercised by December 1 for cash payments totalling $4,500, plus annual rentals, plus royalties on any production. All that was needed was $4,500 and a great deal more to drill a well.

The vehicle for all this was Columbia Oils Limited, incorporated under the BC Companies Act, on November 5, 1932. It was set up in the time-honoured method of financing speculative ventures in oil and mining. Columbia Oils issued 350,000 shares in escrow to Frank McMahon, in return for assignment of the 1,601 acres of leases, and proposed to sell 150,000 public shares at $1 each to finance drilling of the well.

To head Columbia Oils, Frank turned to Owen Thompson and a group of Vancouver investors who had been associated with Thompson in a successful gold-mining venture in the Kootenays. As managing director of Reno Gold Mines, Thompson had brought the gold mine, thirteen miles south of Nelson, into production in 1928 with financial backing from the Duke of Devonshire and other English investors. The mine made its first profit in 1930, and over the following decade it was to pay out more than a $1 million in dividends before the ore finally ran out. Thompson agreed to accept the position of managing director of Columbia Oils, and D.S. Wallbridge, a prominent Vancouver lawyer with the firm of Reid, Wallbridge, Gibson, and Sutton and president of Reno Gold Mines, also became president of Columbia Oils. Wallbridge was an old hand in BC mining ventures, starting out with a mining-brokerage business in the boom town of Sandon in the 1890s. Sutton, a member of the same law firm and secretary of Reno, became secretary of Columbia Oils. Other directors, all prominent Vancouver people, were R.L. Reid, again from the same law firm; A.J. Hendry, a lumberman and director of Reno; W.S. Day, an insurance broker; and F.E. Burke, identified in the company prospectus as an "importer."

Although he was the largest registered owner of shares, Frank

McMahon was not on the board of Columbia Oils. Although the 350,000 escrowed shares were in his name, ownership in fact was shared with the people with whom he had put the deal together. McMahon was involved in two other capacities: as superintendent of field operations, which meant he would spend about nine months a year drilling in the Flathead, and as "fiscal agent," which meant that he and George would spend the rest of the time trying to sell the 150,000 shares to finance the drilling. In a small office on the second floor of the Yorkshire Building, down the hall from Owen Thompson's office, "fiscal agent" Frank McMahon and his brother George set up shop as oil promoters.

Such was the confidence of the "vendors of the property and the original syndicate owners" in "the possibilities of the Sage Creek acreage" that they had agreed to "exceptionally stringent" conditions attached to the escrowed shares, Wallbridge later explained to the first meeting of Columbia Oils' shareholders. Under the agreements, the escrowed shares were to be held in trust by the Yorkshire & Canadian Trust Company until one year after commercial oil production of at least 1,000 barrels per day had been attained, and no dividends were to be paid on these shares until after the other shareholders had fully recovered their original investment. Unless large oil reserves were found, the escrowed shares would be worthless.

A sales brochure put together by McMahon before the end of 1932 claimed that "Columbia Oils Limited offers the investor an opportunity to profitably share in an important phase of the development of Canada's natural resources." It was, said the brochure, "A Speculation of Unquestionable Merit."

Owen Thompson, whose experience was in mining rather than oil, resigned as managing director of Columbia early in 1933, although continuing as a director, to allow the appointment of a veteran oil man as general manager. George Brake had worked in the oil fields of Ontario, the Dutch East Indies, Africa, Venezuela, and Peru for more than forty years. Before retiring to Vancouver in 1930, he had been manager of production and pipeline operations in Peru for International Petroleum, a subsidiary of and principal oil supplier to Imperial Oil.

A steady flow of reports appearing in the *Vancouver Financial News* kept alive investor interest in the progress being made in the remote Flathead Valley. "George W. Brake . . . left Wednesday night for Calgary, where he will inspect the latest type heavy duty diamond drilling plant being acquired by Columbia," the paper reported on May 26, 1933. On June 3, "An eighty-four-foot derrick is on the site, steam power plant ready to go into commission, standard rig made ready. . . . Three hundred cords of wood is available for fuel. . . . Considerable interest has been created in Vancouver by samples of crude oil brought from Sage Creek seepages a few days ago." On July 21, the *Financial News* noted that the earlier test by Crow's Nest-Glacier, "gave every indication that the district overlaid a major oil reservoir." On August 11, "A considerable quantity of oil flowing from the top horizon of the new well . . . has been stored in barrels and gasoline tanks. A 1,000 barrel steel tank has been sent in to supplement the barrels and tanks hurriedly assembled at Columbia Falls." On September 15, "The well is drilling below 902 feet with good prospects being made." In October, Columbia Oils hosted a visit to the drilling site by a group of twenty-six Vancouver investors and journalists. The *Financial News* reported that the company "is making a well-managed attempt to bring into production a field that for thirty years has been begging a real test."

While McMahon was looking for the big oil strike in the Flathead, Charles Shippey was continuing his search for shallow gas on the coast, drilling this time on the US side of Boundary Bay. *The Herald*, in Bellingham, Washington, reported on November 19, 1933, that a well backed by the Bellingham Chamber of Commerce, "with C.S. Shippey, Kansas operator and driller, in charge of the work," struck a gas flow at a rate of 900,000 cubic feet a day from a depth of 172 feet. Although there were reports of renewed interest in the play, the Boundary Bay well apparently turned out no better than the Lulu Island wells.

In its first year of operations, Columbia Oils had sold enough shares to keep the rig drilling throughout most of the winter of 1933-34, with a short break for Christmas. Frank and two other members of the crew were the last to leave the camp on a tractor headed for Columbia Falls where they were to catch a Great Northern Railway train to Vancouver. The tractor tangled with an angry bull moose and lost the battle. With the tractor in the ditch, the three men walked out more than fifty miles to Columbia Falls through snow that was hip deep, a trek that only men in the toughest physical condition could survive.

Drilling resumed after Christmas, but progress was slow. By

early February, seven months after the well had spudded, the hole had reached only 1,570 feet according to the *Western Oil Examiner*. After that, progress was even slower; Columbia Oils had exhausted its funds, and drilling was suspended until more shares could be sold.

With Columbia Oils out of money, the job of fiscal agent and field superintendent was hardly more remunerative than working for the old Crow's Nest-Glacier Oil Company, and the task of surviving the ever-tightening grip of the Depression was as difficult as ever. In Vancouver, McMahon switched from the work clothes of the oil fields to the pressed suit and polished shoes of a salesman and went back knocking on doors. As 1933 ended, he managed to find a short-term contract for one of his stacked diamond-drilling rigs to help demolish a pier of the collapsed Second Narrows Bridge that had spanned Vancouver Harbour's Burrard Inlet.

The inlet pokes its finger into the mountains to form Vancouver Harbour and continues farther inland, so far and through such rugged country that no one has ever built a road from Vancouver to its sister communities across the harbour, North Vancouver and West Vancouver. The harbour narrows at two places called, logically enough, First Narrows and Second Narrows. The first bridge from Vancouver to the north shore was built across the Second Narrows in 1925. Ships kept ramming into it, and five years after it had been built there had been twenty major shipping accidents, with damage and loss claims amounting to $450,000, according to newspaper reports. On September 19, 1930, the log carrier *Pacific Gatherer* knocked out the 300-foot centre span, and work was later started on a new, safer, $3 million bridge.

A new concrete pier was built on the south shore, and McMahon obtained a subcontract from the Foundation Company to drill thirty holes, each 100 feet deep, into the old, steel-reinforced pier. Five thousand pounds of dynamite were packed into galvanized iron tubes, inserted into the holes, and on the evening of March 1, 1934, the charge was detonated. The plan was to set off the explosives at fifteen second intervals and demolish the old pier gently. Something went wrong and the explosions all went off together, rattling windows throughout greater Vancouver and causing "great alarm among the residents," in the words of the *Vancouver News Herald*.

McMahon was not in Vancouver to witness the big explosion. He was in London, looking for money. Shortly after drilling had started at the Second Narrows pier, McMahon left his crew to finish the job, while he sailed to England. What he had in mind was the most extensive search for oil and gas that had ever been undertaken in British Columbia, in the Peace River country more than 600 miles north of Vancouver. The BC government had recently opened the area for exploration by private capital, and McMahon hoped to attract the backing of large English oil interests for a major exploration program.

The great sedimentary basin that stretches from the Mackenzie River Delta on the Arctic Coast to the Gulf of Mexico cuts across the northeastern corner of British Columbia. There it embraces 40,000 square miles, including the rolling farmlands of the Peace River country, its southwestern edge marked by the line of the Rocky Mountains.

Interest in the oil and gas possibilities of the Peace River date back to 1887, when George Dawson of the Geological Survey included the region in his map of the Great Mackenzie Basin. He envisioned it as an enormous petroleum province. Several oil and gas seeps were found on the Alberta side of the region along the banks of the river, and the first drilling started in 1915. On the British Columbia side, in 1919 Thomas Dufferin Pattullo, as provincial Minister of Lands, was instrumental in withdrawing all BC Crown Lands in the Peace River from leasing for oil and gas exploration, a ban that stayed in effect for thirteen years. During the interim, the BC Department of Mines undertook its own geological study of the oil prospects. In 1921-22, the department drilled six shallow test wells, from 1,027 to 2,525 feet, in the foothills of the Rocky Mountains on the southwestern flank of the sedimentary basin near Hudson Hope. All six wells found small shows of natural gas, and three found some oil. Although none of these wells discovered commercially viable accumulations of oil or gas, they did confirm the region as a potential petroleum province. The discovery that most excited McMahon, however, was a gas well drilled in 1922-24 by the Northwest Company, a subsidiary of Imperial Oil, near the Alberta village of Pouce Coupe and within a quarter of a mile of the BC border. The Pouce Coupe discovery flowed gas at rates up to 10 million cubic feet per day from a sandstone formation at a depth of about 3,000 feet. Because there was no ready market for natural gas in such a

36

remote area, Imperial Oil had abandoned its Pouce Coupe well and dropped the leases.

These early exploration efforts in the Peace River country had been widely reported, and geologists had published numerous papers dealing with the petroleum prospects, as McMahon was well aware. He had also talked to two geologists who were particularly impressed by the oil and gas possibilities of the Peace River, Dr George Hume of the Geological Survey of Canada and Stanley Slipper, chief geologist with Canadian Western Natural Gas Company in Calgary.

It was the 1931 Conservative government of Dr Simon Fraser Tolmie that lifted the 1919 Liberal administration ban on leasing provincial oil and gas rights in the Peace River area. "Anyone can now stake for oil," Lands Minister N.S. Lougheed announced on April 19, 1932. "We are putting everything we have got as a province on our shelves, with an open invitation to all to prospect for coal, oil, or natural gas, sure in the knowledge that if rich discoveries are made, the people of British Columbia are fully protected by existing legislation." To McMahon, that sounded almost like a personal invitation.

McMahon's trip to England in search of capital for an exploration program was financed by a man who was to continue to provide important support for his ventures, Colonel Victor Spencer. Joseph Victor Norman Spencer, then fifty-two, was the fifth son of David Spencer, founder of what was then British Columbia's largest chain of department stores. A big man, with the build of a football player and still athletically trim, Spencer was an imposing presence, equally at home in a three-piece business suit or riding on his large Earlscourt Ranch at Lytton. Spencer was something of an adventurer and a business gambler, much to the dismay of his more conservative brothers, but it was his gambles in mining that helped keep the Spencer department stores afloat during the Depression years. At age seventeen he had enlisted as a trooper with a Canadian contingent that served in South Africa during the Boer War, and in the First World War he had served in the infantry, discharging with the rank of Lt Colonel. In 1928, Spencer invested heavily in what was widely thought to be the worthless shares of Pioneer Gold Mines. Off and on for thirty years the company had been trying unsuccessfully to operate a group of gold claims at Bridge River, 100 miles north of Vancouver. With Spencer as president, Pioneer brought a new mine and mill into production. By 1934, at the height of the Depression, Pioneer was paying its shareholders dividends of more than $1 million a year.

Spencer was a natural ally for McMahon. Frank's program included not only British Columbia, but also a large area of northern Alberta and the Northwest Territories. Spencer provided $5,000 for the trip to England, McMahon, in turn, absorbed the travel costs for Vancouver businessman Bill McKenzie whose family had connections with oil interests in England. McMahon also travelled armed with letters of introduction to the Guiness family, the giant brewery concern whose investments would leave an indelible stamp across Vancouver's landscape: the Capilano Golf Course; the British Properties, where expensive homes climb halfway up the mountain on the north shore of the harbour; the magnificent Marine Building that for so long dominated Vancouver's skyline; and Vancouver's premier man-made landmark, the Lions Gate Bridge. The introduction to the Guiness family came from A.J.T. Taylor, the former Victoria machinist who had made and lost several fortunes in mining, engineering, and heavy machinery manufacturing. It was Taylor who had talked the Guiness family into sinking a substantial part of their beer profits into Vancouver real estate development, and who then headed these enterprises.

In early 1934, McMahon and McKenzie boarded the *Ille de France* in New York bound for London. In England, they stayed first in the posh Mayfair Hotel, where the rooms cost $5 a night, and later at the less expensive Cumberland Hotel. Through Taylor's office in London and the Guiness interests, they plugged into the British school-tie network and spent four months calling on every prospect they could find, including such major concerns as Shell Oil and Anglo Iranian Oil (later British Petroleum). The big oil companies were well informed about the oil and gas prospects in the Peace River country, and they were not very interested. The world was swimming in a glut of oil, the sales price was under $1 a barrel, and the last thing the major oil companies needed then was a new source of supply to further flood the market.

Even if the English oil companies had been interested, the plans for a big northern oil play would still have been frustrated, at least in British Columbia. While McMahon and McKenzie were in London, on April 14, 1934, the BC government once more imposed a ban on leasing government owned oil and gas rights in the Peace River. The area had been open for only two years, and no one had rushed in to take out permits. Now the ban was to remain in effect for another thirteen years.

The Conservative government of Dr Tolmie that had lifted the reserve in 1932 was almost annihilated by the Liberal party in the provincial election in 1933. Leading the Liberal party was the former Minister of Lands who had originally imposed the ban in 1919, Duff Pattullo. The diminutive, dapper Duff was a sixty-year-old former newspaperman who had as much faith in the oil prospects of the Peace River as McMahon, but he was dead set against private exploitation of what he considered to be the heritage of the people. With the ban on leasing reimposed, Pattullo would soon launch another government attempt to discover what he was sure would be enormous oil wealth for British Columbians.

McMahon and McKenzie returned to Vancouver empty-handed. They had made some contacts with English investors and brokerage firms that might be of use in raising capital for future ventures, but plans for a big play in the Peace River were completely stalled. Prospects seemed no brighter at home. In August, the officers and directors of Amalgamated Oils, Crow's Nest-Glacier Oil, and Columbia Oils "had a get-together dinner meeting in Vancouver" to review the progress that Columbia was making in developing the Sage Creek oil field and assess future prospects, according to the *Financial News*. It was not the most cheerful review. Columbia had not been able to meet the drilling commitments stipulated in its leases from Amalgamated and Crow's Nest-Glacier: after a year of drilling the hole still stood at only 1,925 feet. Columbia had raised a total of $126,000 from the sale of shares, of which $105,000 had been spent on drilling with the remainder taken up in financing costs. Funds were exhausted again. Robert Wilkinson, the Vancouver-Point Grey member of the BC Legislature, promised the oil men he would look into the matter of a Canadian road access to the Flathead to eliminate the long haul of supplies and equipment from Columbia Falls. The only other thing that appears to have been accomplished at the get-together was that Guy Kirkpatrick, representing Amalgamated, and A.K. Leith, representing Crow's Nest-Glacier, were appointed to the board of Columbia. The expanded board, according to the *Financial News*, "has for its object the keeping of the Sage Creek and Flathead oil fields before the public."

With some financial backing from Victor Spencer, Columbia Oils was able to resume its search in the Flathead. A contract was let with the Diamond Drill Contracting Company of Spokane, drilling at the Sage Creek well resumed in January, 1935, and McMahon promoted yet another venture.

Reflecting the continuing hope for some English capital, the newest McMahon venture was called London Pacific Exploration Co Ltd. Through two controlled subsidiaries, London Pacific obtained a further 6,150 acres of leases from Amalgamated Oil in the Flathead, plus 7,175 acres in Montana. The Montana leases were described in a company advertisement as being "in a direct line with the Tea Pot Dome field of Wyoming and between the famous Cat Creek and Cut Bank fields in Montana." Part of the leases in the Flathead were adjacent to the still-drilling Columbia well. With a few exceptions the board of London Pacific was similar to that of Columbia: Wallbridge was president; Hendry was vice-president; Dr R.B. Boucher, a Vancouver doctor and a director of Spencer's Pioneer Gold Mines, was second vice-president; G. Nelles Stacey, a Vancouver investment dealer, was secretary-treasurer. Other directors were McMahon, who again was fiscal agent; John Anderson, a Scottish financier who had long been associated with A.J.T. Taylor and who was manager of British Pacific Properties Ltd; W.B. Farris, a Vancouver lawyer who was later to become Chief Justice of British Columbia and a brother of Senator John Wallace deBeque Farris who was also to become closely associated with McMahon; and J.T. Trumbull, who was also on the board of Columbia.

In May, 1935, London Pacific made a public offering of half a million shares at twenty-five cents each. It never did drill in the Flathead, but it did spend more than $100,000 to drill a pair of dry holes in Montana. And that was the last of London Pacific Exploration.

The Columbia well at Sage Creek kept grinding slowly ahead, at least whenever the company had enough money for drilling. By July, it was reported at 3,817 feet, the deepest hole in the Flathead, but still not through the Precambrian rocks. By November, it was below 4,800 feet, and the *Western Oil Exami-*

ner reported that, "Oil and water were forced over the top of the derrick." By the end of 1935, Columbia Oils had spent $190,000 and was broke again. In April, 1936, a new financing plan was being arranged, and by June, according to the *Financial News*, the company had "begun hauling in timber for the new 127-foot derrick which will be erected to permit deeper drilling of the test." The newspaper reported that the well was opened after having been shut-in since November, and "oil blew over the derrick and the flow continued for about forty minutes. As a test of the quality of the oil, some of it was used to operate the Delco electric light plant at the camp."

McMahon's attention was again drawn to the Peace River country in 1936. The old Northwest Pouce Coupe gas discovery had been abandoned and shut-in for a dozen years, but it began leaking natural gas. A block of leases surrounding the abandoned well had been taken out from the Alberta government by Calgary interests and Peace River area investors headed by Lee W. Alward, a farmer who was provoked at the high cost of petroleum products and hoped to find a cheaper supply of tractor fuel for the area's growing agricultural industry. Calgary consulting geologist Dr J.O.G. "Pete" Sanderson prepared a report in June for Alward's group, the Canada Empire Crude Oil Syndicate. Sanderson had visited the abandoned Pouce Coupe well and reported that gas was escaping from the shut-off valve at a rate that he estimated at 2 million to 5 million cubic feet per day, an energy loss equivalent to up to 15,000 gallons a day of fuel oil. "There was no timbering over the cellar and no fence or barrier to prevent animals or people from getting into the well," Sanderson wrote. "There are a few old parts of timbers and drilling machinery scattered over the site."

Sanderson, a well respected geologist, was enthusiastic about the possibility of developing a large supply of natural gas and building a pipeline to Vancouver and the adjacent US Puget Sound area, which, he said, was "the largest unserviced market for natural gas in western North America." He pointed to prospects of gas "being present in very large quantities" and estimated that a pipeline could be built to Vancouver "over relatively easy terrain" at a cost of less than $16 million; it might produce sales of $17 million per year. "These figures, although only quoted to show general magnitude and comparisons, indicate that a very attractive commercial venture awaits the enter-

41

prise that will develop this commodity alone," he reported. It seemed "almost certain," he wrote, that the necessary reserves could be "proven by the drilling of three or four wells." There were, in addition, attractive possibilities for the discovery of oil and "a ready market for all the oil that may be produced in this region."

Shortly after Sanderson's visit, the pent-up pressures in the Pouce Coupe well blew out the valve, and the escaping gas caught fire with a roar that could be heard for miles. It was several months before Imperial Oil came back to kill the well and pump cement down the hole to shut off the flow. The flames were still leaping thirty-five feet into the air when McMahon, armed with a copy of Sanderson's report and accompanied by a Vancouver photographer, visited the site for a first-hand look. It had all the markings of an enormous development, and McMahon wanted nothing more than to get in on the ground floor. But the cards were stacked against him. He had failed to find a large pool of capital in England. The London Pacific venture had fizzled out after two dry holes. The Columbia well in the Flathead was still struggling for money and to get through the Precambrian. On the BC side of the Peace River, where Sanderson said the best gas prospects lay, the area was closed to leasing by Duff Pattullo's determination to have the resources developed by government. More than ever, McMahon had a pipe dream, but there was nothing he could do about it.

The directors of Columbia Oils were far more concerned with finishing the job in the Flathead than chasing after smoke signals from the Peace River. They had not lost sight of their objective: "the keeping of the Sage Creek and Flathead oil fields before the public." In September, they invited a blue-ribboned party of fifty-four guests for a tour of the "field." The group included three provincial cabinet ministers, two members of the Legislative Assembly (Robert Wilkinson from Vancouver-Point Grey and Tom Uphill from Fernie), as well as various bankers, brokers, businessmen, and reporters. The party travelled by Great Northern Railway to Columbia Falls and seventy miles by car along the narrow, rutted forestry road where, according to the *Financial News*, one car "plunged over a steep bank. Luckily logs and underbrush broke the fall, saving the occupants from serious injury." Explaining operations to the visitors were Frank and George McMahon; Frank Creasy, Columbia's manager at the well site; and Chester Bartoo, in charge of drilling for the contractor. The wood-fired steam boiler had been replaced by a 250-horsepower diesel, and the *Financial News* reported that, "The steel derrick, diesel-electric power plant and Doheney-Stone drilling equipment put the operation in a class by itself."

The three cabinet ministers were most impressed. Finance Minister John Hart was quoted as saying that, "The oil well project deserves the sympathy, co-operation, and support of the government." Lands Minister Wells Gray went so far as to suggest "the advancing of government funds to complete the well if such assistance should be required." Public Works Minister Frank McPherson said that construction of a forty-mile road from Fernie was "a deserving project meriting early attention when funds are available."

The publicity was great, but it did not generate much money, and by late fall both Columbia Oils and the McMahons were again hard-pressed for funds. Returning to Vancouver after drilling had wound up for the winter, Frank and his family crowded into a small apartment in Vancouver's Devonshire Hotel. Frank, George, and Bain Grant spent endless evenings discussing the possibilities of new ventures. Whoever happened to have the money bought the groceries, and Bain Grant even managed to come up with a few pheasants from a farmer in the Fraser Valley. George was dispatched on the CPR steamer *Princess Margaret* to collect some funds that were owed by a man in Victoria, a sum paid in cash and so large that no one aboard the ship on the return trip would provide change, and George dined on packages of peanuts. Frank, Isobel, and Bain Grant were all waiting at the dock when the ship pulled in, and George stood in the bow, excitedly waving the windfall he had collected, a single $100 bill.

It was, perhaps, a prophetic omen. Within a few months, Frank McMahon had launched yet another oil venture, one that ultimately became the foundation of Pacific Petroleums and Westcoast Transmission, with a cash investment of $100.

CHAPTER FOUR

Eighty Acres Make an Oil Company

If the homes and factories in the Vancouver area had been burning natural gas in 1936, Isobel McMahon probably would not have been standing on the side of the road holding a flashlight on that damp and chilly Saturday evening, November 14.

The fog rolled off the ocean and into Vancouver Harbour, mixing with the belching smoke from burning coal, wood, sawdust, and sulphurous fuel oil, until it was so dense that drivers could not see the side of the road. Passengers had to get out with flashlights to prevent cars from ending up in a ditch. Frank and Isobel were driving out to a small farmhouse near Abbottsford with $100 that had been scraped from the depleted household budget by holding off the creditors a little longer.

The hurried trip to Abbottsford in the fog was the culmination of a chain of events that had started five months earlier with the discovery of a large reservoir of crude oil at Turner Valley, in the foothills southwest of Calgary. For half a century Canada's largest oil field, Turner Valley was actually discovered in three stages. The first was in 1914 when the discovery of oil and natural gas from shallow sands set off the most feverish speculative spree in Canada's history. Within months, 500 companies were formed with authorized capital totalling $400 million, and riots broke out as Calgarians thronged the streets in front of brokers' offices in a frenzy to buy shares. The money came in so fast that it was stacked in wastepaper baskets.

"It was the wildest, most delirious, most uproarious, most exciting time that had ever entered into human imagination to conceive," the *Calgary Albertan* reported. The *News Telegram* commented that Calgary "had a population of 80,000 people, mostly lunatics." By the time the boom was over, only a tiny fraction of the 500 new companies had actually drilled for oil, few of these found any part of the trickle of oil and gas production that resulted, and Calgary's eager investors had been wiped clean of more than a $1 million in savings.

The second Turner Valley boom was triggered in 1924 by the discovery of a deeper and larger accumulation of natural gas made by Royalite Oil Company, a subsidiary of Imperial Oil. This second wave was more substantial than the first, but far more wasteful. The natural gas produced from the deeper Mississippian formation at Turner Valley was accompanied by gas liquids, variously described as naphtha, condensate, and natural gasoline, that could readily be used in place of crude oil to refine automotive gasoline. In fact, these liquids were so volatile that without any refining they fueled some trucks and cars that sputtered and smoked and backfired, but actually ran. There was lots of demand for the liquids, but little demand for the gas. By 1932, more than 100 wells at Turner Valley were extracting nearly 4,000 barrels of liquids per day, while the unwanted gas was being burned off at a rate of 600 million cubic feet per day – enough to supply the present-day requirements of a city the size of Toronto. Calgarians used to boast that on a summer's evening they could sit on their front porches and read their newspapers by the light of the Turner Valley flares, twenty-five miles away.

What the early Turner Valley producers did not realize was that they were wasting more than just natural gas. The sheet of Mississippian limestone that formed this reservoir lay at an angle, dipping to the west. The gas and gas liquids were trapped at the crest of this structure, where the producing wells were drilled. To the west, down-dip on the flank of the structure and beneath the gas cap, lay an enormous and unsuspected accumulation of crude oil. By rapidly producing the gas, the pressure in the reservoir was also being depleted, thereby reducing the amount of oil that could be produced. The amount of gas wasted at Turner Valley by flaring amounted to some 1.8 trillion cubic feet, while more than 300 million barrels of oil were lost due to the rapid reduction of the reservoir pressure. The total amount of energy thus wasted, if it were measured at 1982 prices, amounted to more than $25 billion.

But in the early 1930s no one knew that this oil column lay beneath the gas cap at Turner Valley. One of the first to suspect

45

its presence was Robert A. Brown, manager of Calgary's electric light department and streetcar system. Brown and two associates – *Calgary Albertan* publisher George Melrose Bell and lawyer John W. Moyer – gambled everything they had in a well drilled on the west flank of the structure to find the oil that Brown had become convinced was there. The informed geological opinion was that the well was too far down from the crest of the structure and would find nothing but water. Brown and his associates had formed Turner Valley Royalties Ltd and financed the well by selling royalty units at $1,500 each, for which buyers were to receive 1 per cent of the sales value of any resulting oil production. It took Turner Valley Royalties 2 years and $100,000 to complete the well. Drilling stopped seven times when the company ran out of money, while the promoters tried to flog more royalty units. They eventually sold enough to cover 70 per cent of whatever production they might find, and even then the well was finished only with the help of loans from Imperial Oil and British American Oil. Before the well was completed, Brown had mortgaged his house, his insurance, his car. Bell, who had lost money on earlier wildcat ventures and was losing money on his newspaper, was more than $500,000 in debt. Despite the loss from the depleted reservoir pressure, on June 16, 1936, Turner Valley Royalties Number One struck a flow of oil that ushered in the largest oil field in what was then the British Empire, the first major oil field in Canada, and the third stage in the discoveries at Turner Valley.

In Vancouver, Frank McMahon saw the excitement over the Turner Valley oil discovery as one more chance in his quest for a successful oil venture. With the London Pacific scheme a failure, with hopes dwindling in each foot of Precambrian rock drilled at the Sage Creek well, with any plans to develop a large supply of natural gas frustrated by the policy of Duff Pattullo, McMahon's last hope for success in the oil business could well depend on an opportunity to get in on the important action at Turner Valley. Scouting up all the information and maps on land holdings in the area that he could obtain, McMahon discovered that the oil rights to eighty acres lying less than three-quarters of a mile northwest of the Turner Valley Royalties discovery were controlled by Maitland Shore, the CPR station agent at Abbottsford who lived on a nearby farm. Eighty acres were enough to drill two wells, but they lay west of the discovery well and farther down the flank of the structure. Whether oil or water lay beneath those eighty acres, no one could know, but at least it offered a chance. Frank and Isobel were prepared to gamble their last $100 on that chance.

The deal that McMahon negotiated with Maitland Shore on that Saturday evening in November, 1936, gave him an option on the 80 acres for the $100 cash payment. The purchase price was a further $20,000, plus a gross royalty of 10 per cent. It was the same type of deal he had arranged in the Flathead, and again depended on raising a lot more money, probably more than $120,000, including the cost of drilling the first well.

In less than a month after signing the option with Shore, McMahon had raised the $20,000 from a group of Vancouver businessmen, acquired an additional 600 acres of strictly wildcat leases, and organized a company to take over the properties, West Turner Petroleums Ltd, which was incorporated on December 11. President of West Turner was Robert Wilkinson, by this time no longer a member of the provincial legislature. Frank Burke, a director of Columbia Oils, was vice-president. W.A. Sutton was secretary-treasurer, the same position he had held with Reno Gold Mines, Columbia Oils, and London Pacific. Other directors were Dr R.B. Boucher, also on the boards of Columbia and Spencer's Pioneer Gold Mines; Reg Smith, a Vancouver mining geologist and promoter who was to continue actively involved in McMahon's early oil ventures; John Hunter, formerly secretary-treasurer of the large Winnipeg investment firm of James Richardson & Sons but then retired in New Westminster; and McMahon, who was managing director. It was from this group and their associates that Frank had raised the $20,000 for the lease from Maitland Shore. In return, they and McMahon received a large block of escrowed shares of West Turner. As with Columbia Oils, the terms were such that the escrowed shares would be worthless unless oil was produced. The days when fast promoters could make even faster dollars by selling worthless vendor's shares and not even bother drilling had long since passed. More importantly, McMahon planned to come back to the money well a good many times, and he knew there would be nothing there for him if he failed to give his backers a good run for their money. Convinced beyond any doubt that the lease would prove productive, McMahon's fertile mind was already racing ahead to plan more ventures.

47

One week after West Turner was incorporated McMahon purchased an additional forty-acre lease that adjoined the Shore property. He obtained it from Robert Barker of Vancouver for $5,000 cash, plus $10,000 from production, and a royalty of from 12.5 to 17.5 per cent, depending on the rate of production. The Barker lease was put into a new company, Central Turner Petroleums Ltd, and later assigned to West Turner for 500,000 West Turner shares.

To help raise money for the new venture, both from the sale of shares and royalty units, Frank and George organized an investment firm, British Investments Limited, with George as manager. Early in 1937, West Turner picked up another adjoining forty-acre lease from Robert Kerr of Victoria for 570,000 treasury shares, giving the fledgling oil company 120 acres of leases, or three drill sites, on the edge of the Turner Valley field.

Each of the leases carried drilling commitments, and under the terms of the lease from Shore the first well had to be spudded by April, 1937, or the lease could be cancelled. Finding the money to drill was even more difficult than expected. By early 1937, British Investments had managed to raise some $70,000 through the sale of shares, but that was not enough to start drilling. Because of a shortage of equipment and resultant high prices charged by contractors, coupled with the commitments on each of its leases, West Turner had spent most of its initial funds on the purchase of a drilling rig. McMahon arranged for further financing through an Ontario brokerage house, but the Ontario Securities Commission required that all the company's leases be registered in its name. The snag was that a further $10,000 was payable out of production on the Barker lease, and even though the money was not due until after production had started, the lease could not be registered in West Turner's name until it had been paid. West Turner paid the $10,000, but by the time the arrangements with the Toronto firm were approved by the Ontario Securities Commission, the bloom was already off the boom in western oil stocks, and the Toronto firm backed out of the deal.

To make matters worse, some of the wells near West Turner's 120 acres turned out to be either dry holes or very small producers, and the informed opinion was that West Turner had a piece of moose pasture. In desperation, the West Turner directors tried to sell their leases to Imperial Oil, but Imperial turned them down with the opinion that the acreage was too far west on the structure and would produce only water. McMahon, shunting back and forth between Vancouver and Calgary by train, then attempted to arrange a merger with another small firm that held an adjacent lease, and $70,000 cash on hand, but after two months of negotiations that deal fell through. The future of West Turner looked grim. It had a drilling rig but no money to drill, leases that few people thought would be productive, and the deadline to start drilling on the Shore lease had already passed. Probably the only reason that the original owners did not cancel their leases to West Turner was that no one else seemed interested in drilling on their acreage.

It was at this stage that Victor Spencer put McMahon in touch with the person who, perhaps more than anyone else at the time, rescued West Turner from what seemed certain liquidation. Norman R. Whittall was born in Istanbul, Turkey, of British parents. After a classical education at Cambridge University, he came to Vancouver in 1912 to set up in the lumber business. In the balmy days of 1927-29 when everyone in Vancouver with any spare change seemed to be investing in the high-flying oil companies that were stripping liquids from Turner Valley gas, Whittall was plunging in with the rest. Once the lumber business collapsed on the heels of the 1929 stock market crash, the investment field seemed more attractive, and in partnership with Major J.S. Ross he formed a brokerage business, Ross Whittall Ltd, astutely dealing in mining and oil shares despite the afflictions of the Depression.

Whittall agreed to help raise financing for West Turner. Although not yet a director of the company, he joined Wilkinson, Smith, and McMahon on a company management committee that tried to steer the firm away from the shoals of bankruptcy. Enough money was raised from the sale of shares to spud in the first well on August 6, 1937, nine months after West Turner had been incorporated, but more funds would be needed to finish the hole. Whittall had hoped to involve other brokerage firms in underwriting West Turner shares, but no one was interested. "Under the most adverse market conditions, Mr Whittall took firm commitments on shares of the company and furnished enough money to keep the drilling going for a time and preserve the property," McMahon later wrote in a review of operations

49

for the company's directors. Without these efforts, he added, West Turner "would in all likelihood have lost its leases and the company have gone out of existence."

Prospects brightened in October when in defiance of expert opinions another well being drilled just 600 feet south of West Turner Number One was brought in as a large oil producer. Whittall was then able to reopen negotiations with Imperial Oil, and after two months of discussions reached an agreement whereby Imperial's subsidiary, Royalite Oil Company, would complete the well in return for payments from production.

While finances were being sought for the first well, McMahon had been able to win extensions of the drilling commitment on the forty-acre lease obtained from Robert Kerr and his associates, but now they too were getting impatient. Bill Graburn, a young Calgary lawyer who had set up a trust-company subsidiary for the Calgary investment and real estate firm of Toole, Peet Investments, Limited, was eager to obtain some business from the oil companies. Graburn helped McMahon line up some short-term bank loans and credit from the Oil Well Supply Company. Further financing was arranged with the underwriting of a block of shares and the sale of royalty units covering 25 per cent of the production from the Number Two well by Whittall, Victor Spencer, and McMahon. McMahon had agreed to put up $6,000, money he still had to find. By the end of the year, West Turner was drilling below 5,000 feet at its first well, was moving its own rig to spud in the second well, and had raised $161,000 by selling its shares at an average net to the company of less than seven cents each.

Early in 1938, West Turner issued another 500,000 shares to acquire the forty-acre lease that McMahon had purchased from Robert Barker and put into Central Turner Petroleums. West Turner now had a solid block of 160 acres of leases on the west edge of Turner Valley, and it faced a third drilling commitment. Grandoro Mines, an inactive gold mining company controlled by Victor Spencer, had a bit of cash in its treasury, and it agreed to put up $65,000 toward the cost of the third well in return for one-third of the production income. Further bank loans and credit from the Oil Well Supply Company and drilling contractor Snyder and Head completed the financing.

By mid-February, the directors felt so confident the company would survive that West Turner hired its first full-time employee, Allison Patrick Bowsher, a twenty-nine-year-old accountant from Oyama, British Columbia, who had been with the firm of Helliwell, Maclachlan & Co in Vancouver. In 1937, this company sent him to the offices of Frank and George McMahon in the Hall Building to do an audit on the books of Columbia Oils. By the time he had finished, Pat Bowsher found the books in something less than perfect order and suggested to the McMahon brothers that they could do a better job of keeping track of their complex financial affairs by hiring an accountant to serve as secretary-treasurer. A few months later, George phoned Bowsher and asked, "How much do you want, and when can you start work?" Pat's employer warned him he would not last more than six months with the McMahon brothers and assured him that he could always come back to work for Helliwell, Maclachlan. As it turned out, Bowsher stayed with West Turner and its successor company for more than thirty years, and the day would come when, as senior vice-president and treasurer, he could pick up the phone and in ten minutes negotiate a bank loan for as much as $10 million.

That day was not even imagined, except perhaps by the ebullient McMahon brothers, when the first annual meeting of West Turner shareholders was held in Vancouver in March, 1938. Robert Wilkinson, whose own business affairs had left little time for the fortunes of West Turner, resigned as president, but remained a director, to be succeeded by Norman Whittall. Bowsher was confirmed as secretary-treasurer, and three additional directors were elected to the board. Wendell Farris, the Vancouver lawyer, had served earlier on the board of the ill-fated London Pacific Exploration Company. George Martin, a prominent financier, had handled the sale of the "baby bonds" that built Mayor Gerry McGeer's new, expansive city hall and had promoted construction of the Burrard Street Bridge. In 1931, Martin had purchased the firm of Gillespie, Hart and Todd from John Hart, who had retired from business to enter politics; the company dealt in mortgages, real estate, and insurance. The third new director was Percy McKergow, another Vancouver investment dealer.

West Turner Number One was brought in by Royalite on April 17, 1938, as one of the largest oil wells in the Turner Valley field. From a depth of 7,274 feet it flowed at a rate of more than 1,300 barrels a day during extended tests. At the same time, West

Turner Number Two was drilling below 3,600 feet, and another rig was being moved in to drill the third well. Frank McMahon, it seemed, had at last made it as an oil producer. Before the end of 1938, West Turner had three good producing oil wells and a mountain of debt.

It was not an instant bonanza, however, and the financial affairs of West Turner remained precarious. Its ability to discharge its debts was impeded by a glut of oil on the local market. By mid-1938, the Turner Valley field was capable of producing some 40,000 barrels of oil per day, but the three prairie provinces required a supply of only 17,000 barrels a day. Within two months of the completion of West Turner Number One, the two buyers of Turner Valley oil, Royalite and British American Oil, had cut their purchases to 30 per cent of the available daily supply. To make matters worse, the price of Turner Valley oil had been reduced to absorb transportation costs for supplying refineries as distant as Winnipeg and to meet the competition from imported Montana oil. The price of Turner Valley oil had dropped from $1.55 a barrel in 1936 to $1.14 by 1938.

Aggressive oil promoters, no less than big oil companies, strive to keep as many irons in the fire as possible, because no one can tell which irons the hot coals of fortune will turn white-hot. There were few more aggressive than the McMahon brothers. Even as West Turner was being rescued from the brink, new ventures were being launched. In July, 1937, the McMahons, Whittall, and their associates formed British Pacific Oils Ltd to acquire 1,120 acres of oil leases from the Calgary & Edmonton Corporation. Half of this land was within what was thought might be the limits of the Turner Valley field. The corporation had freehold mineral rights on more than a million acres in southern Alberta from railway land grants that had originally been given to contractors Mackenzie and Mann. Lacking funds to drill all this acreage aggressively, C&E offered leases carrying modest annual rentals and production royalties.

In 1938, McMahon, Whittall, Calgary drilling contractor Clarence Snyder, Vancouver consulting mining engineer Jerry Wood, and Percival McKergow reorganized Central Turner Petroleums into Grease Creek Petroleums Limited to acquire 12,000 acres of leases on the Grease Creek structure 45 miles northwest of Turner Valley. Grease Creek pooled 3,500 acres of its leases with a similar amount held by the Northwest Company, a subsidiary of Imperial Oil, and the two firms committed $150,000 for a wildcat test that started in January, 1939.

During all this activity, McMahon had still not lost sight of his dream of developing a gas supply in the Peace River and piping it to Vancouver. In 1937, he commissioned further preliminary studies by consulting geologist Pete Sanderson, hired Jerry Wood to plot maps of possible pipeline routes, and stayed in contact with the politely interested officials of BC Electric. McMahon was not the only one with this particular vision. In February, 1938, the *Western Oil Examiner* reported that contracts had been signed "by important United States interests for the immediate drilling of a number of wells on the Pouce Coupe structure. . . . The eastern American interests will purchase all the gas obtained at three cents per thousand cubic feet. It is planned to pipe the gas to West Coast cities, one of the largest natural gas markets on the continent." The firm, Guardian Oil Company, did drill a well in the Pouce Coupe field near the old Northwest Company discovery, but no one bought the gas, and Guardian Oil went out of business in the early 1940s.

The lonely well on Sage Creek in the Flathead Valley slowly kept grinding through the Precambrian, but management of the company's activities was assumed by Calgary stockbroker Robert Wilkinson, no relation to the Robert Wilkinson who was the first president of the West Turner Petroleums. The Calgary Wilkinson raised an additional $100,000, was appointed managing director of Columbia Oils, and in October, 1937, drilling resumed at a depth of 5,800 feet. The funds were deemed sufficient to carry the hole to a projected 8,500 feet. The hole reached 8,000 feet the following April, when it was at last abandoned, nearly five years after it had been spudded, and still in Precambrian rock. Like earlier tests, the bit had slanted off at an angle so acute that McMahon once remarked that it might pop up through the surface if they had kept drilling long enough. Again, no one knew what vertical depth the hole had actually reached. It was not, however, McMahon's last attempt to find oil in the Flathead.

As 1938 closed, Frank McMahon could at last call himself an oilman: he had conceived, organized, and promoted a venture that was actually producing oil. But with oil a glut on the market, with prices slashed, with West Turner Petroleums deep in debt, his boast ten years earlier that he intended to become a millionaire seemed more distant than ever. West Turner was certainly not the vehicle that McMahon had hoped to promote for a multi-million dollar exploration program in the north country and a natural gas pipeline to Vancouver. But twenty-five months after it had been incorporated, West Turner was to be succeeded by the organization that would eventually pursue those goals – Pacific Petroleums Ltd.

CHAPTER FIVE

Pacific Petroleums

Saturday, January 14, 1939. In Rome, Neville Chamberlain and Benito Mussolini issued a joint communique confirming "a policy aiming effectively at the maintenance of peace." In Spain, Loyalist forces had "smashed through the rebel lines" west of Madrid, while in China, Japanese forces captured 21,000 prisoners, according to *The New York Times*. In Ottawa, the government announced plans to place guns at the Lions Gate Bridge and Point Grey at the entrance to Vancouver Harbour, "to repel possible raiding enemy ships." English actress Vivien Leigh had just been signed by Selznick International to play Scarlet O'Hara in "Gone With the Wind," while at Vancouver's Beacon Theatre, Sally Rand appeared with "her world famous fan dance." Spencer's Department Stores advertised "freshly minced beef" at six cents a pound; a six-year-old, four-room bungalow in South Vancouver was listed at $1,950, and 200 cubic feet of sawdust for household fuel cost $4.00. Shares of Amalgamated Oil Company had traded the previous day on the Vancouver Stock Exchange at seven-eights of one cent, and West Turner Petroleums had traded, for the last time, at eight cents.

It was the day that shareholders of West Turner Petroleums and British Pacific Oils met in Vancouver and approved the merger that created Pacific Petroleums Ltd. Under the merger plan, Pacific was to issue 800,000 shares for the assets of West Turner and 170,000 shares for the assets of British Pacific.

When the merger was completed, Pacific wound up with three producing oil wells, leases with fifteen more possible oil-well sites in Turner Valley, about 1,000 acres of wildcat leases of dubious value, a pile of debt, and a substantial stock interest in Grease

Creek Petroleums. The interest in Grease Creek was earned in lieu of rental for the Pacific rig used to drill the wildcat on the Grease Creek structure, and its value was strictly speculative.

The first directors of the new board were Norman Whittall (president), Jerry Wood, George Martin, Percy McKergow, and Wendell Farris. McMahon was not a director but was retained as manager to look after the company's field operations, which meant spending about half his time in Calgary.

Not all of the shareholders – or at least not all of the stock-market brokers who represented the shareholders – were enthusiastic about the merger. In the fashion of the day, many of the shareholders of West Turner held only street certificates, while the brokerage firms from which the shares had been purchased remained on the books as the registered owners. It was not considered important to have your ownership registered if the company in which you had invested was not paying dividends. The result was that at shareholders' meetings, the brokerage firms could vote shares they did not own and make their views known.

Recounting the situation a year later in a letter to the directors of Pacific, McMahon noted that the merger had been "severely criticized for several reasons by people ignorant of the oil situation in Alberta. It was considered bad business by these people for a producing company to pay 170,000 shares for the additional acreage acquired in Turner Valley." McMahon stated that subsequent drilling in the field had proven the value of the leases acquired from British Pacific. The criticism, he said, had been prompted by a drop in the stockmarket value of West Turner shares and came from "brokerage firms who had sold the shares to their clients at high prices and at large profits to themselves." West Turner shares had been called for trading on the Vancouver Stock Exchange in December, 1937, and had started out trading in a range of fifteen to seventeen cents, but thirteen months later, at the time of the merger, they had fallen to half that price. Clearly, despite its drilling success, West Turner had not been a winner on the stock market. It had, however, suffered less in a depressed market than many other Turner Valley oil companies that were doing at least as well with their drilling.

As managing director, Frank McMahon had borne the brunt of the criticism, and it was Wendell Farris's suggestion that because of this he should not be represented on the board of

Pacific Petroleums. Farris wanted a new name, and a new image.

Pacific Petroleums did not start life in a frenzy of activity. Its first priorities were to keep down expenses, generate revenue from its three oil wells, and pay off some of the debts. But for a number of pressing reasons the company could not delay further drilling on its Turner Valley leases for too long, in spite of low prices for oil and the field's excess production capacity. The leases carried drilling commitments, and if drilling were postponed, they would be cancelled. In addition, there was always the possibility that the oil under Pacific's leases could be drained by the nearby wells of other companies if Pacific did not get its holes down. General manager Frank McMahon continually pressed the more cautious directors that the company must forge ahead.

Following completion of West Turner Number Three well, now renamed Pacific Number Three, no further drilling was carried out by the company for more than a year. During this period, Whittall and McMahon discussed the possibility of raising money by a bond issue with several investment dealers, including John McMahon who was then working with the Vancouver investment firm of Hal Holland and Company. Whittall tried to interest Toronto investment firms in a share issue, without success.

In June, 1939, the directors approved an option on the sale of 500,000 shares of Pacific to Percy McKergow at a price of fifty cents per share. It was understood that McKergow would try to sell the shares to potential investors in London at fifty-five cents, thus earning a potential fee of five cents a share. The directors cautiously agreed to contribute $5,000 toward McKergow's travel expenses, provided that he sold at least 200,000 shares.

Armed with a detailed file on Pacific's operations prepared by Frank and George and letters of introduction to the contacts Frank had made in England five years earlier, McKergow set sail for London. There he was introduced to a visiting investor from Paris, Andre Moreau. McKergow cabled Whittall that Moreau had offered to buy the 500,000 shares at 55 cents. The deal also included an option until December 1941 on a further 530,000 shares at 75 cents, the balance of Pacific's authorized capital. The deal was subject to a favourable report by French engineer

Andre Fonville, who, McKergow cabled, "must go to Canada immediately." The fee for Fonville's report was to be $6,000, including $5,000 payable by Pacific and $1,000 by McKergow.

Whittall responded by cable: "Holding directors meeting tomorrow. Personally think contribution [to] engineer's expenses very excessive. Suggest travelling expenses only and oppose long option balance treasury." The directors agreed to pay up to $3,000 toward the cost of the report by the engineer and to reduce the size of the option from 530,000 to 300,000 shares. By the time Fonville had completed his report, the Second World War had started, and the deal fell through. Had it not been for the outbreak of hostilities in Europe, control of Pacific may well have been transferred to France.

The implication of the war on the development of Canada's only significant oil field was quickly perceived. "As we go to press Saturday afternoon, Herr Hitler's bombers have been blasting Polish cities for nearly forty-eight hours, Polish troops are holding off Nazi legions on three borders, and Britain, France and their Empires have mobilized to fulfil their obligations to the Poles," Carl Nickle reported in his *Daily Oil Bulletin* on September 2, 1939. What would war mean for Alberta oil? "Increased returns from wells will likely be reflected within a few months in rising stock market values. . . . In the case of oil royalties . . . war will in all probability mean increased monthly returns," Nickle wrote.

The war did create a need for all the oil that Turner Valley could produce, but there were no windfall profits. The federal government moved quickly to put a firm clamp on prices, with rigid controls administered by federal Oil Controller George Cottrelle.

In Calgary, during the late fall of 1939, with the help of Bill Graburn of Toole, Peet Investments, McMahon was still trying to finance the drilling of the company's next two wells on the basis of a bank loan and credit arrangements with the oil field supply companies and drilling contractor Snyder and Head. An application for a $50,000 loan from the Bank of Nova Scotia was turned down by the bank's head office in Toronto. Another application was made to the Royal Bank, where Calgary manager Ernie McLean suggested that it would be better to take out a loan for $150,000 and make the bank the company's sole creditor. But this, too, was turned down by the head office in Montreal. Finally, arrangements were made for a line of credit of $105,000 from the National Supply Company and the Oil Well Supply Company, $50,000 from Synder and Head, and a loan from the Royal Bank for $25,000. With these funds, Pacific was able to move in two rigs to start drilling its fourth and fifth wells in December, 1939.

At the same time, Pat Bowsher moved to Calgary and opened Pacific's first office there, in small quarters in the Toole, Peet Building. The staff then consisted of Bowsher, a part-time stenographer, and the part-time services of McMahon as general manager. By March, the company had paid off its bank loans and the debts to the supply companies and drilling contractor with its first bond issue, a $250,000 issue jointly underwritten by the Vancouver investment company of C.M. Oliver and the Calgary firm of Carlile and McCarthy.

Pacific's first annual meeting of shareholders, held June 19, 1940, in the board room of the Vancouver Stock Exchange, confirmed that ownership of Pacific was widely held, with no one clearly in control. The largest registered shareholder represented at the meeting was Rhea Barrett, with 188,139 shares, or some 20 per cent of the 970,000 issued shares. Rhea Barrett was, in fact, an employee of Ross Whittall Limited, and the shares registered in her name were owned by several hundred investors who had been issued street certificates. It was a mechanism that allowed the board to exercise some measure of control over the company and might help thwart any unfriendly take-over bid, not that anyone was clamouring to acquire Pacific Petroleums. Aside from Miss Barrett, the other major registered shareholders represented at the meeting included Norman Whittall with 47,306 shares (less than 5 per cent ownership), Victor Spencer's Grandoro Mines with 36,441 shares, Frank McMahon with 24,820 shares, and George McMahon with 2,000 shares.

Frank McMahon had been at pains to outline to the Pacific directors how his services as general manager had saved the company large sums of money, as indeed they had. In a memorandum to the directors, McMahon calculated that by purchasing its own drilling rig Pacific had saved $50,000 in drilling its number two and four wells and had also earned 155,000 shares of Grease Creek Petroleums through the use of this rig to drill the wildcat on the Grease Creek structure. Further large savings were effected by supervising the drilling arrangements for the other wells (as opposed to letting turnkey drilling contracts), by the judicious purchase of equipment, and in the operation of the wells themselves. All in all, McMahon estimated that by the time the fifth well was completed his management would save the company a total of $324,000.

Not all the directors, apparently, were that impressed; they figured that even more money could be saved by dispensing with the services of Frank McMahon. The decision was recorded in the minutes of a meeting of the directors held on December 17, 1940:

In view of the risk involved in the company drilling these wells on a cost basis, it was decided that estimates be obtained on a turnkey contract and, if satisfactory, this method be favoured in drilling further wells. At the same time an investigation to be made of the possibility of obtaining a drilling superintendent who could embody the duties and responsibilities of Frank McMahon and Snyder and Head. Inasmuch as on a drilling program of two wells per year, $10,000.00 per year would be paid to Synder, and inasmuch as Mr McMahon's salary and expenses approximate $6,000.00 per year, the directors felt that a good drilling superintendent to cover the duties of the two above-mentioned parties may save the company considerable money. It was acknowledged by all directors that Mr McMahon had carried out his duties in the best interest of the company and given his full efforts in this direction, but it was also acknowledged that the necessity of cutting down overhead and of avoiding unnecessary drilling risks, made the policy above-mentioned imperative, and that as a result the president explain to Mr McMahon, asking his wholehearted co-operation in the matter.

To effect this new policy, the directors approved a contract with Oil Ventures Limited to operate the company's three producing oil wells and supervise start-up and completion of wells four and five.

Before the directors got around to firing McMahon, he tendered his resignation, effective January 31, 1941. "This step has been made necessary by my acceptance of what appears to be a very promising position with a development company operating in Turner Valley," McMahon wrote to the board on December

28. "May I assure you of my willingness and desire to be of assistance to your company at any time in the future."

Neil McQueen, a man who had grown up with Canada's oil industry, took over the job of supervising Pacific's producing and drilling operations. McQueen was born in 1900 in Petrolia, Ontario, where the world's first commercial oil well had been drilled in 1858, one year before Colonel Edwin Drake ushered in the US oil industry at Titusville, Pennyslvania. For a few decades, Petrolia was one of the world's major oil areas, and Neil's father, Alex McQueen, was in charge of production operations for one of the major oil companies there. In 1915, the senior McQueen joined Imperial Oil as vice-president in charge of its new exploration and production department. Under Alex's direction, Imperial was soon drilling for oil from the Montana border to the Arctic, as well as in South America with its subsidiary, International Petroleum Company.

From the time he was sixteen, Neil McQueen spent his summers working on Imperial's geological field parties throughout western and northern Canada. He was the wellsite geologist at Royalite Number Four when it found the big Mississippian gas zone in 1924. In 1927, Neil left Imperial Oil for Vancouver, where he was involved in several mining ventures, and in 1931 he participated, along with a Vancouver group headed by A.C.T. Taylor, in the formation of Bralorne Mines Limited. In 1932, Bralorne put its mine into production in the Bridge River area, next door to Victor Spencer's Pioneer Gold Mines. The Bridge River mine, brought into production for less than $300,000, ultimately yielded more than $90 million worth of gold, and Bralorne's shares jumped from fifty cents in 1932 to $17 in 1934. In the Depression years, the liquid sometimes called "black gold" was seldom as profitable as the real thing.

McQueen did not manage to hang onto the small fortune he made with Bralorne, and after the 1936 discovery of the oil column at Turner Valley he tried his luck with a couple of one-well companies called Deep Oils and Crude Oil. His holding company, Oil Ventures, operated the two wells and performed contract drilling supervision and well operating services with Ken Doze. Oil Ventures' newest client in 1941 was Pacific Petroleums, and it eventually purchased McQueen's companies and hired him as managing director.

Frank McMahon was no longer part of the team running the company he had launched four years earlier with a $100 option on an 80-acre lease. It would be nearly seven years before he would become active again in the affairs of Pacific Petroleums. But he did maintain an association with Pacific: as an investor who still owned about a 2.5 per cent interest in the company, as a participant with Pacific in a number of oil ventures, and by continued close collaboration with Norman Whittall.

Success remained as distant as ever. Any hope of pursuing the vision of a gas line to Vancouver had been deferred by the war. Early in 1941, Frank and George moved to Calgary where the two brothers promoted a string of ill-fated oil ventures, and unwittingly Frank became involved in Duff Pattullo's similarily ill-fated attempts at wildcatting by the BC government.

CHAPTER SIX

Pattullo's Petroleum Pitch

Duff Pattullo was not a friend of the big oil companies. Or even the small ones for that matter.

He campaigned on a slogan of "Work and Wages" to return the Liberal Party to power in British Columbia with an overwhelming election victory on November 2, 1933. A seasoned politician, Pattullo had already sat in the legislature for seventeen years, including twelve as a cabinet minister and five as leader of the opposition.

He was a man of some contradiction. A passionate, and compassionate, champion of the people, he was a loquacious orator, master of "purple, polysyllabic phrases," according to newsman Bruce Hutchison, and deeply motivated by his concern for the Depression's unemployed. Yet he could order riots by unemployed workers quashed with ruthless force. Warm hearted, sometimes impulsive, he was often viewed with affectionate regard, but he was personally reserved and aloof. Short in stature, he was always a natty dresser with a streak of vanity. "I notice from snapshots taken that my clothes give me the appearance of what I am not, namely old," he wrote his tailor shortly after he became Premier of British Columbia. "The kind of clothes that should be built are those which will make one appear as young as one's contemporaries think they are." He was then aged sixty.

Pattullo was uncompromising in his convictions and inclined to be suspicious. He steadfastly refused all pressures to form a coalition government with the Conservative Party that was first suggested to meet the exigencies of the Depression and later to deal with emergency conditions during the Second World War.

After eight years in office, his determined rejection of a coalition led to his forced withdrawal due to the opposition of his own party. He was succeeded by his old friend, the former Minister of Finance, John Hart. It was, Pattullo later wrote, the result of "a constant underground agitation against myself personally," instigated, he was convinced, by the "oil interests."

Pattullo had a life-long conviction that there were large reserves of oil to be found in the Peace River area and that they could be found and developed by the government to the great benefit of all British Columbians. He was not persuaded by the arguments of the oil companies that it was too risky a business for governments. "Oil drilling has been described as a costly and a gambling adventure," he once declared in a prepared statement. "Nevertheless, the oil companies appear to have greatly prospered from this form of gambling. Some of them have enough cold cash and quick assets to pay off the entire debt of British Columbia at one crack."

As Minister of Lands, Pattullo had already instigated the government's first search for oil, withdrawing lands in the Peace River area from leasing in 1919 and following this with a series of six shallow holes in the foothills near Hudson Hope. Dr Tolmie's Conservative government had reversed his policy by reopening provincially-owned mineral rights to private exploration in 1932, but shortly after he had been elected premier, Pattullo once more imposed the ban and looked forward to another government wildcatting program.

Before this next government oil venture got underway, Pattullo was locked in battle with the oil companies on another front: gasoline marketing and pricing. When he reinstated the Peace River leasing ban, Pattullo also appointed Mr Justice M.A. Macdonald of the BC Supreme Court as a one-man Royal Commission to investigate the marketing and pricing of coal and petroleum products. After a three-year study that cost $108,000, Macdonald's 1,447-page report was tabled in the legislature. It claimed that the oil companies were charging too little for their fuel oil, thus unfairly undercutting the coal industry, while charging too much for gasoline. Gasoline was being sold and distributed by wasteful and extravagant methods, including too many service stations, according to the report. The legislature passed the Coal and Petroleum Products Control Board Act in 1937, and Pattullo appointed Dr W.A. Carrothers as the sole member of the new board, giving him sweeping powers to set prices for coal and petroleum products. This appointment marked "the most revolutionary change in the constitutional history of British Columbia since Confederation," thundered the *Vancouver Province*. "Dr Carrothers has been clothed with Supreme Court powers in matters affecting BC's business community, answerable only to the Lieutenant-Governor-in-Council – and not to the Legislature."

Dr Carrothers ordered a reduction of five cents a gallon for gasoline in the Vancouver area, pegging it at 5 per cent less than the wholesale price in Los Angeles and 12 per cent less than in nearby Seattle. The oil companies retained Senator J.W. de B. Farris, appealed the validity of the act to the Supreme Court of Canada, and lost. These companies then refused to supply gasoline in Vancouver, except for such essential services as the fire department, police, and doctors. Within twenty-four hours, all but two of the service stations in Vancouver had run out of gasoline. The embargo lasted a week and was lifted by the oil companies only after Dr Carrothers increased the price by one cent a gallon.

Five days after gasoline deliveries had resumed, the legislature sat in an emergency session called by Pattullo, and on May 10, 1940, it passed the Petroleum Powers Act. The act gave the government, without any further reference to the legislature, the authority to take over all or any part of the petroleum industry in British Columbia. Under the terms of the act, the government could acquire, own, operate, or lease any petroleum refinery or distribution plant in the province; buy shares of any oil company; take over drilling operations; and form a Crown corporation to operate such undertakings. Three Liberal members broke rank with the party to join the Conservatives in voting against the act, but with the support of the CCF party it passed by a margin of thirty-two to ten.

Pattullo told the legislature that, "Gasoline is so vital in the life of our people, it seems unreasonable that its sale and distribution should be at the sole dictation and control of the companies who sell it." He claimed that the act was necessary to ensure supplies of this "essential commodity."

There were two strongly conflicting public views. One side agreed with Pattullo, who accused the oil companies of trying to "set up a sort of gasoline super-state." The other side believed

Pattullo was acting like a dictator. The *Toronto Globe and Mail* declared:

> This sort of thing may be all right in Germany and Russia and Italy where ordinary folk cannot call their souls their own, but it is all wrong in a democratic country like Canada where we still cherish British liberty and justice. There are ways of dealing with injustices here without political dictatorship. . . . Disregard of economic law will destroy the very foundations of democratic freedom. What is the use of fighting totalitarianism abroad if we are going to permit it to rear up its ugly head in Canada?

During the debate in the legislature, Pattullo had said that the bill was introduced solely to deal with the "exigencies" resulting from the gasoline embargo and not to control business in the province. But he also said, "We might need to use this act ourselves. As you know we are now drilling in the Peace River country and expect to find oil."

"Aye, there's the rub," commented Toronto's *Saturday Night* magazine:

> The BC government is drilling for oil in the Peace River and there is more than a sneaking suspicion abroad that all of this discrimination against the oil companies; all this making provision in advance to harass and, if necessary, put private oil companies out of business when the step is deemed necessary, has some very direct bearing on the government's own oil drilling campaign. If, as Premier Pattullo predicts, the government does strike oil before it has bankrupted the taxpayers by drilling wells, it will be very nice – from the government's point of view – to simply eliminate all competition without even having to call on the legislature.

The contractor that was drilling in the Peace River for the BC government was a firm with which Frank McMahon was soon to be involved.

In a memorandum reviewing the history of the government's ill-fated Pine River Well Number One prepared for Premier John Hart in December, 1941, Deputy Minister of Mines John Walker reported that in 1938 he had recommended to Mines Minister J.W. Asselstine that the government open the area to tender for private exploration. Walker had advised Asselstine that if the government were to undertake exploration, it should plan to spend $100,000 to $200,000 for preliminary geological surveys and up to $3 million for drilling. It was not the type of advice that Pattullo wanted to hear. The preliminary field work was undertaken in 1938 and 1939, and the following year the government was ready to let a contract for an exploratory well to test a large structure at Commotion Creek, a tributary of Pine River in the foothills some eighty miles west of Hudson Hope.

In January, 1940, H.R. Milner, chairman of Anglo-Canadian Oil Company Limited, and Grant Spratt, general manager, met with Pattullo and Asselstine in Victoria to discuss a contract proposal prepared by Drilling Contractors Limited, a wholly-owned subsidiary of Anglo-Canadian. Drilling Contractors, then the largest firm of its kind in Canada, offered essentially a cost-plus type of deal which suggested that if no problems were encountered, the well would cost approximately $300,000 to $350,000. Another proposal was then received from Newell and Chandler Limited offering to drill the well to 8,000 feet for $250,000. The contract with Newell and Chandler was signed on January 30, the heavy rig and equipment were moved to the remote drill site during the winter, and the well was spudded in on June 4.

Newell and Chandler Limited had been formed in 1937 by J.F. "Shorty" Chandler, a driller from Montana, and Matt Newell. Newell had been division manager for Canada and the US Rocky Mountain region for Hughes Tool Company, the leading maker of oil-well drilling bits.

Drilling at BC Pine River Number One (also referred to as the Commotion Creek well) was tougher than expected. By the time the hole had reached 5,000 feet, a total of 258 drilling bits had been used, and Newell and Chandler was clearly not making any money on the job. On October 8, according to a memo to Hart, Newell told Walker that, "If they drilled another well, it would have to be on an entirely different contract basis." On October 19, things got a lot tougher. At a depth of 5,084 feet, the drill rods twisted off, and it took eleven months of expensive fishing and sidetracking around the lost bit before the hole was cleared. "The twist-off was due to negligence on the part of the contractor's crew who, shortly before the twist-off, were all found to be asleep on the job," Walker reported to Hart.

The fishing job was still underway when Frank McMahon first

became associated with Newell and Chandler. He had left Pacific in January, 1941, to take a job as vice-president and general manager, as well as a major shareholder, in a new firm, Drillers & Producers Limited. President and managing director of the company was Matt Newell, and other directors were G.E. Watt, Alberta production manager of British American Oil, and Reg Carlile of the Calgary investment firm of Carlile and McCarthy. Drillers & Producers was set up to develop oil production on its own account, as well as to purchase the assets of Newell and Chandler for $460,000. Most of the money was to be paid out of future revenues over a number of years. Newell and Chandler would then operate as a wholly-owned subsidiary of Drillers & Producers; the major shareholders were McMahon and Newell. Shorty Chandler had retired from the business because of poor health and died in Montana two years later. Newell was primarily responsible for drilling at Drillers & Producers, while McMahon handled the production end of the business.

Aside from its agreement to buy Newell and Chandler's rigs, the first venture of Drillers & Producers was an agreement to drill five wells at Turner Valley on sub-leases from Pacific Petroleums. Whittall told a meeting of Pacific directors in January, 1941: "Investigation had shown a serious shortage of drilling equipment in Turner Valley and the vital necessity of speedily drilling the proven leases of the company. . . . The company's revenue is insufficient to develop these leases as speedily as desirable." D&P would put two of its rigs to work to drill these wells. The cost would be financed in part by the sale of royalty units, some of which Pacific had agreed to buy, while others would be sold by the McMahon brothers' British Investments Limited. D&P would wind up with a share of production revenue. In March, D&P completed an agreement with Carlile and McCarthy Ltd for the sale of $500,000 in debentures. British Investments also participated in the public offering of these debentures.

While the Newell and Chandler rigs were busy at Turner Valley, by December, 1941, its rig at the Commotion Creek well in northern British Columbia was standing idle in a contract dispute with the provincial government. A year of expensive fishing and sidetracking had been necessary to clear the obstruction in the hole, and the firm was losing money. Newell refused to resume drilling until he had obtained new contract terms from the BC government, and Deputy Mines Minister John Walker was not in a generous mood. "To sum up our dealings with Newell and Chandler Limited, it now appears to me that they submitted in the first place a low contract for the sole purpose of obtaining the work and that they had no intention of abiding by it unless everything went extremely well in their favour," Walker wrote to John Hart, who had just taken over as premier from Duff Pattullo.

Walker figured that Matt Newell had another reason for seeking more money for the drilling job. He noted that the firm had been taken over by Drillers & Producers:

And unquestionably Newell was trying to get something out of the government so that the $500,000 of 6 per cent, five-year sinking fund debentures, being a specific mortgage on the shares of Newell and Chandler Limited and a floating charge on all the company's present and future assets, could be sold. In plain English, they have taken a licking on the contract and are trying to get compensation from the government to complete the deal with Drillers & Producers Limited, out of which Newell will personally get a considerable amount of cash.

Ultimately, the government completed a hard-nosed agreement with Newell and Chandler to resume drilling. It allowed the firm to minimize its losses but provided no opportunity to earn a profit on the job. The well was finally completed on September 14, 1942, at a depth of 6,940 feet. The BC government's latest venture in wildcatting was a dry hole that had taken two years and three months to drill at a cost of $750,000, three times as much as the original contract price.

With the government's enthusiasm for wildcatting rapidly disappearing down the hole at Commotion Creek, it seemed an appropriate time to enquire whether the provincially-owned oil and gas rights in the Peace River area might be made available for leasing. Still thinking of developing a supply of natural gas for Vancouver, Frank McMahon organized a group of potential investors, including Norman Whittall, Victor Spencer, George Martin, and Pacific Petroleums, to seek exploration permits from the government in Victoria. On March 23, 1942, the Pacific board authorized Whittall "to invest not more than $1,250" in a syndicate "which may be formed to acquire acreage . . . in the Peace River block."

Victoria, however, decided that the suspected large but unproven oil reserves should be developed as a war-time measure by the federal government. The need for additional oil supplies was critical in 1942, and a supply from the Peace River area would be tremendously important to North American defence requirements. Ten thousand troops of the US Army Engineering Corps had already started work on the 1,600-mile Alaska Highway from Dawson Creek, BC, to Fairbanks, Alaska, to defend against possible Japanese invasion. This defence effort would require oil, and nothing could be more handy than a supply at Peace River, virtually alongside the military road then being hacked out of the wilderness.

On April 2, 1942, nine days after the Pacific board approved a maximum of $1,250 to acquire an interest in Peace River acreage, John Hart announced that the BC government was offering the oil rights of the entire area to the federal government, without any provincial taxes, royalties, or other revenue for the duration of the war and one year thereafter. "The province is not desirous of receiving one cent in return from the Dominion Government during the war," Premier Hart announced. "The desire is to make this a forthright gift of British Columbians to Canada's war effort in order to meet the existing shortage of oil and gasoline." He added that the provincial government had decided "to make this offer before considering proposals from any private interests."

Ottawa was vitally interested in seeing an aggressive search for and possibly development of the hoped for Peace River oil supplies, but the two governments could not agree on the terms for undertaking the project. Already stretched to the limit in its frantic war efforts, the federal government did not want to burden itself further by going into the wildcatting business. In fact, it wanted to see the task undertaken by a group of oil companies. That was not what Victoria had in mind. It had hoped that the federal government would undertake the effort itself, then after the war turn over to the province any oil producing business that had been established. It was not eager to forgo royalty and lease revenues if the exploration rights were to be assigned to oil companies.

70

On May 27 and 28, 1942, federal officials led by Oil Controller George Cottrelle and his technical assistant, George Hume, met to discuss the matter in Victoria with Premier Hart, Deputy Minister John Walker, and other provincial officials. Cottrelle presented Hart with a proposal developed by four oil companies: Imperial, Gulf, Shell, and Standard Oil of British Columbia (a subsidiary of Standard Oil of California). These companies proposed to spend $500,000 a year on exploration and drilling over a five-year period. In return, they wanted exclusive exploration rights to an area of 18.5 million acres during this time. After five years they wanted to be able to lease 10 per cent of the area on a long-term basis, with the remaining 90 per cent reverting to the provincial government. The leases, they proposed, would carry an annual rental of ten cents per acre, plus 10 per cent production royalty.

"Mr Cottrelle made it clear that the Dominion Government was not going into the oil business, but that it wanted the Peace River area developed immediately by a strong oil group," John Walker reported in his notes on the meeting. In Walker's view, "It was apparent that the oil companies wanted to tie up all possible structures in the entire foothills area of BC."

The first day of discussions failed to produce any agreement, and the group met again the following day. According to Walker's file memorandum:

The same points were discussed, some more bluntly, and it was made very clear to the Oil Controller that the Government of British Columbia was interested in finding and producing oil and not in putting its potential oil fields away for future use by the oil companies, if and when they might wish to develop them.

British Columbia finally made a counter-offer to the oil companies. The term of the exclusive exploration rights to the 18.5 million acres was reduced from 5 years to 3, the area that could be retained under lease was reduced to 100,000 acres, the annual lease rental was increased from 10 to 15 cents per acre, and the production royalty was increased from 10 per cent to 15 per cent. The oil companies were not prepared to undertake exploration under these terms.

The following month, C.D. Howe, then Federal Minister of

71

Munitions and Supply, wrote to Hart urging a speedy "understanding" to allow an immediate start on exploration:

> If the results of the survey are favourable, we must plan for a reasonably large operation, as a small supply of oil is of little value for our needs. This will involve a very large expenditure on development, and refining and pipeline facilities. Whether the development is undertaken by the Federal Government, as such, or by private interests, or by a combination of both, we must have sufficient acreage to permit the amortization of our investment.

But no understanding was reached. Instead, the Canol project was pushed ahead to supply Alaska's war-time petroleum requirements. Paid for by the US Army, the $134 million Canol project has been described as the largest single construction project of the Second World War. It involved the development of the Norman Wells oil field on the edge of the Arctic Circle in the Northwest Territories, construction of a 600-mile four-inch pipeline across a formidable range of mountains from Norman Wells to Fairbanks, building a refinery at Fairbanks, and laying 1,000 miles of smaller diameter pipeline to carry the refined products to military bases. It may have been just as well that the war effort did not rely on Peace River oil. By 1982, no oil fields had been found within the 18.5 million acres of BC foothills that the oil companies proposed to explore, although large gas fields have been discovered, and oil production has been developed farther east on the plains of the Peace River country.

Failing to reach agreement with Ottawa, Victoria drew up regulations under which it would be prepared to open up exploration along its foothills' belt to any oil companies that were interested. The oil companies still were interested, providing the terms were right. On February 23, 1944, representatives of Imperial, Gulf, Shell, and Standard Oil of BC again met with Premier Hart and his officials to discuss the draft regulations that the provincial government had prepared.

"From the conversation it appeared to me that the companies represented were prepared to undertake a large exploration and development programme and, if the results were satisfactory, to go into the oil business in a big way," John Walker reported in a memorandum on this meeting. "They were definitely not interested in taking up small acreage or developing for the local market." Premier Hart, however, "advised that the province could not give them the large concessions they asked, and though disappointed, they went away understanding the difficulties the government would experience in granting what amounted to the sole rights to develop the oil resources of a fairly large section of the possible oil-bearing territory of the province." The oil companies were not the only ones to be disappointed. "I told Mr Hart it was a good deal for the province, and he agreed," Walker wrote. "However, no one supported the deal in caucus."

Four months later, in June, 1944, British Columbia's new Petroleum and Natural Gas Act came into force. For the first time in twenty years it allowed any oil company to acquire exploration rights in the Peace River area. No oil companies were interested in acquiring acreage on the terms then offered by the government. Moreover, only the foothills' belt was opened for exploration, while the reserve continued in effect on the remainder of northeastern British Columbia, including the area where Frank McMahon suspected there was a large, shallow blanket of natural gas that could supply Vancouver.

Although Ottawa and Victoria failed to reach an agreement for government war-time financing of the supposedly large Peace River oil reserves, Norman Whittall and Frank McMahon did succeed in persuading the government to help finance further development of Canada's major oil supply, the Turner Valley field.

Carl Nickle had been right in his forecast that war would bring a demand for all the oil Turner Valley could produce but wrong in his belief that it would result in greater profits for the oil companies. The cost of drilling a well at Turner Valley had increased to between $200,000 and $300,000 by 1942, but Federal Oil Controller George Cottrelle had allowed the average wellhead price for oil produced in the field to increase by only eight cents a barrel to $1.22. This was twenty-three cents less than in 1936. More wells would have to be drilled if the field was to produce at its maximum rate. There were a great many proven sites still to be drilled, and the extent of the field had not yet been fully defined. Only the larger producing wells could provide enough revenue to recover costs, and investors were reluctant to put up funds to drill on more speculative or marginal sites.

No oil company at Turner Valley seemed more cautious or penny-pinching than Pacific Petroleums. As the company's second annual report to its shareholders noted, its sub-lease to Drillers & Producers on five well sites was made, in part, "to relieve the company of the risks and responsibilities attendant upon continuation of its own drilling operations." Pacific was quite content to allow McMahon's new venture to assume that risk. A further savings of $150 a month was achieved, the company's minute books recorded, "through allowing the secretary [Pat Bowsher] to act as secretary for Drillers & Producers," though Bowsher was cautioned "to assure absolute privacy in matters affecting the operation of our company." At another meeting, Victor Spencer, who joined the board after Wendell Farris was appointed Chief Justice of the Supreme Court of British Columbia, suggested that, "every possible effort be made to further reduce the company's overhead." Whittall responded, "The company's wells were being operated as cheap, if not cheaper, than most wells in the valley." Percy McKergow commented that the company's total salaries of $6,000 per year hardly seemed excessive.

Given Pacific's limited financial resources, the cautious attitude of the directors, and the low price for oil, Whittall advised the directors that it "would be of great value to Pacific Petroleums" if government financing could be obtained for the additional drilling that was required. It was an approach that was not endorsed by all of the Turner Valley producers. "The oil industry doesn't want the government to finance development," Carl Nickle declared in his *Oil Bulletin* in December, 1941. "There is no need for that. . . . The greatest stimulant to oil field development would be the upping of light crude prices to their current competitive level." But Oil Controller George Cottrelle was not about to raise the lid on oil prices, and government financing appeared to be the only way to speed development.

Norman Whittall and Frank McMahon spent considerable time to prepare the brief that Whittall carried to C.D. Howe in Ottawa early in 1942. The result, a year later, was the formation of the federal government's Wartime Oils Limited to advance drilling costs to the Turner Valley oil companies. The funds were repayable from 100 per cent of initial production of any well thus financed and carried an interest rate of 3.5 per cent, plus a nominal royalty. If a well financed by Wartime Oils was a dry hole, however, the loan was not repayable. In 1943, Wartime

Oils spent $4 million to finance the drilling of twenty wells in Turner Valley, including several by Pacific Petroleums.

With its risks carried by Wartime Oils and Drillers & Producers, Pacific Petroleums prospered. Drillers & Producers did not. The end of the war found Pacific with fifteen producing wells at Turner Valley that generated net earnings of $174,000 a year, the debts were paid off, $200,000 was sitting in the treasury, and modest investments had been made in other companies.

The $500,000 bond issue of Drillers & Producers was not a success; its drilling subsidiary, Newell and Chandler, ran into costly problems at more than just the Commotion Creek well, and the company's three producing oil wells generated more revenues for the leaseholders than they did for Drillers & Producers. Early in 1941, McMahon purchased Pacific's drilling equipment for $32,000. But at a directors' meeting nearly a year later it was noted that $20,500 was still owed on the purchase, and "Mr Whittall was authorized to make arrangements for the early liquidation of this account." Another meeting in February, 1943, observed that Drillers & Producers "needed $10,000 very badly."

McMahon appeared before the Pacific directors in July, 1943, seeking help in posting the performance bonds required for D&P to obtain drilling funds from Wartime Oils. "The directors," noted the minutes, "expressed their unwillingness to support such a credit unless the reward was in line with the risk," and Percy McKergow said it looked as though D&P was going to wind up in receivership. But Reg Smith "thought that the business had possibilities of being well worthwhile to the Pacific Petroleums Ltd, and that every effort should be made to assist Drillers & Producers." After further negotiations, Pacific advanced D&P a total of $343,000 in the form of debentures and purchased a one-third interest for less than $16,000. The other two-thirds was owned by McMahon and Newell. McMahon later sold his interest to Matt Newell, and D&P and its subsidiary, Newell and Chandler, eventually went out of business after Pacific had recovered its advances.

From early 1941 to early 1944, Pacific's field operations were being handled under contract by Neil McQueen's Oil Ventures Limited. Pacific then bought out McQueen's interests, including Allied Oil producers Ltd, which by then owned Oil Ventures, which in turn controlled Deep Oils and Crude Oils. At that time, the whole operation held an interest in four oil wells. McQueen was then elected to the Pacific board and appointed managing director, succeeding Norman Whittall, who continued as president.

After the war, the directors of Pacific were faced with an important decision as to the future of the company. There were two basic options. They could simply produce the oil from their Turner Valley wells, pay out all the earnings in dividends, and in due course the company would simply go out of business. That was the safest approach, often followed in the mining business by such companies as Reno Gold Mines and Victor Spencer's Pioneer Gold Mines. The other approach was to try and stay in the oil business by looking for new reserves to replace the declining production at Turner Valley. If successful, in the long run this approach could provide a far greater return to the shareholders, but if efforts to find more oil failed, Pacific could still go out of business without providing any return to its investors. The board was divided, but under the urging of Whittall and McQueen cautiously decided to try the latter approach. The vicissitudes of searching for oil turned out to be a rude shock.

One of the most promising areas appeared to be on the plains of southern Alberta where in 1944 a subsidiary of Standard Oil of California found a small amount of oil near the village of Princess, 110 miles east of Calgary. There was an immediate rush to acquire leases in the area, both from the Alberta government and from the Canadian Pacific Railway that held a large block of oil and gas rights throughout the southern part of the province. In the vanguard of this rush were Frank and George McMahon; they picked up extensive acreage and formed a string of hopeful oil companies: Princess Petroleums, Empire Petroleums, Atlantic Oil Company, and others. Some of these were formed in association with Norman Whittall. Pacific, working with the McMahon companies, joined the play by participating in a number of wells. The Princess area kept teasing the oil men during the next few years with encouraging flows of oil on initial tests at a number of wells. "This at last looks like the real McCoy," California Standard vice-president John O. Galloway declared in November, 1946, when Princess Syndicate Number Three flowed 180 barrels of oil during a 24-hour test. But Princess turned out to be no more than a squirt can in the world of oil, the wells produced more salt water than anything else.

To arm itself for a more aggressive role as an explorer for oil, in early 1946 Pacific raised $227,500 through an issue of 275,000 shares, the first issue since the company was formed in 1939. With this cash and the revenue from Turner Valley, Pacific participated not only in the Princess play, but also in what looked like a foolproof venture in the Cat Creek area of Montana. Neil McQueen picked up some leases in the Cat Creek field, offset on four sides by producing wells, with the nearest one 500 feet from Pacific's property. It looked like Pacific could not miss, and with Whittall's approval McQueen committed the company to drill five wells on the leases at an estimated cost of about $100,000.

When the first three turned out to be dry holes, the Pacific directors were less than enthused. George Martin and Victor Spencer rushed to Norman Whittall's office in Vancouver for a three-man meeting of the board. According to the minutes of the meeting, the directors felt that the affairs of the company were "being conducted in an extravagant manner" and that McQueen "was obligating the company for drilling commitments without first obtaining the approval of the board." Whittall assumed the responsibility for the five-well commitment, but Martin and Spencer were insistent that their displeasure be conveyed to McQueen. Whittall contacted McQueen and urged him to cancel the next two wells, but it was too late, the commitment could not be broken.

After the fifth well was drilled at Cat Creek, Neil McQueen wrote to the board on March 6, 1946, to tender his resignation as managing director and a director of the company:

> This operation has been a great disappointment. . . . I considered the gamble on the acreage which your company acquired in Cat Creek to be the surest gamble of any that I had ever encountered in the oil business in any part of the world, and the phenomenal bad luck of drilling five successive dry holes, four of which were direct offsets to good producers, is the most glaring example, experienced by myself, of the hazards of the oil business. Anyone who cannot appreciate the run that the company has had for the money expended on your Cat Creek leases, and accept such discouraging results, should

not be connected with this business. They have just not got the viewpoint of the oil man.

McQueen urged Pacific to retain its holdings at Princess, "regardless of any disappointing results that may be obtained from any wells that may be drilled in the immediate future," expressing his conviction that, "This area has big possibilities as a potential source of oil and gas." But for Pacific, the Princess play turned out to be not much better than Cat Creek.

If, near the end of the Second World War, Pacific Petroleums seemed to be stumbling a bit in its efforts to build a crude oil empire, the McMahon brothers had certainly fared no better. Frank was still a substantial shareholder in Pacific, but otherwise he was not formally connected with the company. Drillers & Producers had turned out to be a dry hole. The companies the McMahons promoted for the Princess play offered some waning hope, but that was all.

Just as funds were running low and prospects lower yet, McMahon was able to negotiate a large deal with Sun Oil Company of Philadelphia. This armed him with a modest but vital amount of capital with which to renew the quest for a successful promotion. The deal arose out of the first flush of leasing in the Princess area. Among those who picked up acreage was a group of Calgary investors led by D.C. "Skinny" McDonald and stockbroker Cliff Cross. The McDonald group had filed on 517,000 acres of leases from the Canadian Pacific Railway. At that time, the CPR was eager to grant leases on easy terms to anyone who might seem to be interested in exploring. But even with annual lease rentals as low as ten cents an acre, a spread of 500,000 acres was more than the McDonald group could carry comfortably. As hopes waned at Princess, finding the capital to conduct an adequate exploration program became increasingly difficult, and the McDonald group approached McMahon with their CPR leases.

The McMahon brothers, of course, did not have the money, but Frank figured he might be able to find it. Reg Smith, who had moved from Vancouver to San Francisco to pursue a number of mining ventures from there, suggested Sun Oil, then more than 80 per cent owned by the Pew family. Smith knew the patriarch of the clan, John Howard Pew, chairman of the board of Sun, and provided Frank with a letter of introduction. Backed with this and a bundle of maps on which George had coloured in the CPR leases, Frank went to Philadelphia for several weeks of negotiations. Sun bought the leases for $250,000 paid out over five years, plus an overriding royalty on any oil or gas production. It was Sun Oil's first venture in western Canada, initially directed by a twenty-two-year-old geologist, Ned Gilbert. Frank and George got 20 per cent of Sun's payments to the McDonald group.

With the seed money from the Sun Oil deal, McMahon was soon promoting two other ventures, his long dreamed of pipeline from the Peace River and a distillery in Calgary. Jack and Lou Diamond, two Calgary brothers, had been active in the liquor warehouse business during the US Prohibition era. Then, rum-running from Canada was a flourishing business, but only the rum-running was illegal, not the wholesaling in Canada. The Diamond brothers approached Frank with the idea of building a plant to produce industrial alcohols; he rejected that idea but was intrigued by the possibilities of producing booze.

At the time, there was only one distillery operating in Canada west of Toronto, the Vancouver plant of the Reifel family. As McMahon made a careful study of the business, he decided that Calgary had everything required for a flourishing distillery: ample supplies of grain and convenient storage in nearby elevators, large amounts of exceptionally good spring water, low cost fuel in the form of natural gas, and a steady supply of bottles from a large glass factory in Redcliff. McMahon purchased a defunct soap factory from which he salvaged stainless steel tanks, valves, and fittings suitable for use in a distillery. In 1946, he organized Alberta Distillers Limited, and in less than four years he built a $750,000 plant. Associated in the venture were Norman Whittall, who helped raise the money, and three members of the Reifel family: George H., George C., and Harry, who was the general manager of the new plant. The Diamond brothers did not participate, except to buy some of the common stock.

While Alberta Distillers was waiting for its first batch of rye whisky to age five years, McMahon suggested they turn out vodka, a spirit that requires no aging. The catch was that the sale of vodka in Alberta was illegal, because the government of Bible preacher Ernest Manning thought that this colourless, odourless spirit was an insidious danger to the morals of Albertans. Alberta Distillers produced vodka anyway, just as a craze swept New

79

York City for "Moscow Mules" and "Bloody Marys," and the distillery did a landslide export business.

This venture was still on the drawing board when McMahon made his next run at the pipeline from the Peace River. On August 22, 1945, application was made to the BC government for a 700-mile pipeline right-of-way and natural gas permits in the Peace River area by a syndicate comprising Pacific Petroleums, Victor Spencer (identified in the application as "merchant"), Whittall ("broker"), George Martin ("financier"), and Frank M. McMahon ("drilling contractor"). Backed by maps and a study of the potential Peace River gas reserves prepared by consulting geologist Pete Sanderson, the application declared:

Natural gas means automatic heat and an ample supply of hot water for every householder – the poor and rich alike – at a lesser cost than they are now paying. Consider the extra hours of leisure the working man and all householders will be able to enjoy, if they are relieved from the tedious hours of stoking furnaces and carrying out ashes. . . . The dirt and grime which now mars the outward part of the city [Vancouver] and the health of its people would be greatly alleviated. Vancouver, one of the most beautiful cities in its natural state, is already one of the dirtiest on the continent. During much of the year a heavy fall of oil soot hangs over the city. At times it enshrouds the industrial, business, and residential areas. After every winter the city emerges with its buildings and its homes disfigured and smeared, both inside and out, with the soot that belches forth from the soft coal and fuel oil now in use. In vain has the city tried to enforce its smoke by-law.

The application requested gas permits in an area of 256,000 acres near the Alberta border, including the BC side of the Pouce Coupe field. As well, it asked for exploration rights on an additional 1 million acres out of which, if gas were found, permits could be selected on 640,000 acres. Because "the purpose of the applicants is to discover and develop an area for the production of natural gas, and not petroleum," any wells that found oil would be turned over to the government at cost.

The applicants proposed an initial five-well exploration program at a cost of $150,000. If successful, it would be followed by an additional ten-well program at an estimated cost of $545,000. If sufficient reserves were found, the group estimated that the entire project would cost some $80 million, including $40 million for the pipeline to Vancouver, $20 million to drill the necessary producing wells, and $20 million for urban gas distribution systems. The project, it was said, "would have a tremendous effect on the whole economy of the province, as an abundant supply of power and economic fuel is the basis of practically all industry." Finally, the applicants pointed out that, "It would obviously be impossible to contemplate the expenditure of the monies required to establish the existence of a supply of natural gas" without first having a franchise to build the pipeline.

Uncertain what its policies ought to be, and with Duff Pattullo still declaiming against awarding any oil or gas rights to private companies, the government was far from ready to issue the requested permits. Before there was any opportunity to launch the venture – in fact, even before the Alberta Distillers plant had been financed – attention was diverted by the most significant oil discovery in Canada's history. In its wake, Pacific Petroleums and Frank McMahon would emerge as two of the leading players in the drama of the Canadian petroleum industry.

CHAPTER SEVEN

Atlantic's Rogue Well

Canada emerged from the Second World War with still only one major oil field, and its output was declining. Turner Valley production peaked at 10 million barrels in 1942 and, despite the drilling of additional wells, declined to 7 million in 1946. More than 90 per cent of the country's oil requirements were imported, principally from South America and the United States, at a cost of more than $500 million a year, a heavy burden for the Canadian economy.

Imperial Oil had long been the leader in the search for new oil fields in the enormous sedimentary basin of western Canada. Born in the Petrolia oil fields of southwestern Ontario in the 1880s, Imperial had become a subsidiary of John D. Rockefeller's Standard Oil Company (now Exxon) when it had been unable to find capital elsewhere. Imperial, by 1947, had spent thirty years looking for a big oil field in western Canada. All it had to show for its $23 million in exploration expenditures were 133 dry holes, some shut-in gas wells, and the Norman Wells field at the edge of the Arctic Circle that was too remote to be economically produced. So frustrating was the search for oil that Imperial was considering building a plant to manufacture synthetic oil from the more abundant supplies of natural gas. Before committing itself to this costly endeavour, Imperial decided to make one more try in its search for oil and picked a site near the farming village of Leduc, eighteen miles southwest of Edmonton.

On February 3, 1947, Leduc Number One tested a Devonian limestone formation at a depth of 5,085 feet, sending a black plume rising into the air half the height of the 136-foot drilling derrick and drenching the crew with oil. Leduc was the kick-off of an industry that would produce more than $100 billion dollars worth of oil and gas in the following three-and-a-half decades and transform the Canadian economy in the process.

More immediately, though, Leduc started a mad scramble for leases in the area by nearly every oil company, operator, promoter, lease hound, and speculator in Alberta. Most of the nearby government rights had already been blanketed by Imperial, but there were still pockets of "freehold" leases to pick up. Until 1887, any homesteader acquiring land in western Canada from the federal government also acquired the sub-surface mineral rights, including oil and gas. After 1887, ownership of sub-surface rights was retained by Ottawa, and in 1931 this was transferred to the three prairie provinces. The Alberta government wound up owning the oil and gas rights under about 85 per cent of the province. Freehold rights to the rest of the province were held in large blocks by the Hudson's Bay Company, the Canadian Pacific Railway, other railway land grantees, and individual farmers lucky enough to own land that had been granted before 1887. The farmland around Edmonton had been settled fairly early, so that a number of the farmers there owned the oil and gas beneath their lands. After the Leduc discovery, these freehold owners suddenly found themselves ardently courted by cheque-waving oil men.

The McMahon brothers already had a fistful of irons in the fire: the Peace River syndicate, Alberta Distillers, Princess Petroleums and its string of sister companies. Some were no more than paper companies. But that did not slow them down in the race to pick up leases anywhere within sight of Leduc.

George McMahon was president and managing director of Princess Petroleums. A month prior to the Leduc discovery he announced that the company would participate in the drilling of six wells in the Princess area, where it held an interest in 12,000 acres and a few small oil wells. By late April, two months after the Leduc discovery, Princess had picked up two petroleum and natural gas reservations totalling 260,000 acres in the central plains of Alberta and eight quarter-sections (1,280 acres) in the general Leduc region, the hot spot on every oil map. Two of these freehold quarter-sections were within six miles of the Leduc discovery well, where Imperial Oil now had four rigs drilling, and the other six were thirty miles to the southeast.

Pacific Petroleums was induced to take a joint interest in the new properties acquired by Princess. To finance drilling, these companies then made a deal with another firm that the McMahons had formed two years before but had never activated. Perhaps because they had hoped to rival the success of Pacific Petroleums, the McMahons had named their new venture Atlantic Oil Company. Atlantic issued 1.1 million escrowed shares for the properties in which it now held a half interest, with Pacific and Princess sharing the other half. Atlantic then made a public offering of 2 million shares at twenty-five cents each to raise a drilling fund of nearly half a million dollars after brokerage commissions. "The company's acreage cannot yet be regarded as being in a proven area, and an investment in its shares must be considered as speculative," Atlantic's prospectus cautioned. Atlantic, however, was soon to acquire what turned out to be the most valuable proven lease in the Leduc field.

By July, 1947, the Leduc field had sprouted eleven producing oil wells out of twelve holes drilled, and the daily rate of oil production already surpassed the declining output at Turner Valley. In the heart of the Leduc field, one mile northeast of the discovery well and surrounded by producing wells, lay a quarter-section large enough for four wells that was tangled in the legalities of a complicated estate.

Bronislaw and Rose Rebus had arrived at Leduc from their native Poland to take up farming at Leduc in 1897. The bush and buffalo wallows out of which they carved a rich farm included 160 acres of sub-surface mineral rights. When Rebus died in 1940, the estate fell to his widow, three daughters, and seven sons. Imperial Oil had taken a lease on the quarter-section from Rose Rebus. Imperial, somehow, had erred. Under the terms of the uncertain will, it was not the widow Rose, but the eldest son John Rebus, who was farming that particular quarter-section and held the right to lease the oil and gas title.

When Frank found out about the situation, he hired veteran lease broker Norman "Bus" Lacey to negotiate a deal with John Rebus. Rebus did not want anything to do with any oil company. All he wanted was to be left alone to farm his land. He was afraid that the oil companies, with their big drilling rigs and their pipelines, would destroy his farm. It took all the charm and persuasion that McMahon and Lacey had to convince Rebus that they would not ruin his land. After the drilling was finished, they promised, the farm would be just as it was before, except for the valves sitting on four small concrete pads, and Rebus would be able to continue to work the land to within twenty feet of each of these wells. To help persuade Mrs Rebus, Frank offered to replace the old wood-burning stove in the Rebus kitchen with a new, effortless natural-gas range.

John Rebus and his wife were ardent movie fans. Bus Lacey invited them to stay at his apartment in Calgary, and he took them out to movies every afternoon for a week while discussions continued. Lacey had a good reason for this. He wanted to keep John Rebus away from Imperial Oil, because Imperial had every reason to approach Rebus to fix up the faulty lease. On July 2, Rebus was finally persuaded to sign an option for a lease on the 160 acres to Frank McMahon. The option was exerciseable for a cash payment of $200,000, plus the standard royalty of 12.5 per cent on the total sales revenue of all oil and gas produced.

When the rest of the Rebus clan heard about the deal that brother John had signed, they were so irate that Lacey was more than a little apprehensive about visiting Leduc again. Yet, in order to clear up any dispute about the tangled affairs of the lease, there were still more negotiations to be completed. McMahon persuaded Imperial to drop its uncertain interest in the property in return for 100,000 barrels of oil to be provided out of production from the lease. The rest of the Rebus family finally agreed to accept the arrangement.

McMahon assigned the lease to Atlantic Oil Company, which then had a proven piece of property with significant oil reserves. By early September, 1947, a contractor was moving in two rigs to start drilling on Atlantic Leduc Number One and Number Two.

The members of the Peace River syndicate were, at the same time, pressing ahead with their efforts to obtain the long-sought gas permits and the franchise to build a gas line to Vancouver. By 1947, a sixth partner had joined the syndicate, Frank Ross. The son of a Scottish shepherd, Ross had made a fortune in shipbuilding in New Brunswick before moving to Vancouver and would later become Lieutenant Governor of British Columbia. In its annual report for the fiscal year ended February 27, 1947, Pacific noted that its share of expenses as a member of the syndicate totalled $4,000, suggesting that the total expenditures to that point amounted to $24,000.

The syndicate's main expenses then were for the consulting services of Dr Stanley Slipper, the former chief geologist of Alberta's two principal gas utilities who had prepared a number of studies of reserves, markets, and economics, as well as for Senator J.W. de B. Farris. The brother of Wendell Farris, Chief Justice of the Supreme Court of British Columbia and former director of Pacific, the senator had long been a powerful figure in the BC Liberal Party and one of its principal fund raisers. The senator was retained by the syndicate as legal counsel; he also acted as their lobbyist.

The first break for the Peace River syndicate was on March 28, 1947, when the government of Premier John Hart introduced still another petroleum and natural gas act into the legislature. The act would finally open the province's oil and gas rights in the Peace River area for filing, in permit blocks of up to 25,000 acres. The act was speedily passed, but regulations had to be framed first before applications could be accepted, and it was another seven months before the first permits were issued.

In April, McMahon and other members of the Peace River syndicate called on Del Grauer, president of the BC Electric Company, in Vancouver to outline details of their planned gas project. BC Electric had been supplying Vancouver with gas manufactured from coal since before the turn of the century, but it was an expensive fuel. Grauer was "intensely interested in our proposed plans," McMahon later wrote to Senator Farris in Ottawa.

The McMahon group also learned at this meeting that they might face some competition. For a period of several months, officials of BC Electric had been meeting with representatives of other manufactured gas utilities serving Seattle, Portland, Tacoma, and Spokane to consider a proposal to pipeline gas from Alberta, Wyoming, and Montana to the US Pacific Northwest and Vancouver. "They explained to us that it was of utmost importance to the major cities of the northwest and Pacific coast that an ample supply of natural gas be made available as expeditiously as possible," McMahon wrote to Farris. One of the sponsors of this plan was Shell Oil; it had discovered the large Jumping Pound gas field west of Calgary in 1944.

McMahon asked Farris to meet with Premier Hart, who was scheduled to be in Ottawa for a conference, "as undoubtedly he will be approached some time later concerning the importation of natural gas from Alberta and the United States fields, and it is not likely he will look upon this favourably until such time as he is convinced there is or is not sufficient gas in British Columbia to supply at least the British Columbia market. . . . We believe if he is familiarized with what is going on and its importance to British Columbia, he might assist us in various ways in getting our program underway immediately."

Farris met with Premier Hart on May 9, 1947, and reported back to McMahon that he "found Premier Hart very much interested in the proposal" and "very anxious to see the work go ahead, as he believes it would be in the interest of the province." Farris noted that he had briefed Hart and his officials "on more than one occasion. . . . Although at first they were rather skeptical, I am satisfied now that they believe the proposal is a practical one and that the men behind it know what they are doing. I think we may expect from the government full co-operation to the extent they believe is consistent with the public interest." Farris urged McMahon to proceed immediately with applications for the necessary gas permits, even though "You will have to put up a substantial amount of money in advance for rentals."

In August, when the government was finally ready to accept applications, McMahon was first in line on the steps of the Legislative Building in Victoria to file with the Department of Mines for permits one, two, and three, covering 750,000 acres. Next in line was Phillips Petroleum of Bartlesville, Oklahoma, which took out permits four, five and six. But the government continued to move with maddening slowness, and it was an additional three months before the first permits were actually issued. Before then, the McMahon group was indeed faced with a strong rival bid.

The Peace River deal and the joint venture interests with Atlantic Oil and Princess Petroleums were steadily bringing the McMahons into closer relationship with Pacific. In July, the Pacific directors brought the relationship even closer by approving the "joint supervision" of Pacific, Princess, Atlantic, "and when it takes effect, the Peace River gas deal." The arrangement envisioned supervision of exploration activities by Stan Slipper, "a competent production petroleum engineer under him," and Pat Bowsher in charge of financial affairs. This group was to locate in the suite of offices occupied by the McMahon brothers in Calgary's Toronto General Trust Building, while the McMahons would move across to Pacific's offices farther east on Calgary's Eighth Avenue. The arrangements, the Pacific minutes

87

added, would result in the release of two Pacific employees, which "should bring about a saving in the current Pacific Petroleums overhead."

While the Pacific directors were still pinching pennies, a new proposal to supply Vancouver and the US Pacific Northwest was disclosed. The earlier plan involving Alberta, Wyoming, and Montana gas had apparently fallen through. But on July 15, 1948, Northwest Natural Gas Company announced plans to build a grid of gas gathering lines in Alberta and a 900-mile mainline from the southeast corner of British Columbia. The mainline would be built through the Crowsnest Pass, across Idaho and Washington, to Seattle and north to Vancouver at a cost of some $80 million. Northwest Natural had been organized after some two years of preliminary studies by A. Faison Dixon, a partner in the firm of Brokaw, Dixon, and McKee, consulting geologists and engineers of Dallas, Texas, who had been associated with some of the earliest and largest gas transmission projects in the United States. Financial backer was the venerable US investment house of Morgan Stanley and Company. Canadian interests associated with the project included Vancouver timber baron H.R. MacMillan and Calgary lawyer Eric Harvie, whose freehold leases in the Redwater field northeast of Edmonton were soon to make him the wealthiest man in Canada. Dixon announced that Alberta appeared to have far more gas than it needed and that it would no more pay the province to hoard this gas than it would to refuse to export its wheat. Alberta's oil producers agreed. "Export of gas would add great impetus to the Alberta oil hunt," commented the *Calgary Herald*. "Previously a gas well has been little better than a dry hole." With the optimism endemic to every pipeline promoter, Dixon announced that he hoped to have the planned pipeline completed before the end of 1949.

It was clear that the Peace River syndicate faced a strong rival, but there was not much they could do to further advance their proposal until the BC government got around to issuing the requested 750,000 acres of permits. Frank McMahon, however, was determined to build an organization that could fight in the same league with Northwest Natural, and the key to this lay with Atlantic Oil and its 160-acre lease in Leduc. It was a tiny enough block on which to build, but McMahon figured to use it as a fulcrum that would provide great leverage. Atlantic Leduc

Number One was brought into production early in November, 1947, at an initial rate of nearly 2,900 barrels of oil per day, followed by Number Two well at a rate of 2,600 barrels a day. Carl Nickle was moved to comment in his *Oil Bulletin* that the purchase of the Rebus lease for the highest price then paid at Leduc was "looking more and more like a bargain."

On November 19, the Pacific directors met to consider a deal that would put McMahon in the driver's seat of Pacific, the company that he had been instrumental in forming with the eighty-acre lease at Turner Valley a decade earlier. The proposal was to offer 700,000 shares of Pacific in return for 2.1 million shares of Atlantic. This arrangement would give Pacific two-thirds ownership in Atlantic, but it would also provide the McMahon brothers with ownership of the largest single block of Pacific shares.

Whittall and the directors of Pacific reviewed Stan Slipper's report which estimated the recoverable oil reserves under Atlantic's lease at 3.2 million barrels. Discounting this estimate by one-quarter, "in order to be conservative," Whittall calculated that the lease would yield some $4 million in net earnings after taxes, of which Pacific's share would be two-thirds. In effect, Pacific was offering 700,000 shares for anticipated future earnings of more than $2.5 million. Whittall described it as "a very favourable deal." The shareholders apparently agreed, and at an extraordinary general meeting in Vancouver on December 19, 1947, it was approved. Of the shares that Pacific issued for its interest in Atlantic, Frank McMahon received 137,833 and George McMahon, 81,500. That gave the McMahons about 15 per cent ownership in Pacific. It was far from control, but the block was large enough to win some influence.

In November, before the offer to Atlantic had been approved, the Peace River syndicate finally obtained the permits from the British Columbia government to explore the area stretching west from the Alberta border to the BC side of the Pouce Coupe field. The permits were assigned to a new company, Peace River Natural Gas Company, entirely funded at this point by the six members of the syndicate: Pacific, McMahon, Martin, Spencer, Whittall, and Ross.

In a tenuous way, Frank McMahon now had control of his future oil and gas empire – from the Pacific to the Atlantic, as it were. But it was not part of McMahon's plan to simply sit with some measure of control over a profitable, growing, but still

89

small oil company. It was becoming increasingly clear that the planned gas pipeline from the Peace River would require the backing of a large corporation, and it had to be put together in a hurry. If Pacific Petroleums was to be the spearhead of the pipeline and the related exploration and development program, it would need buckets of money. Even before he was appointed to the Pacific board, McMahon set out to find it.

The search began in Los Angeles, where McMahon ensconced himself in the posh Biltmore Hotel with a three-room suite fit to conduct business, entertain, and establish that air of affluence considered necessary for anyone in search of millions. Reg Smith had given McMahon some introductions to start: one to Walter Seligman, a New York broker, and another to Edwin A. Parkford. Parkford had worked a long time with J. Paul Getty and had been instrumental in assembling many of the oil deals that made Getty the wealthiest man in the world. According to a 1960 biography, *The Richest American* by Ralph Hewis, Getty believed that Parkford could have been just as wealthy:

E.A. Parkford of Palm Springs needed $3,500 a month to exist. He liked luxury – caviar, champagne, fast cars, and comfort. Consequently his problem has always been to find $100,000 a year for living expenses. He has never at any time been worth more than a million. Yet he has had some of the most valuable oil properties in the United States. If he had hung on and developed his oil properties – instead of selling them – he would have been worth at least $500,000,000 and ranked as one of the richest men in the United States.

Both Parkford and Seligman were anxious to arrange deals that would back Pacific with substantial funds. Whittall joined the Los Angeles negotiations and reported to the board on March 8, 1948: "It appeared to the meeting that the negotiations with Parkford would prove more interesting as the meeting did not particularly favour the idea of disposing of the assets of Pacific Petroleums for stock in a US company. The president was instructed to proceed with his negotiations." At this point, the directors of Pacific approved the election of Slipper and McMahon to the board.

On the same day as this appointment, March 8, Atlantic Oil Company's third well on the 160-acre Rebus lease roared out of control to become the most famous wild well in Canada and a bonanza for Pacific and Atlantic. The well had barely punched into the main producing reservoir a mile below the surface when a mighty surge of pressure shot the drilling mud up through the pipe and 150 feet into the air. As the ground shook and a high-pitched roar issued from the well, the mud was followed by a great, dirty plume of oil and gas that splattered the snow-covered ground. Drillers pumped several tons of drilling mud down the hole, and after thirty-eight hours the wild flow was sealed off, but not for long. Some 2,800 feet below the surface, the drill pipe had broken off, and through this break the pressure of the reservoir forced oil and gas into shallower formations. As the pressure built up, the oil and gas were forced to the surface through crevices and cracks. Geysers of mud, oil, and gas spouted out of the ground in hundreds of craters over a ten-acre area around the well.

The Alberta Oil and Gas Conservation Board stepped in to take over operations to kill the wild well. Production from the other sixty-one wells in the field was shut in as the flow from the ground around Atlantic Three mounted to rates of up to 15,000 barrels per day – twice the field's normal production – together with gas flows at rates between 50 million and 100 million cubic feet per day. Dikes were built to pond the oil in a huge lake, and all available pipeline and railway transportation facilities were pressed into service to handle the production from this forty-acre valve. The Conservation Board brought in Texas wild-well fighter Myron M. Kinley to direct operations, but the rogue defied all efforts to tame it. Drillers pumped down tons of material that they hoped would seal off the flow: feathers, sawdust, mud, 10,000 sacks of cement. All of it simply disappeared without a trace, and still the oil kept gushing out of the ground in hundreds of geysers that shot up from a few inches to as high as fifty feet.

Imperial Oil pumped 700,000 barrels of water from the Saskatchewan River down a nearby well into the oil producing reef in the hope that the water would find its way to the wild well and choke off the flow. Instead, the water simply increased the reservoir pressure, and the oil and gas began spouting up at the surface at an even faster rate.

With the air saturated with natural gas, the danger of explosion and fire was extreme. Aircraft were not permitted to fly over the site. Police set up a cordon to keep out all unauthorized visitors. Any workman found with matches or cigarettes had them confiscated. One worker managed to sneak off to a nearby outhouse for an illegal smoke. An explosion blew the door off and badly burned the offender. "I wasn't smoking," he pleaded. "It was spontaneous combustion."

Visiting the site, McMahon was greeted by an irate John Rebus. "You promised me this drilling would not interfere with farming," Rebus claimed. "Look at the land. It's covered with oil. It's all ruined." McMahon promised that the land would be restored and that it could be farmed again. It cost a lot of money, but eventually it was.

Two relief holes were drilled under the supervision of Imperial Oil, one 700 feet to the west of Atlantic Three, and the other 700 feet to the south. The relief holes were drilled at angles to intersect the producing well a mile below the surface, where water, mud, and cement would be pumped down to seal off the rampaging flow of oil and gas. It was slow drilling. Measurements had to be taken almost constantly to ensure that the holes were being slanted at exactly the right angles to reach the precise target. Drilling stopped whenever a shift of wind threatened to blow in escaping gas and create a danger of explosion.

As the relief holes neared their objectives, a large and growing crater neared the 136-foot derrick. The derrick shook as the cratering increased, and large chunks of rock shot into the air. The derrick began to tilt to the south, threatening to collapse into the crater. If it fell, it might set off a spark that would ignite the whole area into a roaring inferno. A twelve-man crew rushed in to jack up the leaning derrick, then even more rapidly rushed back to safety. An hour later the derrick was leaning again, in the opposite direction.

At one AM on Labour Day, September 6, 1948, the derrick collapsed into the crater, taking with it two large boilers, pumps, and other heavy equipment. By daylight they had all disappeared from sight. Miraculously, the fall of the derrick did not ignite the escaping gas and oil. But seventeen hours later something did – perhaps a rock hurled against the derrick or steel striking against steel as the twisted derrick settled farther and farther into the hole. At 6 PM that evening, a ball of fire danced for an instant over the crater, then a great roaring flame wooshed more than 600 feet into the air. A column of smoke mushroomed like an atomic bomb explosion 7,000 feet into the sky, spreading a dirty plume a hundred miles to the east. Two days later, and after six months of work, Atlantic's third Rebus well was finally sealed off by the two relief holes.

The rampage of Atlantic Three was not the disaster it might have been. No one was killed, and most of the oil had been salvaged. There were, in fact, some benefits. Accounts of the wild well and fire, with dramatic photographs, were published in newspapers and magazines around the world. Newsreels publicized Alberta's embryonic oil boom like nothing else before. The notoriety attracted the attention of thousands of large and small investors. More importantly, it was a vivid demonstration that Leduc was no small oil field. The well had flowed oil at an average rate of nearly 10,000 barrels a day for six months. At the end of that period, there was no drop in the reservoir pressure, no decline in the rate of flow, and the flow had not turned to salt water. Here was proof that this was not yet another false hope, another flash in the pan, another Princess.

Atlantic Three was a financial blessing to Atlantic Oil Company. When all the accounts were settled, it was found that 1,317,840 barrels of oil produced at the wild well had been salvaged. Of this, nearly 250,000 barrels had been pumped back into the producing reservoir through Atlantic One and Two, and nearly 86,000 barrels had been delivered to Imperial Oil under the terms of the Rebus lease. That left just 1 million barrels of oil to sell for $2.9 million. Of this amount, $1.4 million went to pay for bringing the well under control, restoring the land so that it could be farmed, and damages. The Rebus family collected $366,544.17 in royalty payments, and Atlantic Oil found its treasury enriched by $1,139,145.16. In McMahon's quest for funds to launch his other ventures, it was a good start.

While Atlantic Three was bubbling oil all over the ground, McMahon kept Pacific bubbling with a steady stream of plans, all of which depended on securing the necessary capital. At the annual shareholders' meeting in Vancouver in June, 1948, Whittall reported that, "While the present resources and current earnings of the company were sufficient to carry out a normal development plan, they would not permit the intensive development program" that was contemplated, including "an intensive exploration of the gas area in the Peace River block." He further reported on negotiations to sell "a large block of shares at prices in excess of the current market and that these negotiations if successfully completed, would place at the disposal of the company technical and financial resources greatly to be desired in such a program."

After the shareholders' meeting that day, the directors appointed McMahon managing director of Pacific, the position from which he had been fired nearly eight years before. They also appointed a three-man management committee with broad powers to conduct the affairs of the company, consisting of McMahon as chairman, Whittall, and Smith.

In Los Angeles, McMahon continued negotiating with Parkford, who was really the middleman in a contemplated sale of Pacific shares to Sunray Oil Corporation, a fair-sized independent firm headquartered in Tulsa, Oklahoma. The head of Sunray, Clarence Wright, was the son of an Oklahoma cotton farmer, who began his career as an errand boy for a general store at age ten, quit that to sell popcorn, and had been in business for himself ever since. In 1912, he opened a clothing store in a small Oklahoma town, expanded it into a chain of stores, and bought and sold properties with the acumen of a horse trader. Wright once swapped a piece of property for an expensive set of diamonds, which he then took to New York and traded for a stock of ready-to-wear merchandise. Wright also invested in oil leases, and in 1930 he sold the clothing business to become president of Sunray. Wright typified the country-boy style of management: aggressive, shrewd, thrifty, and always down to earth. He seemed the last type of person that could be charmed by McMahon's gracious manner and showmanship. "I've got Clarence Wright flying here from Tulsa," Parkford warned McMahon one day. "You better get rid of this big hotel suite. If Wright sees it, he'll have a fit thinking about what it cost."

McMahon moved into a less pretentious room in the Biltmore Hotel and quickly demonstrated that he was as good a salesman as Clarence Wright. The two hit it off immediately and became life-long friends. Intrigued by the glowing prospects of wildcatting in Canada that McMahon laid out, Wright decided to fly to Calgary in Sunray's aircraft to see for himself. Wright spent a couple of weeks studying the reports on Pacific's properties, visiting the shut-in gas wells at Pouce Coupe, flying over the route of the proposed pipeline to Vancouver. Sunray agreed to participate with Pacific in its exploration ventures, bought what was for a time effective control of the company (600,000 shares

94

purchased through Parkford for nearly $1 million, plus an option on a further 700,000 shares), and helped Pacific organize one of the largest exploration plays launched in western Canada up to that time.

This wildcat play was to be operated by a new firm, Bear Oil Company Limited, along with twenty-three subsidiary companies. The idea for the Bear Oil play had originated with Dr Theodore Link, formerly chief geologist with Imperial Oil, who had left that firm to establish a geological consulting practise. One of his first clients was Pacific Petroleums. Ted Link's theory was that the billions of barrels of bitumen in the tar sands some 200 miles northeast of Edmonton had originated deeper in the basin and migrated upward in a northeasterly direction to form the tar-like mixture of sand and very heavy oil found near the surface at Athabasca. Link reasoned that large deposits of lighter gravity oil might still be found at comparatively shallow depths in a region between Edmonton and Athabasca.

An effective exploration program for these suspected deposits would require a block of holdings of several million acres. The Alberta government, however, had recently changed the rules to limit the amount of provincial oil and gas reservation rights that could be acquired by any one company to a maximum of 200,000 acres. But there were no restrictions on the ability of a company to transfer its interest in a reservation to another company. Therefore, McMahon organized the 23 subsidiary companies, each of which would file on a 200,000-acre reservation selected by Link. The total 4.6 million acres was to be explored by Bear Oil Company.

The plan to file on this large spread of reservations had already been informally discussed with Alberta's Superintendent of Land and later Deputy Minister of Mines, Hubert Sommerville, by late August, 1948, when Pat Bowsher was attending a conference of accountants in Edmonton. At his hotel one evening, Bowsher received a phone call from George McMahon in Calgary, and he was instructed to file on the reservations the next day. Bowsher was to issue a personal cheque for the required fees, and Pacific would credit his bank account in Calgary with the necessary funds.

When Bowsher arrived at Sommerville's office at ten minutes before nine the following morning, another man was already standing there, waiting for the office to open. The door opened promptly at nine, and Hubert Sommerville stepped out. "Oh, yes, Mr Bowsher," he said, "we have an appointment." Bowsher walked into Sommerville's office, signed the documents, wrote out a cheque for $586,500, and left the office with the reservations in hand. As Bowsher was leaving, Sommerville turned to the man who had been waiting first in line. "I'm sorry," he said, "but all that land has been taken." "Those were the days," Pat Bowsher later recalled fondly, "when the oil business was operated on the basis of a handshake."

Bear Oil Company now had one-third of the total oil and gas rights that had been issued by the Alberta government. All it needed was some wealthy partners to share in an aggressive exploration program. Wright and Parkford were instrumental in persuading Getty to take a piece of the action, and two Getty companies, Pacific Western Oil Company and Tidewater Associated Oil Company, acquired a 40 per cent interest. It was the first substantial participation by the Getty interests in Canadian oil exploration. The balance of the interest in Bear Oil and its exploration program was divided 20 per cent each to Sunray and Pacific, 5 per cent each to Princess Petroleums and Anglo Canadian Oil Company, and 10 per cent was taken up by Toronto mining promoters General Donald Hogarth and John Frame. The eight participants put up $5 million for the exploration play.

An exploration team was rapidly assembled to conduct operations for both Bear Oil and Pacific Petroleums. From Imperial Oil, W.L. Falconer was hired as field superintendent, and Ivone Burne signed on as manager of the land department. W.T. "Scotty" Tosh, formerly drilling superintendent for Drilling Contractors Limited, was hired in the same capacity for Bear Oil and Pacific. Before the end of 1948, two drilling rigs had been moved in to start the series of shallow wildcat holes. In due course, Bear Oil spent the entire $5 million without finding a drop of oil and surrendered the reservations. Much later, other companies went back to the same region and found some significant oil fields. It was not an unusual experience in the business of exploring for oil.

More successful was Pacific's venture in the Redwater field mounted through the purchase of "Crown Reserve" leases. Under Alberta's system of administering the province's oil and gas rights, half of any petroleum and natural gas reservation could be retained, after exploration, in a checkerboard of leases that had to be selected before any production was allowed. The other half was returned to the government, and they were put on the block periodically, selling for the highest sealed bid. Pacific participated with a group of partners – Sunray, Princess, Calvan Petroleums, Atlantic Oil, and others – in its first Crown Reserve sale on November 12, 1948. The group, with Pacific holding a 25 per cent interest, successfully bid for two quarter-sections near Imperial's new Redwater discovery. This was a Devonian reef oil find twenty-five miles northeast of Edmonton, that was even larger than the Leduc field. The Pacific group paid $384,006.76 for the 320 acres and eight possible well sites.

The Redwater field was to turn into an important source of financing for Pacific during the next decade. Early seismic work by contractor Cec Cheshire, combined with geological deduction by Pacific's chief geologist, Art Nauss, gave Pacific confidence that it had a good picture of the big reef that was eventually found to contain nearly a billion barrels of recoverable oil. Nauss figured that the best wells might be drilled along the edge of the reef, and because they were at the edge, there was a chance that they could be purchased at the Crown sales for less than more proven leases. The risk, of course, was that these leases might turn out to be just off the edge, in which case the wells would find nothing but salt water. It was a calculated gamble that McMahon was willing to take. During a two-year period starting with the sale on November 12, Pacific and its partners successfully bid for sixteen quarter-sections at Redwater, for which they paid a total of $5,542,391.53, and on which they drilled more than fifty oil wells. For Pacific, with its average interest of nearly 25 per cent in these leases, they were as good as money in the bank. Using the oil in the ground as security, Pacific was able to obtain multi-million dollar bank loans, time after time.

At the same time that Bear Oil was starting its $5 million exploration program and money was being gambled for edge leases at Redwater, Pacific, Peace River Natural Gas, Sunray, and Atlantic started drilling on both the Alberta and BC sides of the Peace River area in search of the gas supplies for the contemplated pipeline to Vancouver.

Not all the directors of Pacific were enthused about the bold directions in which Pacific was being led by the three-man management committee of McMahon, Whittall, and Smith. On October 15, 1948, the directors met in the offices of Whittall's

97

brokerage firm in Vancouver. Before the minutes of the previous meeting "could be read or any business for which the meeting was called could be discussed, Mr Spencer stated that he was not in accord with the power given to the management committee . . . and as a result felt he no longer wanted to act as a director of the company. Mr G.A. Martin voiced the same opinion."

Spencer and Martin walked out of the meeting, and the other directors took this as notice of resignations, "to take effect immediately." It was a dramatic break in the relationship of two of the earliest backers of McMahon's ventures and original sponsors of the Peace River syndicate. In time, however, the breach was healed. Martin and Spencer later both joined the board of the pipeline company, while Martin rejoined the Pacific board.

The final meeting of the directors in 1948, held on December 15, completed the transformation of Pacific's board and management. Four directors resigned: George McMahon, Pat Bowsher, Stan Slipper, and Jerry Wood. Three new directors were appointed: Sunray president Clarence Wright, Sunray geologist William W. Porter, and Parkford. Whittall resigned as president, because "the position should be held by an official able to devote his full time to the operations of the company;" he was appointed chairman of the board. Frank McMahon became president, managing director, and chief executive officer. If the events in the affairs of Pacific Petroleum had been hectic during the past two years, they were nothing compared with what was to come.

Drilling for Columbia Oils at Sage Creek in the Flathead Valley, BC, 1934. George McMahon at far left and Frank McMahon second from left. Photo courtesy Frank McMahon.

Francis Joseph McMahon, his daughter-in-law
Isobel McMahon, and grand-daughter Marion,
at Barkerville, BC, 1936.
Photo courtesy Wm. McMahon.

Col. Victor Spencer at Columbia Oils'
Sage Creek well in the Flathead Valley,
September 6, 1936.
Photo courtesy Frank McMahon.

Visitors at the Sage Creek well, September 6, 1936. Left to right: Morley Sellers, Arthur J. Hendry, Col. Victor Spencer, Hon. John Hart (later BC Premier), Guy Penney, and F. E. Wilson.

Norman Whittall, soon to become the first president of Pacific Petroleums. Photos courtesy Frank McMahon.

London Pacific Exploration's first unsuccessful wildcat drilling on the
Winifred structure in Montana, 1936. Photo courtesy Frank McMahon.

Drilling at Columbia Oils
Sage Creek No. 1 well, 1936.
Photo courtesy Frank McMahon.

A spray of oil and gas
from Columbia Oils' Sage
Creek well, June, 1936.
It was not enough to make
a commercial oil well.
Photo courtesy Frank McMahon.

Below: The well that attracted
Frank McMahon's attention to
the natural gas possibilities of
the Peace River area. Burning
gas out of control in August,
1936, at abandoned Pouce
Coupe well drilled by Imperial
Oil subsidiary.
Photo by D. McAllister.

West Turner No. 1 well, later re-named Pacific Petroleums Turner Valley No. 1, being brought into production, April, 1938. Photo courtesy Petro-Canada.

Wild well Atlantic 3 on fire, September, 1948. Out of control for six months, Atlantic 3 spewed out nearly 1.5 million barrels of oil, and caught fire two days before it was shut in. Photo courtesy Glenbow Archives, Calgary.

Drillers and Producers Number 2 well at Turner Valley. Photo courtesy Frank McMahon.

Official opening of the most northern natural gas pipeline in the world,
at Dawson Creek, BC, October 31, 1950. At the microphone is George McMahon.
H. Pollard photograph courtesy Westcoast Transmission.

Representatives of Westcoast Transmission and Pacific Northwest Pipeline at Tulsa, Dec. 13, 1954, signing agreement that paved the way for construction of both pipelines. Back row, left to right: Frank McMahon, Charles Hetherington, and D. P. McDonald of Westcoast; Bill Whaley (Sunray Oil); Robert Herring, and Leon Payne (Pacific Northwest). Front row: Paul Talleferro (Sunray); Dick Williams, and Ray Fish (Pacific Northwest), and Clarence Wright (Sunray). Photo Hopkins Photography, Tulsa, courtesy Westcoast Transmission.

Frank McMahon and Dr. George Hume at Fort St. John, BC, late 1950s. Photo courtesy Westcoast Transmission.

BC Premier W.A.C. Bennett officially opens the
Westcoast pipeline at Vancouver, October 8, 1957,
while Frank McMahon looks on. Photo courtesy
Westcoast Transmission.

The three McMahon brothers, John, Frank, and George, at Vancouver,
October, 1957. Photo courtesy Westcoast Transmission.

Laying pipe on the Westcoast main line, 1957. Photo courtesy Westcoast Transmission.

Construction of Westcoast's aerial crossing of the Fraser River
at Flood, BC, in 1957. Photo courtesy Westcoast Transmission.

The Westcoast gas processing plant and Pacific Petroleums refinery at Taylor, near Fort St. John, 1961. Photo courtesy Westcoast Transmission.

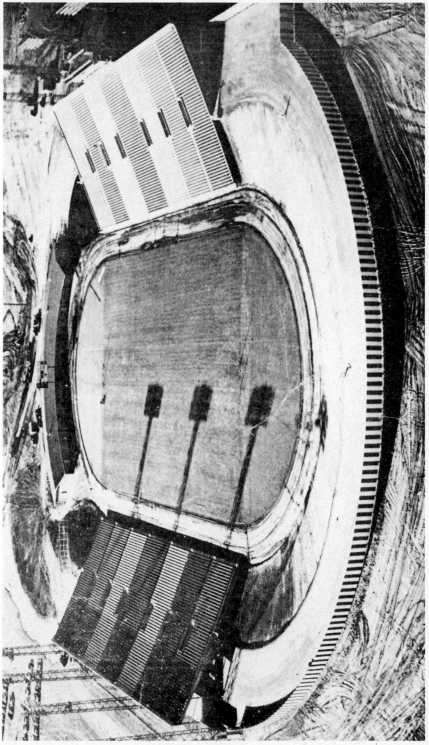

McMahon Stadium, home of the Calgary Stampeders Football team, under construction in 1960. Pacific Petroleums photo courtesy Petro-Canada.

HRH Princess Margaret accompanied by Frank McMahon on visit to Fort St. John gas field. Photo courtesy Westcoast Transmission.

Pacific Petroleums service station at Banff, Alberta.
Photo Bruno Engler, Banff, courtesy Petro-Canada.

Kelly Gibson headed Pacific Petroleums and Westcoast
Transmission during period of greatest expansion.
Photo Jack Lindsay, Calgary, courtesy Petro-Canada.

Frank McMahon in 1980. Photo, Bert & Richard
Morgan Studio, Palm Beach, Florida.

CHAPTER EIGHT

Prelude to the Pipeline Debate

The great pipeline debate that rocked the House of Commons in the spring of 1956 was perhaps the most bitter and tumultuous fray in the history of Canada's Parliament. The issue was the government's handling of plans to pipeline Alberta gas east to Ontario and Quebec. But the stage had already been set, the issues framed, and the outcome cast by a debate that had started seven years before over a scheme to pipeline gas west to Vancouver and the United States.

"Canada first," was the issue that defined the western pipeline debate. The question was whether natural gas from Alberta and northeastern British Columbia would be moved by an "all-Canadian" pipeline, or whether the claimed cost savings of a route across the United States would prevail. This same issue later shaped the debate about the shipment of Alberta gas to the east.

In the case of westward movement, geography and economics appeared to lie on the side of Canada first. In the case of moving Alberta gas to Ontario and Quebec, it was not at all clear that these factors supported this political stance. No matter, because by that time the western pipeline debate had already established the Canada first policy as politically mandatory.

The first skirmish in the fight to move gas to the West Coast was joined in 1947. McMahon and his group wanted to move northern gas through most of the length of British Columbia by an all-Canadian route to supply Vancouver and, it soon turned out, US Pacific Northwest markets as well. Faison Dixon and his Northwest Natural Gas Company – and later others – wanted to move gas from southern Alberta, across the states of Idaho and Washington to Seattle, with a stub line north to Vancouver.

Before the end of 1947, the basic issue in this contest had been clearly seen by George Hume, the Federal Deputy Minister of Mines. Writing in *Western Business and Industry* in November, just months after the Leduc discovery, Hume was already predicting that, "Petroleum self-sufficiency is in sight." He envisioned not only the development of large oil production, but also saw some inkling of the natural gas pipeline network that would span Canada from Vancouver to Quebec with more miles of pipelines than railway tracks in the country.

"In addition to the gas reserves and prospects in southern and central Alberta, there are the gas and oil prospects of the Peace River area of northern Alberta and northeastern British Columbia," Hume wrote. Then he went on to define what would soon become the focus of the issue:

> It would seem highly improbable that a gas pipeline southeastward from the Peace River area to Edmonton would be feasible in view of the gas supplies already available there and at Athabasca. On the other hand, an outlet to Vancouver has many desirable features, such as a large market and the obvious advantage from the national standpoint of greatly assisting in the development of the whole Peace River country. Such a plan would also have the further advantage of leaving the large gas reserves from central and southern Alberta available for other enterprises, and if the reserve was found to be adequate, it might be piped down even as far as the industrial part of Ontario, supplying various prairie cities, including Winnipeg, en route.

It would take more than a decade to accomplish this, but George Hume had just laid out the scenario for the development of Canada's multi-billion dollar natural gas industry.

The advantages of the McMahon plan to supply the West Coast with gas from northern Alberta and British Columbia were clearly seen by 1947. Four advantages were perceived. It would provide an outlet for northern gas that might otherwise lay bottled up for decades. It would supply natural gas to communities throughout most of the length of British Columbia, which the alternative proposals could not. It would escape the supposed political and regulatory perils of having Canadian consumers rely on the stub end of a pipeline through the United States and subject to US jurisdiction. And it would free the gas reserves in central and southern Alberta for consumers from Saskatchewan to Quebec.

Against this, the proposal to ship southern Alberta gas to the West Coast offered the advantage of merely saving money. It offered a source of supply closer to West Coast markets, particularly in the United States, which would result in lower transportation cost. But if providing service to the greatest possible number of communities, and making maximum use of available resources were considerations, it had some obvious disadvantages.

"The Peace River deal," as the minutes of a Pacific meeting called the plan to ship northern gas south and west, was soon to face competition from yet another proposal: a plan to pipeline gas from the southwestern United States to the US Pacific Northwest and Vancouver.

It would take nearly a decade of corporate, political, and regulatory battles fought in Victoria, Calgary, Edmonton, Ottawa, Washington, and elsewhere to declare the winner. As still more competitors joined the fray, a map of the alternative and constantly changing proposed pipeline routes began to resemble a highway map of western North America. If the basic issues had seemed simple enough at the outset, they were soon to be highly confused in the dense cloud of argument and counter-argument.

For the McMahon group, the battle was fought on several fronts. There was the campaign to find an adequate supply of Peace River gas. There was the fight, both in Canada and the United States, to win political and regulatory approval of the planned pipeline project. And there was the task of building an organization with the resources and muscle capable of sponsoring one of the largest resource development projects in Canada. On each of these fronts, there were surprises in store.

Based on the theory that a gas-bearing sandstone formation blanketed a large part of British Columbia's Peace River area, stretching west from the Pouce Coupe wells just across the Alberta border, it was thought that it would be a simple and inexpensive task to punch a number of shallow holes and prove a large supply of gas. No time was lost in testing this theory. The 750,000 acres of BC permits had been acquired by the six members of the Pacific syndicate on November 5, 1947, and turned over to Peace River Natural Gas Company in return for shares in that firm. Peace River Natural Gas, then still a private company, spudded its first well on Christmas eve, just on the BC side of the Pouce Coupe field. By January 18, it had completed the first commercial gas well drilled in British Columbia, and the first hole on the BC side of the Peace River financed by private capital. But the next half dozen wells were dry. The theory that gas would be found in a blanket of sand covering a large area had been shattered.

This did not necessarily mean that British Columbia's Peace River region was without large gas reserves. It meant that if they existed, they would be found in a number of separate structures that could require years and millions of dollars to discover.

Although the initial results were discouraging, it had become clear that the required supply would be greater than first anticipated. The initial intention had been to build a small-diameter pipeline to supply Vancouver and the BC interior towns along the route. Further study soon showed, however, that in order to transport the gas at an economically feasible cost it would have to be moved in much larger volumes than Vancouver and the interior towns could use. This meant a larger pipeline to supply the cities in the US Pacific Northwest as well.

The effects of this on immediate planning for the pipeline to Vancouver were profound. It looked for awhile as though most of the gas would have to come not from British Columbia, but from Alberta; and not from the Peace River, but from farther south in the region north of Edmonton, where greater volumes of gas had already been found.

Nevertheless, the search for gas in the Peace River was continued. Sunray Oil Company, with a half interest, and Peace River Natural Gas and Pacific Petroleums, with 25 per cent interest each, jointly undertook the search on permit holdings that had been increased to more than 2 million acres in both British Columbia and Alberta. Oil was the main prize for most explorers, and as the search for oil fanned out from Leduc, other companies later joined the play in the Peace River.

Peace River Natural Gas had relied on its six sponsors for drilling funds up until 1949 when it raised its first public financing. Pacific Petroleums provided additional funding that eventually exceeded $5 million and wound up with more than half the ownership of the company. Once the magnitude and risks of the project became clear, most of the original backers of the Peace River deal backed out, leaving the McMahon brothers, Norman Whittall, and Pacific Petroleums to carry the ball.

The McMahon group of oil companies would have to be expanded rapidly if it was to provide the support necessary to see the pipeline through. That meant large financing.

In 1948 and early 1949, Pacific sold nearly a million shares for some $1.5 million, nearly two-thirds of these being purchased by Sunray. The first US public offering of Pacific shares was arranged in 1951 by Lloyd Gilmour of the New York investment house of Eastman, Dillon, and Company, the firm that also acted as investment underwriters for Sunray. While these shares sold for $1.50 in 1948 and 1949, by 1951 the price had quadrupled; Eastman, Dillon underwrote an issue of 700,000 shares at $6.37. This brought Pacific's capital to 4.5 million shares, but they were so widely held that no one clearly controlled the company. The largest block was held by Sunray, but that was less than 20 per cent. In 1952, Pacific sold a portion of its interest in Atlantic in a public offering that netted nearly $4 million for an investment that had cost it only $500,000. At the same time, Atlantic was merged with Princess Petroleums and Allied Oil Company, the firm that had been acquired from Neil McQueen and later reactivated by Whittall. These three firms were combined to form Canadian Atlantic Oil Company, with Reg Smith as chairman of the board, and it raised some $4.5 million through a public sale of its shares.

In total, the three McMahon companies – Pacific, Peace River, and Canadian Atlantic – raised some $15 million in public financing during the five-year period 1948-52, in addition to $5 million for the Bear Oil project. It was a substantial sum of money for that time and a dramatic change from the financing struggles of the 1930s and early 1940s.

The boards of the three McMahon companies were almost interchangeable. By the end of 1948, every director on the Pacific board was new, except for the chairman, Norman Whittall, because when Frank McMahon had taken over with plans to spend big money, all the other directors had fled.

With the addition of Bear Oil, the operations of all four related companies were handled by a single staff. In the fall of 1948, the staff of the Pacific group jumped from a dozen employees to 150 within a few weeks.

In the first years of the boom that followed Leduc, landmen were the kings of the oil patch. The first requirement to enter the Canadian oil play was a spread of land, or more accurately, the oil and gas rights beneath the land. The larger the land spread the better, and competition for the best land was keen. It was not surprising, then, that in July, 1948, Pacific hired a landman as general manager. He was John Maberry, who had been assigned to Calgary a few months earlier as general manager of Sunray's Canadian operations.

By nature, a landman must be an outgoing person equally at ease negotiating with a company president or a farmer. The ideal landman can play gin rummy with a company president on an aircraft, pitch horseshoes with a farmer, drink beer with the roughnecks from a drilling crew, or present a talk to the high school class in Eyebrow, Saskatchewan. John Maberry, an Oklahoman with a howdy-do smile as big as the open spaces, seemed to combine all of these abilities. His career with Pacific, however, was short.

Raising money, negotiating deals, and promoting a pipeline, McMahon was constantly travelling: Calgary, Edmonton, Los Angeles, New York, Toronto, Ottawa. A company aircraft seemed appropriate, and in the fall of 1949 Pacific purchased a used twin-engine Lockheed Lodestar from the government company that C.D. Howe had launched, Trans-Canada Airlines. At 7:20 AM on Friday, November 6, the plane was preparing to take off from Calgary's municipal airport on its maiden flight for Pacific Petroleums. Its destination was Chicago where several thousand oil men gathered every year for the annual meeting of the American Petroleum Institute. Aboard were the pilot, the co-pilot, and six passengers: John Maberry and his wife; *Daily Oil Bulletin* publisher Carl Nickle and his wife; Harry Bass Jr, manager of Can-Tex Drilling Company; and Robert Curran, western division manager of Imperial Oil.

As the pilot, Jack Bowman, later described it for the *Calgary Albertan*, the aircraft on "taking off on a north-south runway, had attained a speed of 75 miles an hour when the plane skidded sideways for several hundred yards, the left wing-tip struck the field and the craft burst into flames. Passengers and crew quickly made their escape through the door of the craft just as the fuselage was enveloped in flames." Pacific purchased a new Lockheed Lodestar and hired another chief pilot, Don Brady, who was to fly for McMahon for the next two decades.

There were other changes, too. Stan Slipper, who joined Pacific in 1948 to head its geology department, left in less than a year and later worked as a consultant on the rival project of Northwest Natural Gas. Slipper was succeeded by Art Nauss, who in turn left in 1951 to join Ted Link's consulting practice, but as part of the firm of Link and Nauss he continued to work with Pacific. Maberry also left Pacific, as well as Canada, in 1951. Les Clark, an Oklahoma geologist with Shell Oil who had spent more than twenty years looking for oil in most corners of the globe, succeeded Nauss as vice-president of exploration. Under Clark's direction Pacific encountered its greatest success in the search for a supply of northern gas.

Substantial quarters were needed to house this growing empire. In September, 1949, ground was broken on Calgary's Ninth Avenue for a seven-storey office complex to be called the Petroleum Building. Within a few years this grey concrete structure was followed by the adjacent, ten-storey Pacific Building. Three decades later, downtown Calgary is studded with fifty-storey glass and steel towers of the oil companies, standing as thick as Douglas firs in a BC forest, but in 1950 the six-storey Petroleum Building was one of the more impressive office towers in a foothills' city of fewer than 90,000 people.

FROM CRAMPED QUARTERS

It was not in the Petroleum Building, but in cramped quarters in Calgary's Toronto General Trust Building where in January, 1948 three engineers from the New York firm of Ford, Bacon & Davis Incorporated discovered the offices of Pacific Petroleums and Westcoast Transmission. The engineers were C.S. Whittelsey, Charles Hetherington, and George White. Whittelsey was soon to become the president of Ford, Bacon & Davis, Hetherington was chief engineer, and White was in charge of a pipeline construction subsidiary. It was McMahon's style to seek the services of the most highly regarded and most expensive people, and Ford, Bacon & Davis was the world's foremost firm in engineering, design, and planning of natural gas pipelines. The three

FBD representatives came to take a look at McMahon's plans for a gas pipeline to the West Coast.

They arrived, after a three-day trip by train from New York, in the midst of one of Calgary's worst winter storms, with temperatures minus 30 degrees Fahrenheit. McMahon put them up in the largest suite in the Palliser Hotel, stocked the room with the best brands of Scotch and bourbon, and provided his guests with buffalo coats and fur hats. "Frank's office," recalls Hetherington of the Toronto General Trust Building, "was up this flight of steps. At the entrance there was a list of oil companies as long as your arm. We had to walk past Pat Bowsher's desk, past the desk of his assistant, Len Youell, and the last desk was Frank's. And that was the whole organization."

Ford, Bacon & Davis had been in the gas pipeline business a long time. One of its earliest projects was the construction of 170 miles of 16-inch line from the Bow Island field to Calgary in 1912, then the longest gas pipeline in the world. Hetherington, who held a Doctorate in chemical engineering from the Massachusetts Institute of Technology, had joined the firm in 1946 following a stint with Shell Oil and war years with the US National Defence Research Committee. At FBD, he was responsible for the design of such systems as the $100 million Michigan-Wisconsin pipeline from Texas to Detroit and the Algonquin Gas Transmission line from the US Gulf Coast to Boston.

Whether it was the hospitality at the posh suite in the Palliser, the gifts of Canadian bacon that the three engineers took back to New York, or the appeal of McMahon's bold idea, Ford, Bacon & Davis agreed to provide preliminary planning services for the proposed pipeline and to defer charges until and if McMahon put together an organization that could handle the task. For more than a year, McMahon thus had the advice of a top-flight firm that was willing to gamble "on the come," as oil men say.

It was more than just hospitality and charm, however, that persuaded Ford, Bacon & Davis to contribute its services in anticipation of a piece of future action. McMahon had approached the firm as a result of his negotiations with Clarence Wright of Sunray and Sunray's investment banker, Lloyd Gilmour. Gilmour was a member of Eastman, Dillon, and Company which also did the financing for several gas companies in which FBD was involved. Through them FBD was persuaded that McMahon's plan was worth a small gamble.

106

Interest in possible gas exports from Alberta had been intensified by the December, 1947, discovery of what appeared to be Alberta's largest gas field at Pincher Creek. Located in the Rocky Mountain foothills at the southwest corner of the province, the find was some forty miles east but on the other side of the mountains from the Flathead Valley where Columbia Oils had drilled. The Pincher Creek region had been the site of the first drilling for oil in Alberta, starting in 1901, and more than two dozen holes had been punched down within a twenty-five-mile radius. None went deep enough to find the reserves that lay there, until Gulf Oil Corporation entered the play. Gulf had spent five years and $4 million in extensive geological and seismic surveys in Alberta. In early 1947, it selected a large structure at Pincher Creek that its seismic studies had revealed as its best drilling prospect. Gulf's Pincher Creek well cost more than $1 million, but at a depth of nearly two miles gas was found, accompanied by large volumes of liquids and sulphur. Within three years, Gulf had drilled another three deep tests at Pincher Creek, and the company estimated the field's recoverable reserves at some 2 trillion cubic feet of marketable gas, more than 7 million tons of by-product sulphur, and 70 million barrels of gas liquids. In total, the estimated reserves represented potential gas worth some $560 million at 1952 prices (more than $25 billion at 1982 prices). Pincher Creek became the foundation for nearly all plans to pipe Alberta gas to markets from Vancouver to Montreal. It was not until a decade later, after all the vital decisions had been made, that these reserves were found to be only one-third as large as Gulf had first estimated. By that time, so much gas had been discovered in other fields that it did not really matter.

Six months after the Pincher Creek discovery, in June, 1948, the Federal Bureau of Mines released a detailed study of Alberta's gas supply prepared by George Hume and Alex Ignatieff. Completed too early to include the Pincher Creek find, the study estimated Alberta's discovered gas reserves at 1.4 trillion cubic feet proven, with an additional 0.8 trillion probable. "If large markets and a reasonably attractive price warranted an intensive search for gas, further quantities would be found in amounts far exceeding those now proven and probable," Hume and Ignatieff predicted.

Faced with increasing pressures to authorize the export of gas from Alberta, in late 1948 the provincial government appointed

107

Robert Dinning chairman of a commission to study the province's future gas requirements. Faison Dixon of Northwest Natural Gas and McMahon both appeared before the Dinning hearings in Calgary in January, 1949, with some conflicting views about how Alberta's gas ought to be handled. Northwest Natural's brief claimed that, "There was no route whereby it would be possible, except at prohibitive cost, to construct a pipeline entirely across British Columbia to the coast, nor would it be certain, if such a pipeline were built, that it could be maintained in repair throughout the winter months." The only feasible way to move Alberta gas to the waiting markets on the West Coast, according to Northwest Natural, was by way of its proposed pipeline across Idaho and Washington. "Furthermore, it is a shorter route than any possible route in British Columbia."

"It is our firm conviction that in the export of gas from this province, a Canada first policy should be adopted," McMahon told the Dinning Commission. "By putting a pipeline through to Vancouver in a Canadian route, that object will be accomplished and Vancouver will receive priority." McMahon derided his rival's claim that an all-Canadian route would be physically impossible, prohibitively expensive, or impossible to maintain. "The answer to these suggestions is simple," he said. "We are prepared to do it."

McMahon's brief was presented on behalf of the companies that were prepared to do it: Pacific Petroleums; Peace River Natural Gas; Sunray; the two Getty companies (Pacific Western Oil and Tidewater Associated Oil); and Eastman, Dillon, and Company.

It seemed as though nearly everyone in Alberta, except for the oil companies, told the Dinning Commission that no gas should be exported from Alberta until the province had enough gas to look after its own needs for fifty years. There was widespread concern that export would mean higher prices for Alberta users and a depletion of their supplies. Moreover, it was argued that if Alberta kept all of its own gas, then large industries would be forced to locate within the province, rather than using the gas elsewhere. With the stage set by the Dinning hearings, the question of whether Alberta should allow any gas to escape from its borders became the hottest political issue in the province.

Within weeks of the Dinning Commission report – which failed to make any specific export recommendations – the

McMahon group had incorporated two firms to build the planned gas pipeline: Westcoast Transmission Company Ltd and Westcoast Transmission Company Limited. Westcoast Ltd was incorporated first, as an Alberta company. Westcoast Limited had to await the passage of the Pipe Lines Act by Parliament before it could be incorporated under a federal charter. By that time McMahon had lost more of his supporters; the two Getty oil companies dropped out of the picture.

The Pipe Lines Act, introduced in Parliament by Transport Minister Lionel Chevrier, stipulated that any company proposing to construct a pipeline that would cross provincial boundaries, or enter the United States, had first to be incorporated by a special act of Parliament. Such companies could then apply for leave to build their pipelines to the Federal Board of Transport Commissioners, and public hearings would be held.

Six firms were already waiting to seek incorporation when debate on the Pipe Lines Act opened in the House of Commons on April 6, 1949. Three hoped to build oil lines: Interprovincial Pipe Line (which initially proposed to move Alberta oil as far east as the head of the Great Lakes for tanker shipment to Toronto), Trans-Northern Pipe Line, and British American Pipe Line Company. The three others wanted to build gas lines: Westcoast Transmission, Western Pipe Lines (which proposed to move Alberta gas as far east as Winnipeg), and Alberta Natural Gas Company (a subsidiary of Faison Dixon's Northwest Natural Gas Company).

The plans of Dixon's Alberta Natural Gas and its parent Northwest Natural Gas to move Alberta gas via the US route to the West Coast started the debate in Parliament. Howard Green of Vancouver said that the Conservatives approved the principle of the bill, but opposed Dixon's plans. "We believe that oil and iron can form the foundation upon which Canada could become a great world power," Green declared. However, he insisted that, "The oil and gas should be used in Canada as much as possible," and claimed that the "main purpose" of Dixon's proposal "is not to pipe gas to Vancouver but to pipe it to Seattle and Portland." Such a scheme, he said, would be "primarily for the western United States rather than for British Columbia."

Howe tried to point out that the incorporation of a pipeline company by a special act of Parliament did not give it the right to build any pipeline, merely the right to apply to the Board of

Transport Commissioners. It would then be up to the BTC to decide what pipelines could be built over what routes. But MPs from the West Coast had little inclination to leave that decision in the hands of any regulatory board.

At this stage, it was a short debate. Parliament was in a hurry to finish its business so the country could face a national election. The Pipe Lines Act was rushed through, followed by bills sponsored by individual MPs for the incorporation of the pipeline companies. On April 30, just minutes before Parliament was prorogued, five of the six private members' bills obtained final clearance. The only one of the six proposed firms that failed to win incorporation was Dixon's Alberta Natural Gas. When the next Parliament met later in 1949 – with the Liberals again in office – renewed efforts were made to incorporate this company, as well as other proposed firms that had emerged in the interim. The Parliamentary debate was truly launched; it was a show that would run for nearly seven years.

The first directors of Westcoast were Frank McMahon, lawyer Harold Riley from Calgary, and four prominent Vancouver financiers: Ronald Graham, Fred Brown, George Martin, and Norman Whittall. Despite who might be on the board, an agreement dated May 15, two weeks after Westcoast was incorporated, stipulated where the financing would come from until the hoped for government approvals were obtained. Funds for the preliminary studies and regulatory proceedings were to be provided by Pacific Petroleums, Sunray Oil Company, Eastman, Dillon, and Company, Frank McMahon, and A.E. Parkford.

Six days after Westcoast Transmission Company Limited was incorporated by special act of Parliament, the firm retained as general counsel the brilliant, scrappy lawyer Peter Douglas McDonald. For the next five-and-a-half years, he would lead the legal battle before regulatory bodies in Canada and the United States. Like McMahon, the forty-four-year-old McDonald was a man from the Kootenays. Better known as D.P., he was born in Rossland where his father had been a carpenter working in the mines, later a union leader, and mayor of the small mining town before the family moved to Trail.

McDonald would lead Westcoast's long legal battles with the competitive drive of an athlete. At Trail he had played hockey, baseball, and lacrosse. It was not until he attended the University of Alberta in Edmonton that he saw his first football game, and after that he played right end for five years. A bantam-weight five-foot-ten-inches, D.P. may have been the smallest player on the university's football team. He also played on the hockey team. After university, McDonald played semi-professional football for one year and semi-pro hockey for five years. When he finally retired his hockey sticks and goalie pads in 1934, he became an active member of the Alberta Amateur Hockey Association, serving as president in 1937-38, and later headed the Western Canada Senior Amateur Hockey League from 1945 to 1950.

McDonald's first contact with the oil business came when he became a partner in Bill Fisher's Calgary law practice. Fisher had been fighting for years to finance Model Oils, which was then drilling north of the gas and condensate wells at Turner Valley. Fisher's well came in as a large producer in 1929, shortly after McDonald had joined the law firm. With a steady source of oil revenues, Fisher promptly turned over most of his legal work to McDonald. In the 1930s, McDonald represented the small oil companies at Turner Valley in hearings before the province's new Oil and Gas Conservation Board which were designed to determine the field's allowable production rate. By the mid-1940s, he had been associated with the McMahons' Princess Petroleums as secretary of the firm. In 1947 and early 1948, he served as counsel for the Dinning Commission hearings that examined Alberta's future gas requirements.

Following the Dinning hearings, McDonald's services were sought by both McMahon for the Westcoast project and Faison Dixon for Northwest Natural Gas. Despite the strong financial backing of Morgan and Stanley, McDonald figured that Dixon's proposal faced political obstacles that were just too great and elected to join forces with Westcoast.

After securing incorporation from Parliament, Westcoast lost no time in seeking Alberta's approval to ship gas from the Peace River country and in launching a high-profile campaign to win support for its all-Canadian route. "Natural gas for the Pacific coast will result in a new era of development and progress for northern Alberta and BC," Westcoast proclaimed in a June, 1949, series of advertisements in small-town newspapers throughout northern Alberta and British Columbia. The $100 million pipeline, the ads declared, "will encourage and assist the greatest possible development of northern Alberta and British

111

Columbia, and at the same time bring the convenience, efficiency, and economy of natural gas to the greatest number of Canadian communities, industries, and homes."

The program included a little campaigning for BC's coalition government, then headed by Byron "Boss" Johnson. Johnson became premier when John Hart resigned at the end of 1947, shortly after the first BC oil and gas permits had been issued in the Peace River country. Under the coalition banner, the Liberal and Conservative parties faced a tough election challenge from the socialist CCF party, and there was no doubt about which side Westcoast supported.

In a confidential letter to BC Attorney General Gordon Wismer, on June 4, 1949, George McMahon reported on a recently completed tour along the proposed pipeline route by Westcoast public relations man Jack Grogan, accompanied by *Toronto Globe and Mail* correspondent Sidney Norman. George wrote that Grogan and Norman saw all the towns along the route – Prince George, Dawson Creek, Hope, Chilliwack, Lytton, Ashcroft, Quesnel, Kamloops, Williams Lake – and visited with boards of trade, newspaper editors, service clubs, and "all of the political leaders for both Conservative and Liberal parties." McMahon informed Wismer:

> Our representatives made it abundantly clear that only in the event that a stable government was maintained in British Columbia could such an undertaking, involving approximately $175 million of private capital, be possible. They stressed the program of the coalition government in British Columbia and had long talks with all of these editors about the platform as set out by the premier and left no doubt in their minds that it was the only practical and sensible program for British Columbia to follow.

McMahon offered Wismer copies of a booklet that Westcoast had prepared on the pipeline project, "together with the use of two films for use by coalition candidates during the current election." Screening of the films, George McMahon wrote, could be arranged through Ralph Farris, Vancouver financier and son of Senator Farris, who was still retained as counsel for Westcoast.

Whether or not it was helped by the efforts of Westcoast, the coalition government did win in 1949, the last election in which it was victorious.

112

Fresh from campaigning in the field, Westcoast appeared before the Federal Board of Transport Commissioners in Ottawa on June 21 for a hearing on its application for approval to build the pipeline from the Peace River to Vancouver. Counsel for Westcoast at the hearing was Duncan MacTavish of Ottawa. The crusty chief commissioner, Mr Justice M.B. Archibald, vented his displeasure over "thirty or forty telegrams here that have come in in the last few days, from oil companies, boards of trade, and towns. . . . They are all supporting the application. I just wish to observe that if some over-energetic representative of the company is going around getting people, and municipalities, and what not to send us telegrams, he is pretty well wasting his time. This board does not operate as a result of favourable telegrams or unfavourable telegrams."

MacTavish acted properly shocked at the suggestion that his client, Westcoast, would actually lobby: "I hope that your lordship has not been embarrassed," MacTavish said. "If it has emanated from my clients I shall see that it ceases." Archibald replied, "We are not embarrassed, we are reasonably thick-skinned, as far as that goes."

This first session before the Board of Transport Commissioners lasted less than ten minutes. Westcoast did not have a permit from Alberta to remove the gas from that province, and without the Alberta permit the federal board was not prepared to hear the application. The hearings were adjourned for six weeks in the hope that in the interim Westcoast would secure a provincial export permit. It was a wildly optimistic hope. Westcoast's quest for an Alberta export permit required not six weeks but two years.

Despite strong popular opposition to any Alberta gas export, Ernest Manning's Social Credit government favoured the plan, but it moved through this political minefield with methodical caution. In July, a special session of the legislature passed the Gas Resources Preservation Act, which stipulated that only gas deemed to be surplus to Alberta's foreseeable requirements would be authorized for export and that permits to any aspiring exporters would be issued only after public hearings by the province's Oil and Gas Conservation Board.

Three applicants were already waiting at the door: McMahon's Westcoast, Dixon's Northwest Natural Gas and Alberta Natural gas companies, and Western Pipelines, with its plans to move southern Alberta gas to Winnipeg and then south to the US midwest.

Manning sought to cool the ardour of the export applicants with a prepared statement issued on July 19. When enough gas surplus to Alberta's requirements had been found, Manning said, "The government will then permit the surplus to be made available for use outside the province, with the understanding that Canadian requirements will be given first priority." However, Manning added, "This condition definitely does not exist at the present time and is not likely to exist for some time to come."

Frank McMahon was undeterred. He figured that Peace River gas was too remote to be of use to most Alberta consumers; they could get gas at less cost from the province's southern gas fields, leaving northern gas for shipment to Vancouver. Manning's statement, McMahon wrote to Allan Williamson, Vancouver vice-president of Wood Gundy Limited and one of the backers of Western Pipe Lines,

> is purely for public consumption and it has, I believe, soothed the nerves of a lot of people who were of the opinion that gas was going to be exported in such quantitites that it would leave Alberta "high and dry." I have since had meetings with Mr Tanner [Mines Minister Eldon Tanner] and Mr Maynard [Attorney General Lucien Maynard], and they advise me that they will arrange long-term contracts with the operators and the transmission companies from certain specific areas. They further advised me that the areas we were developing and expecting to take gas from would in their opinion be the first to receive the blessing of the government.

Meanwhile, the expenses for putting the Westcoast proposal together were mounting. On August 18, 1949, McMahon wrote to Lloyd Gilmour of Eastman, Dillon, noting that Westcoast's preliminary expenditures had already exceeded $130,000. "I am of the opinion that the total cost will probably be not over $200,000," McMahon added. That estimate proved to be about as wildly optimistic as the hope of getting an Alberta gas permit in six weeks.

These were heady days in Alberta's oil business, with companies from around the globe flocking to Calgary to join one of the hottest hunts on the globe. As the excitement mounted, so did the breadth of McMahon's vision. "There is no question about it, we are in an oil boom," McMahon wrote to Henry Judd of Standard Oil Company of California in San Francisco. "I have seen a few, but none as big as this one. We have Oklahomans, Texans, Californians, etc. by the bundle, all great people and full of enthusiasm."

In his August, 1949, letter to Judd, McMahon revealed that he was thinking of building his pipeline from the Peace River not just to Vancouver and the adjacent US Puget Sound area, but also as far south as California. This, he wrote, "would have many further advantages, and considerably more gas would be consumed in the northwest areas due to the cost reduction which would be effected." Moreover, "Our own geologists . . . do not think there is any question about there being enough gas to supply the line to California."

Even more boldly, McMahon was thinking about building not just a gas pipeline, but also an oil pipeline from Alberta to Vancouver. Westcoast's charter from Parliament allowed it to apply for approval to build both oil and gas lines. "It is the considered opinion of the oil fraternity that eventually an oil line will be constructed to the Pacific Northwest," McMahon wrote. "Our route again lends itself to such a plan both politically and economically."

An oil pipeline was built from Edmonton to Vancouver and the US Puget Sound area. It was completed in 1953, but not by Westcoast. Trans-Mountain Oil Pipe Line Company was backed by the Bechtel Corporation of San Francisco, a large engineering and construction firm, and by the major oil companies with production in Alberta. This represented financial support that Westcoast could not hope to match. After filing a preliminary application, Westcoast withdrew its bid for an oil pipeline, and instead Pacific Petroleums joined in sponsoring the 700-mile, $80 million Trans-Mountain line, taking a 4 per cent interest.

Progress on the gas pipeline, meanwhile, was not keeping pace with McMahon's leaping imagination. Westcoast had still not obtained the Alberta export permit when it next appeared before the Board of Transport Commissioners in Ottawa on September 12, 1949. Unlike its arch rival, Northwest Natural, Westcoast had not even finished assembling the massive documentation necessary to support its application before the Alberta board. But that did not prevent it from bringing its big guns to the hearing, including Frank McMahon, Senator Farris, C.C. Whittelsey, and Charles Hetherington from Ford, Bacon & Davis. British Columbia's Attorney General, Gordon Wismer, was there to argue that the hearing before the board should proceed even without the Alberta permit. "The government of British Columbia is very, very strongly supporting the proposal to export gas from northern Alberta through British Columbia and to Vancouver," Wismer told the commissioners. If the board continued to insist that it would not hear the Westcoast application without the Alberta permit, Wismer argued that, "Then I am afraid that British Columbia's very justifiable desire to develop the northern part of the province is not going to go ahead for a very long time."

But Chief Transport Commissioner Archibald was insistent that Westcoast must have the provincial permit before it could present its case in Ottawa. Senator Farris was a bit upset. He had come all the way from Vancouver to present Westcoast's opening argument before the board, and it appeared that he was not even going to be allowed to speak. "I have been practising law a long time," the senator said. "I have never had this experience before."

"Well, of course, experience comes first to a lot of us," Archibald responded. "I suppose, Senator Farris, you can make your statement," Archibald continued, but added that until the Alberta permit had been obtained, "we will not hear any evidence."

The senator made his speech, and that was the end of the hearings in Ottawa on Westcoast's application, for the time being.

CHAPTER NINE

The Pipeline Fight in Canada

From late 1949 until 1952 the race for the right to transport natural gas from Alberta and northern British Columbia was fought by a growing number of contestants on battlefields across the continent. In Calgary, two new groups joined Westcoast Transmission, Northwest Natural Gas and Western Pipe Lines, in the contest before the Alberta Oil and Gas Conservation Board. Trans-Canada Pipe Lines, sponsored by wealthy Texas oil man Clinton Murchison, proposed the longest gas pipeline in the world, an all-Canadian route stretching 2,200 miles from Alberta to Montreal. Prairie Transmission Pipe Line Company, sponsored initially by a Toronto promoter and Edmonton investors, wanted a line from southern Alberta to the West Coast via a US route similar to that proposed by Faison Dixon's Northwest Natural Gas.

In Washington, DC, another bid to supply the US Pacific Northwest and Vancouver area, this time with natural gas from the US southwest, was advanced before the United States Federal Power Commission by Pacific Northwest Pipeline, backed by veteran pipeline builder Ray Fish. In addition to moving gas from as far as the Gulf Coast of Texas more than 2,000 miles to Seattle and Vancouver, Fish also proposed to supplement this with southern Alberta gas. For the purpose, his organization took over Prairie Transmission Pipe-Line Company.

In Edmonton, the plethora of proposals to pipe the province's gas across nearly the breadth of the continent stirred a political storm for Ernest Manning's Social Credit government.

In Victoria, the BC Legislature passed resolutions demanding that any pipeline to supply Vancouver with gas follow an all-

117

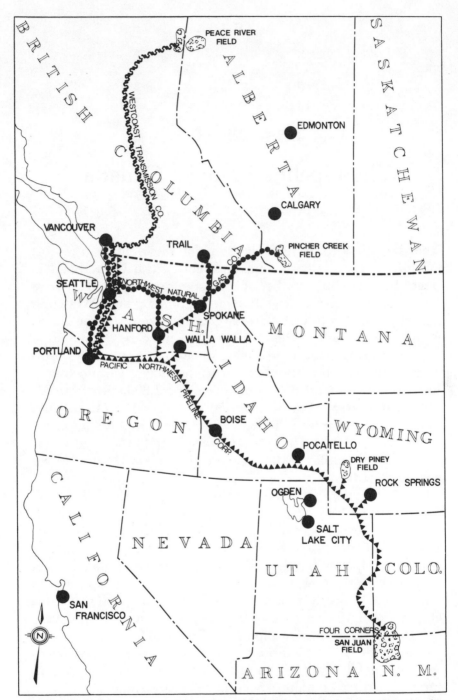

Proposed pipeline routes of firms seeking the right to supply natural gas to the west coast of Canada and the northern United States in the early 1950s.

Canadian route the length of the province. This meant only the Westcoast pipeline.

In Ottawa, renewed attempts to incorporate Faison Dixon's Alberta Natural Gas Pipe Line Company, as well as what became Ray Fish's Prairie Transmission Pipe Line, created another storm in which Liberal MPs from British Columbia broke party rank to oppose the pugnacious C.D. Howe.

Just to complicate matters more, there were proposals for an integrated continental approach to gas marketing. Alberta and BC gas would be shipped southwest to US markets, while gas from Texas and Oklahoma would be shipped northeast to supply Ontario and Quebec. In the Peace River, the Pacific Petroleums-Sunray-Peace River Natural Gas team was joined by others in a search for gas that lagged one step behind anticipation. Finally, in the southeast corner of British Columbia, Frank McMahon led Pacific back to the Flathead Valley in a final effort to find the treasure of oil and gas that was thought to be lurking beneath the cover of Precambrian rocks.

THE FILIBUSTER IN OTTAWA

Two issues were at stake in the Parliamentary battle over incorporation of Dixon's venture and Prairie Transmission. The first was the all-Canadian pipeline issue. The second was who was to decide which lines would be built where. The opposition parties were determined that any pipeline would be built on all-Canadian routes, and that this decision was to be made by Parliament. The government and Howe did not necessarily favour Dixon's proposal, but argued that these were decisions to be made by government and its regulatory bodies; by hard-headed administrators and bureaucrats. As far as the opposition parties were concerned, the matters were too important to be left to any regulatory boards. As far as Howe was concerned, they were too important to be left to politicians.

The renewed effort to seek incorporation of Dixon's venture and Prairie Transmission got underway in October, 1949. After the first bill for ANG failed to obtain passage before the June election, the second bill of incorporation was sponsored in the House of Commons by Ralph Maybank, Liberal Member for Winnipeg South and Parliamentary Assistant to Mines Minister George Prudham.

119

Dixon lined up powerful political support. In Vancouver, he retained Defence Minister Ralph Campney's law firm. For the hearings before the Alberta board, the Dixon companies were represented by H.G. Nolan, chief counsel of the Calgary law firm founded by former Prime Minister R.B. Bennett. In Ottawa, the counsel was John Connolly, a man of considerable influence in the Liberal Party who was later appointed to the Senate where he served as government leader. On the business side, backers included Vancouver timber baron H.R. MacMillan and Calgary oil men Eric Harvie and John Moyer. Despite this support, the private members' bills to incorporate both Alberta Natural Gas and Prairie Transmission were filibustered for another seven months by the Conservatives, the CCF, and a number of Liberals.

The Canada-first faction had already lost one battle to C.D. Howe over the Interprovincial Pipe Line, which was built to move Alberta oil 1,170 miles from Edmonton to the head of the Great Lakes at Superior, Wisconsin, with a later 645-mile extension across Wisconsin and Michigan to Sarnia, Ontario. Progressive Conservative leader George Drew had strongly opposed the US route, declaring that, "Our first obligation is to supply our own centres with that vital fluid by means of a pipeline." Howard Green of Vancouver had said that the oil pipeline should follow an all-Canadian route "regardless of cost."

Howe had staunchly defended the shorter and less costly route through the United States, because he said it would result in higher prices for Alberta oil. "I think the plan is to sell a great deal of oil in the United States," Howard Green declared in the midst of the debate over Interprovincial. "Is there anything wrong with that?" asked Howe.

When it came to natural gas, however, the insistence on an all-Canadian route mounted into a political groundswell that in the end even C.D. Howe could not withstand. The irony is that the cheapest route is more crucial to a gas pipeline than an oil pipeline; measured by the energy content, it costs three times as much to ship gas through a pipeline than oil.

In the year-long filibuster of the bills to incorporate Alberta Natural Gas and Prairie Transmission, the same arguments were played over and over again, much to the chagrin of Howe who was far more interested in doing things than in debating things. Howe's supply of patience over Parliamentary debate was revealed in a remark he once blurted out in the House: "Don't let this degenerate into a debate."

In introducing the second bill to incorporate Alberta Natural Gas, Maybank stressed that this would merely give the company the right to compete with others for an Alberta export permit and, if successful there, to seek a pipeline permit from the Board of Transport Commissioners. "When first one group and then another are granted the right to endeavour to persuade the transport board to permit them to construct pipelines, it is hardly fair to refuse the same right to others," Maybank argued.

That was not the way opposing MPs saw it. Doug Harkness, Conservative Member for Calgary South, argued that Dixon's route through the United States would leave Vancouver's gas supply at the mercy of US regulatory authorities, and in the event of any shortfall in supplies Canadian consumers would be the first to be cut off. "I do not think there is much question that the gas, once it is in the United States, would go to United States cities," Harkness stated.

George Cruickshank, the Liberal Member for the Fraser Valley who had sponsored the bill incorporating Westcoast, argued that the ANG bill "is designed to disrupt the economy of Canada as no other bill ever brought before us was designed to do."

Howard Green accused Howe of lining up on the side of US interests. "It is obvious that his policy on this question is the same as the policy of the United States oil and gas interests," Green declared. "We do not expect, therefore, very much help from the Minister of Trade and Commerce in seeing that this pipeline goes through British Columbia before going to the United States."

Howe argued that refusing to incorporate Alberta Natural Gas and Prairie Transmission would result in monopolies for Westcoast Transmission and Western Pipe Lines in the western and eastern movements of Canadian gas and usurp the role assigned to the Board of Transport Commissioners to determine the best pipeline routes. Howe would have none of it. "If these bills continue to be talked out in the limited time permitted for private bills, the government will ask the house to suspend the rules and provide whatever time is required to finish the discussion and to obtain a vote on such bills," Howe warned, foreshadowing the closure rule that would be applied six years later at the climax of the debate.

121

Howe's policy of allowing Alberta and the Board of Transport Commissioners to determine pipeline routes did not sit well with opposing MPs. "Whether pipelines should be laid in United States soil in order to serve other parts of Canada is far too important a question to be settled by any board set by the government," according to Green. George Drew added that if it had been left up to the transport board rather than Parliament, the Canadian Pacific Railway would never have been built across Canada.

The Canada first group received further support on March 16, 1950, when the BC Legislature unanimously endorsed the route, then proposed by Westcoast, from a starting point near Edmonton to Vancouver via the Yellowhead Pass through the Rockies (the route of the Canadian National Railway), "with provision for the extension of the line to the Peace River block . . . when sufficient supplies of petroleum and natural gas are available in that area."

So intense was the political support for an all-Canadian route that backbenchers of the Liberal Caucus in Ottawa demanded that the government adopt the position. Prime Minister Louis St Laurent was moved to observe in the House that newspaper reports of the caucus rebellion "must be the writer's guesswork," but did not deny it. Only four of twelve Liberal Members from BC – Ralph Campney, Tom Goode, William Mott, and J.L. MacDougall – supported the government's position. For their pains they were censured by a motion of the Vancouver Liberal Association for "talking in favour of the natural gas pipeline going through the US before going to Vancouver."

In the midst of this furor, Howe paid a visit to Vancouver, where he walked into an ambush set by Sydney Smith, the Kamloops Member of the BC Legislature. Four days before Howe's arrival, Smith sent a telegram to four other Members along the pipeline route:

Mass meetings being held in our district Monday and Tuesday to promote dispatch of hundreds of telegrams from individuals and organizations to Hon. C.D. Howe at Hotel Vancouver May tenth, eleventh, and twelfth. Have quantity of telegraph forms printed as follows, quote: I or we endorse pipeline resolution unanimously passed by British Columbia Legislature. Unquote. This will be signed at meetings and charges collected. Would suggest you take similar action.

When Howe arrived at the Vancouver airport, he was greeted by reporters. According to the *Vancouver Sun*:

Reporters stepped up and asked Howe if he would grant an interview then or wait until morning.

"No, it's alright," he said. "What would you like to know?"

"What is your stand on the pipeline to BC, Mr Howe," a reporter asked.

Immediately Mr Howe's face darkened.

"Go to hell," he said. "Don't talk to me anymore. We've talked enough about that back east."

Later, safely back in Parliament, Howe told the House, "It is one of my proudest possessions that I have the right to tell any one just what I told that reporter when he steps over the line." Howe acknowledged, "Yes, I got telegrams. I got 476 telegrams." He said they could be read "in fifteen seconds, because they are identical." Howe laid the blame for the telegrams on Sunray Oil Company, which he had discovered from a report now controlled Westcoast Transmission and Pacific Petroleums. "They are good operators, but I did not read anywhere in the report that Sunray follows the principle of Canada first. I looked for it but it was not there. . . . The matter of routes has been brought in as a red herring to cover up the effort to shut off competition for this United States pipeline company." Howe never did find out how the telegrams had been organized.

The campaign by the opposition parties and the Liberal members from British Columbia failed. "I am afraid that while we have fought the good battle that the Honourable C.D. Howe's influence was a little too strong for us," George Cruickshank wrote to Sidney Smith in Kamloops in May, 1950. "I can assure you that I stuck my neck out on a line in carrying on the campaign that I did," Cruickshank added. "You, as a Member, will realize that there can be retaliation as to grants, etc., for your riding when you cross such men as Howe."

A few days later, on May 22, the bills incorporating Alberta Natural Gas and Prairie Transmission were passed by Parliament. In the process, however, the Liberal government all but abandoned its policy of supporting the shortest, most economical pipeline routes in favour of the all-Canadian principle. Prime Minister Louis St Laurent spelled it out in the House a few days before the two bills were passed:

I am not going to suggest that the protracted debate in this Parliament about the desirability of an all-Canadian pipeline for the gas and oil of Alberta has been a waste of time. It has aroused public opinion as to the desirability of doing that, if it is possible. I would expect that they [the arguments for all-Canadian pipeline routes] would not be lost upon the Board of Transport Commissioners or that they are going to lightly disregard the unanimous desires of Canadians that their own territory be used to the greatest possible advantage. I would expect that when they get an application and before they approve anything they will want to be shown that there is no practical way of doing it without going outside of Canada.

It was Howe who had earlier led the fight against the all-Canadian pipeline principle in favour of the shortest, cheapest routes. But Howe now became the champion of this very principle and pushed it with such vigour and determination that six years later it landed him in the middle of Canada's greatest Parliamentary storm.

AN EAR FULL OF GAS

The first public provincial hearings on an application to export natural gas from Alberta opened with a prediction that Albertans would soon be swamped with so much gas that it would be running out of their ears.

The export applicant was Westcoast Transmission, and the hearings opened on Monday, January 30, 1950, in Calgary's three-storey sandstone courthouse building before the province's Oil and Gas Conservation Board. Behind the bench overlooking the courtroom, its rows of oak benches jammed with lawyers, engineers, and newspaper reporters, sat the three members of the board. The chairman was a sombre Scot, Ian McKinnon. He had joined Alberta's Department of Mines as an accountant when the province acquired ownership of its resources from the federal government in 1931, and he had risen to become deputy minister, as well as chairman of the Conservation Board. Later, he would become the first chairman of the National Energy Board. On McKinnon's right sat D.P. Goodall, one of the board's first petroleum engineers. Red Goodall had been in charge of the board's conservation measures in the Turner Valley field during the 1930s, and he was to sit through years of gas export hearings hardly ever uttering a word. But when Goodall did speak or ask a question, it was clear that nothing had slipped by him. On McKinnon's left sat dapper Dr George Govier, the board's third member and professor of chemical engineering at the University of Alberta. Born in Turner Valley and raised with the oil business, Govier had been a consultant to the board since it had been established. In the hands of these three rested many of the hopes of those lining up to ship Alberta gas across nearly the width of the country.

Two days after the hearings opened, Westcoast witness Dr John F. Dodge, a former petroleum consulting engineer for the State of California, told City of Calgary counsel L.H. Fenerty that Albertans could stop worrying about their future gas supplies. "If this country has the oil future that you up here think it has, and that the world seems to think it has, then you will have more gas than you will know what to do with," Dodge testified. "Gas is automatically produced in producing oil. You will have gas running out of your ears. You should be more worried about what to do with the gas. . . ."

Nearly two years later, the cautious Conservation Board was still holding public hearings to determine whether there was enough surplus to permit any to be exported, and H.R. Milner, chairman of the province's two major gas utilities, was still concerned about the future supplies for his customers. The plans of the export applicants, Milner told Northwest Natural Gas counsel H.G. Nolan, may "have changed a little bit since those halcyon days when gas was flowing out of their ears."

"What was flowing out of their ears?" Nolan asked.

Milner: "Gas."

Nolan: "I have known it to flow from other orifices."

Throughout 1950, the board held hearings not only on the applications of Westcoast, but also the other four major export applicants: Prairie Transmission, Northwest Natural Gas, Western Pipe Lines, and Trans-Canada Pipe Lines.

It was not only the five export applicants who were worried about Alberta's slow and cautious decision-making process. In Ottawa, Trade Minister C.D. Howe, who was in fact the nation's premier post-war promoter of industrial development and big projects, was chomping at the bit; he was eager to see some of these pipeline projects get off the drawing boards, par-

ticularly a gas line to Vancouver. On September 16, Howe wrote
to Alberta Mines Minister Eldon Tanner urging Alberta to hurry
up, because otherwise it might miss out. Howe indicated that he
had been advised by the head of the US Munitions Board that it
was "seriously concerned about the lack of fuel in the Pacific
Northwest" and hoped to get some Alberta gas to help meet this
shortage. But, wrote Howe, if supply from Alberta was not
available:

> Immediate steps will be taken to supply the area from Texas
> sources of natural gas. You are aware that an application has
> recently been filed with the Federal Power Commission of the
> USA for a permit for a pipeline from Texas to the Pacific
> Northwest. This government is in the position that we cannot
> answer the question until Alberta decides whether gas from
> that province will be made available for export outside the
> province. There would seem to be great urgency for a decision
> one way or the other. . . . I see little prospect of a line being
> built from Alberta and the Canadian northwest unless that
> line can be extended from Vancouver southward to serve the
> Pacific coast cities.

Implied in Howe's reference to extending a line from Vancouver south into the United States was the all-Canadian line of
Westcoast Transmission, rather than the competing lines of
Northwest Natural and Prairie Transmission that would extend
from Seattle north to Vancouver. Howe may have fought to have
these firms incorporated by Parliament so that the Board of
Transport Commissioners could make the decision, but in his
own mind he appears to have already decided which way it was
to go.

The pipeline from the Texas Gulf Coast to Seattle referred to
by Howe was proposed by a couple of pipeline promoters named
Fish and Herring. Ray Fish was president of the Fish Engineering Corporation of Houston, and Robert Herring was senior vice-
president of the firm. The vehicle they proposed for the line was
the Pacific Northwest Pipeline Corporation, the company that
filed an application for the system with the US Federal Power
Commission in Washington in July of 1950.

Ray Fish was a twenty-five-year veteran in the gas pipeline
business. During the Second World War, he had been vice-president in charge of engineering design of the Tennessee Gas Trans-

mission Line, one of the first US "big-inch" lines. After the war, he formed Fish Engineering, which did the engineering and construction for a number of other large-diameter gas pipelines. His firm had the turnkey contract for the design and construction of what was then the world's longest pipeline, nearing completion at that time. It was the Transcontinental Pipe Line System, being built from Texas to New York at a cost of $250 million. In addition to the engineering and construction contract, Fish personally held a 2.5 per cent interest in the 1,840 mile Texas-New York line. The proposed pipeline from Texas to Seattle would be 2,175 miles.

In addition to moving Texas gas north to Seattle, Fish wanted to supplement the plan with a supply of gas from southern Alberta by a line from Pincher Creek to Seattle on a route similar to that proposed by Faison Dixon. So cocky was Fish in his bid that in announcing the project he warned Alberta: "Unless applicant can immediately be assured of obtaining its minimum requirements from Canadian gas fields, then it must of necessity purchase all its gas requirements from the United States' fields, thus excluding the province of Alberta from participating in this market." Later, in an appearance before the Alberta Conservation Board hearings in Calgary, Fish said. "We have come all the way from Texas up here to see if we could get a little gas to add to our proposed Pacific Northwest pipeline system."

To advance his proposal, Fish acquired control of Prairie Transmission Pipe Line Company from a group headed by Hales Ross, a seventy-six-year-old Edmonton lumberman, who also controlled a number of small oil companies. Ross later told the Conservation Board how the deal with Fish came about.

Prairie Transmission had been formed by Toronto lawyer and promoter Glenn Wilton, and it was later backed by Hales and his associates. The company, according to Hales, was "going along in the usual way" of getting its application ready when, "We finally saw in the paper that Pacific Northwest were going to build a line from Texas to the border to serve the territory which we figured that we would serve. . . . We were a little annoyed, I may say." Fearing that they would be left out in the cold by the plans of the Texans, Hales and his partners arranged to sell out to Fish in exchange for shares of Pacific Northwest Pipeline.

Frank McMahon's group seemed far less concerned about the threat of Fish's proposed line from Texas. In a letter to Clarence

127

Wright of Sunray, Lloyd Gilmour of Eastman, Dillon noted that, "The arithmetic is simple enough, because the distance that Frank would carry the gas is one half the distance that Fish would carry it." Gilmour concluded, "If Canada wants to export gas, I cannot see how Fish could build his line, as the cost would preclude him getting into that market competitively." Gilmour said he had asked the engineers at Ford, Bacon & Davis what they thought Fish's chances were, "and the lowest odds were fifty to one against it. After all, these people are experts and their opinion is of some value."

While the hearings in Calgary inched on throughout 1950, Westcoast proceeded to build what was then the most northerly natural gas pipeline in the world and the first to export natural gas from Alberta. It was not what pipeliners would call a big-inch system: just eighteen miles of four-inch diameter pipeline, built at a cost of $200,000, from the Pouce Coupe field straddling the Alberta-British Columbia border to Dawson Creek, a village of 4,000 people. The gas was supplied by two wells drilled in the Pouce Coupe field by Peace River Natural Gas Company.

The fact that the field lay in both Alberta and British Columbia, combined with the minuscule amount of gas involved, had sped Alberta's approval, with far less than the customary red tape, and approval by the Federal Board of Transport Commissioners for construction of the first inter-provincial gas pipeline. In applying to the transport board, McMahon said that the cost would be "purely put up" by the backers of Westcoast without any public sale of shares. If the board wanted any further financial assurances, "I could file any undertaking that is necessary," McMahon said. "I mean, I could cover that without any question for you. I would do that personally, as far as that is concerned."

The Dawson Creek line may not have been a big project, but it was still a bold gesture aimed at winning political and public support by demonstrating Westcoast's commitment to supply gas. And it paid off well.

"With a mighty roar a fifty-foot flame leapt into the zero air in this northern village to signal the opening of the first inter-provincial gas pipeline in Canada," the *Vancouver Sun* reported on November 1.

The dedication ceremonies were staged on an outdoor platform alongside the zero mileage marker of the Alaska Highway in Dawson Creek. BC Agricultural Minister Harry Bowman

turned the valve opening the flow of gas, while Alberta Municipal Affairs Minister C.D. Gerhart lit the flame. "The clear,
bright torch that soared skyward warmed the whole square and
melted the snow for yards around," the *Sun* reported. On a hill
at the back of the town, an even larger flare from the main-gate
valve of the pipeline "belched out a 300-foot flame . . . and the
roar of it deafened all else in Dawson Creek," according to
Alaska Highway News editor Margaret Murray. "The flame
which was lighted there will add to the already warm hearts and
useful hands of the people of this Peace River country," Murray
wrote. Bowman promised that it marked only the start of gas export from Alberta. "Providing we have enough gas for our own
use, the rest of the world can have all the rest," he said.

The four-inch pipe for the Dawson Creek line had been salvaged from the war-time Canol Oil pipeline. Later, Westcoast
was to use more four-inch pipe from the abandoned Canol line
for a similar but longer system, costing more than $1 million, to
supply Grande Prairie and four other small villages on the Alberta side of the Peace River area. Salvage was relatively easy,
because Canol was just about the only oil pipeline built in
Canada where the pipe had been laid on the surface rather than
buried. It operated for only one year before being shut-down
after the war. The abandoned pipe was shipped by barge up the
Mackenzie River, across Great Slave Lake, and up the Peace
River.

Using salvaged pipe, however, was not without problems, particularly on the longer line to Grande Prairie. The Grande
Prairie line was supplied from a small gas discovery that Pacific
Petroleums had drilled near the village of Ryecroft, and the pipe
was laid in winter. Charles Hetherington, the Ford, Bacon &
Davis engineer who later joined Westcoast, was in charge of
engineering for both the Dawson Creek and Grande Prairie lines.

When the line to Grande Prairie was ditched, it was pressure
tested with gas from the Ryecroft wells. Several sections blew up
during testing and caught fire. "We'd just shut off the valve and
let it drain, then dig it up and replace the broken pipe," Hetherington explained. "We'd replace that section, test it again, and
some times it would blow up again. I figured if we kept blowing
it up and replacing the bad sections of pipe, eventually we'd
wind up with a good pipeline. We must have blown it up more
than half a dozen times."

Hetherington sent samples of suspect lengths of pipe to the Batelle Memorial Institute at the Massachusetts Institute of Technology for testing and analysis.

The report from Batelle indicated that the pipe had been hit with something in various places, so that it tended to break where it had been stressed during the cold of winter construction or later blow up during pressure testing.

Years later, Hetherington spoke to a US Army officer who had been involved in the construction of the Canol line and who explained the mystery of the faulty pipe. When the line was abandoned it had been drained, but pockets of oil collected and lay in the pipe wherever the ground dipped. To get rid of this oil, the army had sent out soldiers with .306 rifles to shoot holes in the pipe and let the oil run out. No one then seemed to have heard about the environmental catastrophy of oil spills. Some of the rifle shots had merely ricocheted off the pipe without piercing it, and that was what had caused the Grande Prairie pipeline to keep blowing up during pressure testing.

As the Calgary hearings continued throughout 1950, Westcoast was still wavering as to the source of supply and the route for its proposed line to Vancouver. The first plan had been to tap Peace River gas, starting out at Pouce Coupe and following the Pine Pass across the Rocky Mountains to Prince George and south to Vancouver. The first disappointing drilling results in the Peace River area shifted attention some 450 miles southeast to an area a bit north of Edmonton and a route across the Rockies, through the Yellowhead Pass to Prince George, and then south to Vancouver. By late 1950, attention again reverted to the Peace River as a result of a number of northern gas discoveries, particularly one by Shell and British American Oil Company at Whitelaw.

In a letter to Hetherington on October 17, McMahon said that the Whitelaw discovery "looks very big" and described the Pine Pass route as "the very best one to Vancouver." He added that, "The crux of the whole matter is whether we can produce enough gas reserves and deliverability in the Whitelaw area to warrant the line originating in the Dawson Creek district."

A week later, McMahon wrote to Alberta Mines Minister Eldon Tanner:

Westcoast has done the engineering work on a revised pipeline route in the form of a "Y," one branch commencing in the

130

vicinity of the Pouce Coupe field to Pine Pass to Prince George; another branch commencing in the vicinity of Edmonton and the Yellowhead Pass up the Fraser River to Prince George. This line will traverse the more direct and cheaper to construct route and will assure the northern area of an outlet on the best possible terms.

The first round of the Conservation Board's hearings finished in November, and McMahon seemed confident of approval. "I do feel that we are sitting in the driver's seat and that a decision will be handed down in the near future favouring our proposal," he wrote to Senator Farris on November 13. "I am not sure, of course, how many export permits will be granted, but I am hopeful that there will be only two – one to take gas east from the southern part of the province and one to go west from the area north of Edmonton."

The Conservation Board's recommendations on the export applications were tabled in the Alberta Legislature by Premier Manning on January 25, 1951, almost exactly a year after the hearings on the Westcoast application had started. All the export applications were rejected, but Manning did his best to keep the industry's hopes alive. The board estimated that the remaining discovered natural gas reserves in Alberta amounted to 4.439 trillion cubic feet and a reserve of about 4.5 trillion was needed to meet Alberta's own needs over a 30-year period. Thus, said Manning, "These reserves should be further increased before the export of gas is approved." At the same time, Manning said his government "concurs fully" with the board's recommendation, "That as quickly as additonal reserves are established it will be in the best interests of the people of Alberta to make surplus gas available for sale outside the province." Such exports, said Manning, would encourage development of the province's oil and gas resources, as well as more rapid industrial development, and "make gas available to Alberta communities which otherwise could not be served." Manning's announcement said that the export applications would be deferred for eight months, until September 4, 1952, when the Conservation Board would resume hearings to determine whether reserves had increased enough to permit an exportable surplus.

Most of the export applicants and the oil and gas companies expressed disappointment and attacked the government's decision in statements issued to the newspapers. In the House of Commons, Howe hinted that Alberta should approve gas exports immediately. "I think the time has arrived," Howe said, "as it has for some time, when the Premier of Alberta should make up his own mind as to whether he wants to export gas. I assure him he will never receive that request from me." But Frank McMahon told the *Vancouver Sun* that he was encouraged by Alberta's decision and agreed completely with setting aside the reserves of central and southern Alberta for Alberta requirements. Westcoast's plans, McMahon said, were in line with the government's policy, because the gas the company proposed to export was in northern Alberta and beyond the economic reach of Alberta consumers. Because the government had supported the principle of gas export, McMahon said that Pacific and its associated companies would continue to "diligently pursue" exploration for gas in the Peace River area.

By the time the hearings resumed in the fall, Westcoast had amended its application and now sought two export projects: one from the northwest corner of Alberta and a second from the southwest corner of Alberta. It had dropped its proposed line from Edmonton through the Yellowhead Pass in favour of the route from Pouce Coupe through the Pine Pass to Vancouver for its mainline. In addition to British Columbia cities and towns, this line would also supply those markets in the US northwest lying west of the Cascade Mountains. For centres east of the Cascades in the states of Washington, Idaho, and Montana – the Inland Empire, including Spokane and Trail, BC – Westcoast proposed a second, much smaller project to deliver gas from the Pincher Creek field. But ever cautious of closing its options, Westcoast added that if exports were not available from Pincher Creek, then it could serve the Inland Empire with a spur off its mainline from the Peace River.

Westcoast was hoping that its plan would commit Pincher Creek gas to Inland Empire and Alberta markets, so that it would not be available for the West Coast. Its plan involved only the construction of a short line to the US border, where the gas would be sold to Montana Power Company, which in turn proposed a 600-mile distribution system.

The Inland Empire could absorb only a part of the gas supply available from the big Pincher Creek field, but under the plan developed by McMahon the rest would be available for use in Al-

132

berta. The Conservation Board report in January had suggested that some of the Pincher Creek gas might be required by Calgary in the future, but that presented a problem. Because of the need for expensive processing facilities to remove the hydrogen sulphide present in the gas, it was felt that the Pincher Creek field could not be economically produced for the small supplementary supplies that Calgary might need. McMahon's idea was that by exporting part of the Pincher Creek gas, the rest would be made available for use in Alberta at an economical price.

In promoting this proposal, McMahon got caught in an embarrassing dispute with a consulting geologist in California, one who wound up seizing Pacific's aircraft. To advance the idea, Westcoast arranged for a trio of California consultants to prepare, "An economic analysis of the relation of orderly development of natural gas to the industrial progress of the province of Alberta." The economics part of the study was prepared by Dr Nathanel Engle of the University of Washington and O.R. Angelillo, a consulting engineer in Pasadena, California. The part dealing with geology and gas reserves was prepared by another Pasadena consultant, Florent H. Bailly.

McMahon did not like the assessment of Pincher Creek in Bailly's study. Bailly had said that the large reserves estimated for the field could not be counted on until further wells had been drilled, and because of the need to remove the hydrogen sulphide the gas "would certainly be too expensive to export." Bailly's report was thrown out, and a new study on Alberta's gas reserves, prepared by Calgary consultants Link and Nauss, replaced it in the report that Westcoast filed with the board. Link and Nauss took a more optimistic view of the Pincher Creek reserves and concluded that the hydrogen sulphide would lower the cost of the gas, rather than increase it as Bailly had suggested. Removal and sale of sulphur, claimed Link and Nauss, "is a very lucrative business, and in spite of the capital necessary in the construction of sulphur removal plants, the profits from this operation will either help to decrease the cost of the gas to the consumer or add to the income of the operation."

Bailly was furious that his study had been rejected, and McMahon, equally annoyed, refused to pay the full price Bailly had charged for his report. The dispute was still unresolved when McMahon flew to Pasadena for a quick business trip. Returning to the airport for the flight back to Calgary, McMahon found that Bailly had obtained a court order and had the aircraft seized. Not until after McMahon had settled Bailly's account with a cash payment was the aircraft released.

In the end, McMahon's play to pre-empt the Pincher Creek gas supply did not work. Gas for Calgary was found much closer than Pincher Creek, and Gulf Oil was far more attracted by the offer made by Faison Dixon's Northwest Natural Gas for its Pincher Creek gas. In early November, Gulf contracted to sell its gas to Northwest Natural, which in turned secured sales contracts with the Seattle Gas Company and Portland Gas & Coke Company. McMahon's Peace River pipeline still faced competition for the vital US West Coast markets from both southern Alberta and Texas gas.

The Peace River pipeline, moreover, still seemed tenuous, resting on a northern gas supply that consisted more of hope than discovered reserves. But the Pacific group of companies was aggressively drilling in the north in a determined effort to turn that hope into reality. In a submission to the board in October on behalf of Pacific, Peace River Natural Gas, and Canadian Atlantic Oil Company, George McMahon stated that the group and its partners had already spent $22 million in Alberta, including $11 million for the purchase of Crown leases and the balance for exploration, drilling, and production equipment. In Alberta and British Columbia, the group had drilled 171 wells, including 111 oil wells, 22 gas wells, and 38 dry holes. In the Peace River area, where they held oil and gas rights on 5.5 million acres, the group had drilled 16 gas wells and 20 dry holes and had 6 drilling rigs searching for more gas. No other export applicant had a similar program underway to prove up the gas it hoped to export. "We certainly believe that the area can and will produce, under export stimulus, almost limitless gas reserves," George McMahon declared.

Westcoast's Alberta export request amounted to less than 2 trillion cubic feet of gas, less than half the amount needed to fill the pipeline it proposed to build. It was counting on yet to be discovered reserves on the BC side of the Peace River to fill the other half. That hope was strengthened with the discovery of the Fort St John field. Completed early in November, 1951, the Pacific Atlantic Fort St John Number One well recovered 960 feet of oil in the drill pipe on a test of a formation below 5,000 feet. The well was initially greeted as a major oil find. "Discovery of oil in

British Columbia at Fort St John is expected to herald a great new era in the province's industrial economy," blared the *Vancouver Sun* under a front-page banner headline in type size usually reserved for the outbreak of world war or a Grey Cup victory by the BC Lions. "This," said the *Sun*, "is the first real oil ever found in BC." Oil stocks boomed, the British Columbia Department of Mines was swamped with applications for more oil and gas permits, and Duff Pattullo's thirty-year-old vision of BC oil wealth was said to be vindicated at last. "It only goes to show that there is oil in BC," Pattullo commented.

The only note of caution was in the final paragraph of the news story. "Findings of water in the Fort St John well, along with the oil, may not be particularly significant," said the *Sun*, "because a water flow can be shut off and oil brought out before it."

With the excitement generated by this assumed oil discovery, a public offering in New York of 500,000 shares of Canadian Atlantic Oil Company was over-subscribed within hours, raising more than $3 million. There turned out to be far more water than oil at the Fort St John discovery, but it did disclose a fair-sized natural gas field. Most of the gas was in a sandstone formation completely separate from where the oil show had been found. The Fort St John field became the backbone of Westcoast's initial gas supply, a supply that would prove none too adequate for the pipeline's needs. But it also provided the stimulus that did lead to the discovery of truly large gas reserves.

The Westcoast sponsors were gambling on a long-shot, and if their horse came in, they expected it to pay off accordingly. By early 1951, the four sponsors – McMahon, Pacific, Sunray, and Eastman, Dillon – had spent more than half a million dollars advancing the Westcoast proposal, in addition to several million dollars searching for gas. Astute betters would not have given any odds in Westcoast's favour. It was an upstart against established pipeline interests, as well as some of the biggest oil and gas producing companies, and Alberta had just rejected its export bid. Drilling had so far failed to find the needed gas supply. Even if it won approval in Canada to build the line and sell gas to the United States, there would be stiff opposition before US authorities biased against the importation of Canadian gas.

If they won, the payoff would come in a block of shares, the same way that promoters had sought rewards for their efforts

135

and risk for more than a century. The hoped for payoff was provided for in an agreement dated April 30, 1951, under which the sponsors gave themselves an option – exercised two years later – on a block of 500,000 Westcoast shares at slightly less than five cents each. McMahon, Pacific, Sunray, and the partners of Eastman, Dillon were each alloted 118,750 shares, while E.A. Parkford was granted 25,000 shares for his role in bringing the partners together. Some six years later Westcoast shares would be offered for sale to the public at a price 100 times greater than the sponsors had paid, and the five-cent shares would create a political storm.

THE LAST FLATHEAD VENTURE

At the same time that his companies were developing oil production at Leduc and Redwater, looking for gas in the Peace River, and promoting the Westcoast line, McMahon embarked on one more venture in the Flathead Valley of southeastern British Columbia, that graveyard of promoters' hopes where he had started out in quest of his oil fortune nearly two decades before. For Colonel Guy Kirkpatrick of Amalgamated Oil Company, it would be even more the final test of a faith in the Flathead that had been kept burning for close to four decades. In June, 1950, Pacific, Atlantic, and Sunray arranged a farm-out from Kirkpatrick on 60,000 acres of oil rights held by Amalgamated; the Pacific companies would earn a 75 per cent interest in return for drilling the first thorough wildcat test in the valley.

Following completion of seismic work, Pacific Atlantic Flathead Valley Number One started drilling in October, 1951. It was the first to drill a straight hole through the Precambrian rock that overlaid the hoped for pay zone. Some 5,700 feet of Precambrian was penetrated before reaching the Mississippian, the same formation that was the basis of Turner Valley, Pincher Creek, Jumping Pound, and a string of other fields on the eastern slopes of the Rocky Mountains. At a depth of 5,400 feet, the well tested natural gas flowing at a rate of 250,000 cubic feet per day, and McMahon reported the encouraging omen to George Hume in Ottawa. The well, wrote McMahon, was "contacting conditions now that are absolutely different from anything we have seen before. . . . It certainly looks as though we are getting close to something, and evidently we are still on top of it. The Flathead and the north country are the two places you have always recommended, so here is hoping we are all right." At a depth of 7,700 feet, the well encountered even more gas, this time flowing at a rate of more than 1 million cubic feet per day.

The Pacific Flathead well proved that there was, if not oil, at least natural gas beneath the Precambrian in the Flathead, but the amount was not great enough to pay for the high cost of drilling. On January 22, 1953, drilling was stopped at a depth of 10,500 feet after working continuously for more than fifteen months at a cost approaching $1 million. The abandoned Pacific well snuffed out the final hopes of Kirkpatrick and Amalgamated Oil, and the source of the oil seeps first reported by George Dawson of the Geological Survey in 1885 still remains a mystery. In a review of the history of the Flathead published in the *Bulletin of Canadian Petroleum Geology* in 1964, George Hume concluded that there remained "the very practical question as to whether large oil fields do still exist" under the overthrust Precambrian rocks in the Flathead Valley.

GREEN LIGHTS FOR WESTCOAST

The gas export hearings that had resumed before the Alberta Conservation Board in September, 1951, finally drew to a close in January, and the board's recommendations were again tabled in the provincial legislature. The board concluded that in the year since its previous report, the province's gas reserves had increased nearly 50 per cent (from 4.7 trillion to 6.8 trillion cubic feet). But the projected 30-year needs of the province had increased almost as much (from 4.2 trillion to 6.5 trillion cubic feet), so that once again there was virtually no surplus gas available for export. All of the export applications were rejected – except for Westcoast's. The board found that there was a surplus of 300 billion cubic feet of gas available for export by Westcoast from the Alberta side of the Peace River country and added that, "No other gas is now estimated as surplus to the 1952-1981 requirements of the province." In recommending export from the Peace River, the board concluded:

The Peace River area is remote from other settled areas in the province and does not lend itself readily to an integrated province-wide gathering and distribution system. Accordingly, the board is of the opinion that it would be to the advantage of the Peace River area, and without danger to the protection of other areas of the province, to permit the applicant to remove gas from the province subject to stringent conditions for the protection of the province and the residents of the area.

In the legislature, where Manning's Social Credit government commanded an overwhelming majority, the Liberal and CCF opposition members bitterly opposed the government's motion to permit even this limited volume of gas to leave the province. "The day the government's motion is passed will be one of the saddest days in this province's history," Liberal Leader Harper Prowse predicted. "The government will make a quick profit today by selling gas, instead of having the gas available for our own use tomorrow. . . . We may be getting a little chickenfeed in the treasury, but look at what is being taken away from us and our children." The opposition members had just enough power to keep the legislature up in a couple of all-night sittings before they were steam-rollered by Manning's majority. The motion to approve the Peace River gas export by Westcoast was approved by a vote of forty-one to four.

Equally unhappy with the government's decision was Gulf Oil. Approval of the Westcoast plan to supply Vancouver and the US northwest with Peace River gas and the rejection of Faison Dixon's proposed line from southern Alberta meant the loss of gas sales to the biggest, closest, best-paying market for Gulf's Pincher Creek field. Shutting-in Pincher Creek, warned Gulf, would shut in natural gas sales worth some $65 million, preclude sales of by-product sulphur and gas liquids worth some $300 million, and represent lost royalties for the Alberta government of more than $200 million. "The rate of discovery of new gas reserves would be seriously affected if Pincher Creek and the remainder of the large reserves in southern Alberta are denied a market," Gulf observed. "This would clamp a tight lid on the search for additional gas fields in the area where the largest reserves exist."

Frank McMahon, however, saw it in a completely different light. Writing to Mines Minister Eldon Tanner, McMahon commented:

Needless to say, we are tremendously enthused about the decision that the government has handed down. . . . Had an export permit been granted the Northwest Company to take gas

138

from Pincher Creek to the Pacific coast markets, the Dominion Government would have lost millions and millions in income tax, and I am sure it would have retarded the development in northern Alberta and British Columbia for a long and indefinite period. All the operators in the north are very pleased with the decision, and I am sure as a result not only more gas will be discovered but also much more oil.

The export permit that Alberta issued contained conditions that would later present difficulties for Westcoast. The permit authorized Westcoast to export gas from a specified area during a period of twenty-two years, but allowed only the volume of gas required for the first five years. Moreover, the Alberta government retained the right to divert the export gas at any time that it was urgently needed in the province.

Because of the catches in the export approval, and the sparse reserves available to it, Northwest Natural counsel H.G. Nolan remarked to D.P. McDonald that Westcoast had "just won a permit to commit suicide."

Next stop for Westcoast was the Board of Transport Commissioners in Ottawa, where former chief commissioner Judge Archibald had been succeeded by John Kearney, a Montreal lawyer and career diplomat who had been Canadian Ambassador to Argentina prior to his appointment. "Naming Mr Kearney to the transport post readies the government for momentous policy decisions," the *Financial Post* reported, "namely, how best to distribute the vast new resources of gas and oil now growing daily in Canada's west." The pipeline decisions, said the *Financial Post*, "may be as far-reaching in the implications for Canada as the construction of the first transcontinental railway in the 1880s."

The *Financial Post* article discerned a growing reluctance in Ottawa to accept "the oft-mooted continental approach to oil and gas pipeline transportation," which on the surface could have resulted in enormous cost savings by shipping Canadian oil and gas to the western United States and US oil and gas to Ontario and Quebec. Instead, Ottawa appeared to be leaning toward an all-Canadian oil and gas development policy that would favour construction of a gas line from Alberta to Montreal as proposed by Trans-Canada. This attitude was reinforced by the difficulty Ottawa was then experiencing in working out a plan

139

with the United States for the joint development of the St Lawrence Seaway, and the recent decision by the US Federal Power Commission rejecting the export of American gas to Union Gas Company in southwest Ontario because of the needs of US consumers. Still, Ottawa could not push a go-it-alone policy too hard, because development of Peace River gas depended on access to US markets. More than anything else, however, it was probably the demands of the opposition parties in Parliament and the weight of public opinion that inclined the federal government and Howe to champion the all-Canadian principle, if not for oil lines, then at least for natural gas.

It was against this background that Westcoast Transmission appeared before Judge Kearney and two other Transport commissioners on June 11 to 13, 1952. The proposed line included 683 miles of 24-inch-diameter pipeline from Pouce Coupe to Vancouver and a nearby border export point; 277 miles of 20-inch line to be built in the United States by a wholly-owned subsidiary (Westcoast Transmission Inc) to take gas to Seattle, Tacoma, Portland, and other US northwest centres; and a branch line through BC's Okanagan Valley to Trail and to the US Inland Empire.

Westcoast counsel D.P. McDonald presented the board with letters of intent to purchase gas from Westcoast provided by BC Electric, Portland Gas & Coke, and other gas utilities. The only cloud on the horizon appeared to be cast by Henry Gellert, president of Seattle Gas Company, who had written to Westcoast the day before the Ottawa hearings opened: "After nearly four and a half years of effort to get gas from Canada, and the incessant delays, we have naturally become discouraged with the prospect of ever getting gas from Canada." Gellert's firm had earlier contracted to buy Pincher Creek gas from Faison Dixon's proposed Northwest Natural Gas pipeline, but now that Dixon's project appeared to be almost dead, Gellert had signed a tentative contract to buy southwestern US gas from Ray Fish's proposed Pacific Northwest Pipeline and had rejected Westcoast's bid for support.

Judge Kearney did not seem particularly worried about this development. "I think it is abundantly clear," he commented during the hearings, "that on the Pacific West Coast there is a big demand for gas; in fact, they have been crying for it for years. I do not think our board has any worries about whoever gets the certificate and gets there first getting the orders for gas. We are not very much worried about that."

On the witness stand, McMahon told Kearney about the millions of dollars that Pacific and its partners were spending to find and develop northern gas resources.

"So far you have had no return on it?" Kearney asked.

McMahon: "No return yet, sir. The only chance we have is the line."

Kearney: "Well, if it were not for men of your type, I think that a lot of natural resources would remain undeveloped."

After just two days of hearings, Kearney announced that the board was satisfied with all aspects of Westcoast's application, subject only to further study of the gas reserves available in the Peace River area. The research was conducted by George Hume, then Director General of Scientific Surveys in the Department of Mines and Technical Surveys, and Alex Ignatieff, a senior engineer in the department.

The Hume-Ignatieff study, completed three months later, estimated the Peace River area gas reserves available to Westcoast at some 2.5 trillion cubic feet, of which nearly 1.6 trillion was on the BC side. The largest field was Fort St John, estimated at 1.3 trillion. Westcoast had spent three years seeking approval for a gas supply from Alberta, but as a result of the exploration efforts of Pacific and its partners, British Columbia had now emerged as the principal supply and Alberta the supplementary source.

With the confirmation provided by Hume and Ignatieff, the board issued the certificate approving construction of the Westcoast pipeline on October 10, 1952. Shortly after, C.D. Howe, as Minister of Trade, issued the required permit to export gas to the United States. Like the Alberta permit, though, it contained conditions that would present difficulties for Westcoast. Under the Electricity and Fluids Exportation Act, the export of gas could be authorized only on a year-to-year basis, while financing of the pipeline and US regulatory approvals required firm assurance of a twenty-year flow of gas. These, however, appeared to be details that could be cleared up later.

Westcoast had won the battle in Canada. Now the action would shift to Washington where even fiercer competition for US authorization could be expected. Playing in the US league would be some heavy hitters. Once again, opposing McMahon's bid would be Faison Dixon, whose planned Northwest Natural pipeline from Pincher Creek had been badly wounded but not quite killed by failure to obtain Canadian export authorization; and Ray Fish, whose planned Pacific Northwest pipeline from the San Juan Basin to Seattle and Vancouver remained very much alive.

Other players in the US action would turn out to be powerful allies for McMahon. Among them:

Gardiner Symonds, who headed the world's largest natural gas pipeline system, Tennessee Gas Transmission. TGT had joined forces with The Consumers' Gas Company of Toronto in a plan to ship US Gulf Coast gas to Ontario.

Clint Murchison, one of the richest oil men in Texas, whose planned Trans-Canada Pipe Lines from Alberta to Montreal would be the longest in the world.

Western Pipelines, Trans-Canada's rival, that planned to pipe Alberta gas as far east as Winnipeg and then south to Northern Natural Gas Company for markets in the US Midwest.

The Canadian authorization that Westcoast had won from the transport board gave it more than three years, until December 1, 1955, to secure US approval to import the gas into the United States, arrange financing, and complete construction of the pipeline. That seemed to be ample time.

CHAPTER TEN

The FPC Battle: Round One

The article in one of the early March, 1952, issues of *Life Maga-zine* was entitled "A Brawling, Bawling Industry," and one of the photographs showed a pumpkin-headed businessman with a cookie moustache and balding pate. He was H. Gardiner Symonds, forty-eight, of Houston, Texas, president of one of the two largest US natural gas pipeline firms, Tennessee Gas Trans-mission Company. Its arch-rival was the other major US gas pipeline company, Texas Eastern Transmission Corporation, headed by Reginald H. Hargrove, also of Houston. Symonds and Hargrove were locked in battle for the right to supply natural gas to the New England states.

D.P. McDonald was flipping through the issue of *Life* while sitting in Frank McMahon's suite in the Carlton Hotel in Wash-ington, waiting for others to arrive for a business conference. "The interstate transporters of natural gas are probably the most tempestuous and discontented lot in US industry," the article claimed:

> They bawl and they brawl (one of them knocked an FPC of-ficial to the floor last October and is now being sued in a federal court). They are suspicious of each other and some of them maintain elaborate spy systems to keep tabs on rivals. . . . Brutal fights are waged for gas reserves, for access to new markets or for favored positions within markets too big for one supplier. A high proportion of top executives in the business are Texans; and even if they were not born with an aptitude for cutting throats they perforce acquire it.

> Growth of the gas industry in the United States had exploded

143

after the Second World War, and in the competition to build the big pipelines that spanned the nation, no rivalry was more intense than that between Symond's Tennessee Gas and Hargrove's Texas Eastern. Symonds, who had started his career as a Chicago banker, directed construction of the 1,300-mile Tennessee gas line from Texas to West Virginia with government priorities and financial help to provide fuel needed during the war, and he rapidly expanded it thereafter. He had also leased two government-built, war-time oil pipelines, called the Big Inch and the Little Inch, and converted them to gas. But when the government actually put the two lines up for sale in 1946, Symonds lost out in the bidding to Hargrove.

Both firms applied to the Federal Power Commission to extend their systems into the New England states. The FPC suggested they should combine forces for a single project, but Symonds refused. So the FPC awarded half the New England market to TGT and half to Texas Eastern. Symonds again applied to the FPC for the whole New England market and was turned down without a hearing. By 1952, both TGT and Texas Eastern's subsidiary, Algonquin Gas Transmission Company, were laying pipe to New England. The Algonquin system was built by Ford, Bacon & Davis, with Charles Hetherington in charge of design and engineering. It had been estimated to cost $31 million but wound up costing $56 million.

As McDonald sat reading the *Life* article, Symonds had already launched a court action to overturn the FPC's approval of the Algonquin line, arguing that TGT's request for the whole pie had been turned down without a public hearing. Few paid much attention to Symond's appeal to the court, because it was felt that in the first go-round before the FPC he had, in effect, already had his day in court. But before the end of 1952, the courts were to rule that the FPC had acted illegally in issuing a permit to Algonquin without first hearing TGT's appeal. The result was that Algonquin found itself with a nearly completed $56 million pipeline that had to stand idle for almost a year, at a cost of $32,000 a day, until the complex issues in the case were finally settled. In launching the court action Symonds explained that Algonquin had "delayed us for two years . . . and made all the trouble they could. I'm just vindictive enough to want to do the same thing to them."

Much later, the Algonquin case was to provide a useful precedent for Westcoast in its protracted battle before the FPC for permission to deliver Peace River gas into the United States. But there was no intimation of that on March 8, 1952, as McDonald read the article in *Life* and people trooped in for the start of a two-day meeting. The man with the pumpkin head walked in and sat down beside McDonald, who looked at the face, then at the photo in the magazine, then turned to Gardiner Symonds and said, "Hey, that's your picture in here." Symonds grabbed the magazine and read the article with dismay. He was not amused.

The Washington meeting was being held to "co-ordinate" a number of applications for natural gas projects that were about to be filed with the FPC. In effect, it was an effort to divvy up natural gas markets in Canada and the United States on a continental basis that would fly in the face of the growing political demand in Canada for the all-Canadian principle. The firms represented at the two days of discussions in New York included:

– Westcoast Transmission, represented by Frank McMahon; his executive assistant, George Peters; D.P. McDonald; Westcoast's Washington counsel, Charles Shannon; and Charles Whittelsey, president of Ford, Bacon & Davis. Westcoast was still months away from obtaining its authorizations from Edmonton and Ottawa, but Westcoast Transmission Company Inc, the US subsidiary, was preparing to apply to the FPC to import gas from Westcoast Transmission Company Limited.

– Western Pipe Lines Limited and Northern Natural Gas Company of Omaha, Nebraska. Western was pursuing its planned pipeline from Pincher Creek to Winnipeg and south into the United States where it had a contract to sell to Northern Natural.

– Tennessee Gas, represented by Symonds and vice-president Richard Freeman, and The Consumers' Gas Company of Toronto, represented by general manager Ed Tucker. TGT and Consumers' planned to supply Toronto with gas from southern Louisiana. Consumers' had contracted for the purchase of the gas, and TGT would haul it to the Canadian border at Niagara Falls. This would require an expansion of the TGT mainline, plus a short extension from Buffalo to Niagara Falls, where it would cross the river on an aerial suspension bridge, much to the dismay of the local tourist industry and the state park authorities. From Niagara Falls a pipeline was to be built to Toronto by

Niagara Gas Transmission Company, which would be owned 65 per cent by Consumers' Gas and 35 per cent by Symonds and his associates.

The effect of these independent but co-ordinated applications would be an international gas exchange. As TGT's counsel later explained it at the Federal Power Commission hearings:

> If Westcoast supplies the Pacific Northwest with Canadian gas, and Tennessee supplies eastern Canada and Ontario with American gas, the two nations have, in effect, swapped reserves, the advantage to each lying in the fact that its own market is supplied out of the nearest accessible and available reserves. This exchange of reserves is one which will greatly favour the United States.

There were advantages, too, for Westcoast and Western Pipe Lines in advancing their projects against competing proposals. If the Pincher gas were shipped east to Winnipeg, it would not be available to either Faison Dixon's Northwest Natural Gas or Ray Fish's Prairie Transmission, thus eliminating this competition to Westcoast's plans. For Western Pipe Lines, supplying US gas to Ontario would pre-empt the market required by the competitive proposal of Clint Murchison's all-Canadian Trans-Canada Pipe Lines which was planned to stretch from Alberta to Montreal.

The applications were filed with the FPC on March 18, 1952. On the following day McMahon wrote to the editor of the *Vancouver Province*, stating that each of the companies involved:

> have agreed to act together in a friendly way for the purpose of presenting a comprehensive scheme whereby all the areas will receive natural gas at the minimum cost and in the shortest period of time. . . . Each of the companies and each of the applicants is independent. In the case of our own project, we will continue to advance our applications to transmit gas from northwestern Alberta, together with gas from the fields recently discovered in northeastern British Columbia, via the all-Canadian route through the interior of British Columbia.

This group of companies, acting in a friendly way, was not the only one to propose a gas swap. Ray Fish's Pacific Northwest Pipeline by this time had modified its planned pipeline to Seattle; it was to start from the San Juan gas basin in northwest New

Mexico, rather than the Gulf Coast of Texas. The effect was to shorten the distance from nearly 2,200 miles to just under 1,500 miles. Even at that, it was still half again as long as the pipeline proposed by Westcoast to supply the same cities. In addition to West Coast markets, Fish also proposed to supply gas to eastern Canada. He had secured an option on a large gas supply in southwestern Texas from a subsidiary of Standard Oil of New Jersey (now Exxon) that he proposed to ship by existing pipelines to Windsor, Ontario. From Windsor, a 580-mile line would be built to Toronto and Montreal.

One other firm to apply to the FPC for permission to import Canadian gas was Trans-Northwest Gas Inc. This company proposed to buy gas from Westcoast for distribution throughout the Inland Empire in eastern Washington and Idaho. Under the plan, Westcoast would build a lateral from its mainline that would take off near Kamloops, snake through the Okanagan Valley to the US border at Osoyoos, and there the gas would be picked up by Trans-Northwest.

Trans-Northwest was the brainchild of Paul Graves, a Spokane lawyer who figured that he had found a law that would allow him to swipe the gas market in the Inland Empire from under the nose of Northwest Natural. Northwest's planned line from Pincher Creek passed through the middle of this area, and the company naturally counted on supplying it with gas. The State of Washington required that any utility, such as a pipeline, had to obtain permits from the counties involved in order to cross state roads. This was a requirement that Northwest Natural had either overlooked, or possibly intended to get around to at a later stage. Paul Graves, however, hustled around and got county permits to lay a gas line across state highways throughout much of Washington and thus, in effect, had close to an exclusive franchise on the business of carrying gas across the Inland Empire. This seemed like such a strong impediment to the plans of Northwest Natural that Pacific Petroleums put up three-quarters of Trans-Northwest's costs in presenting its application to the FPC. Before the case was decided, Trans-Northwest would prove to be a valuable ally for Westcoast.

The applications of Westcoast, Pacific Northwest Pipeline Corporation, Northern Natural Gas Company, Tennessee Gas Transmission, Niagara Gas Transmission, and Trans-Northwest

Gas were all filed by the end of April, and consolidated hearings on them opened before Federal Power Commission presiding examiner Glen R. Law on June 16. It was the same day that Alberta issued its export permit to Westcoast, although Ottawa's approval was still four months away.

More than seventy lawyers, pipeline executives, some of the army of experts who would later testify, newspaper reporters, and other assorted observers crammed into the main room of the Washington FPC building at 1800 Pennyslvania Avenue for the start of the hearings. In addition to the applicants, close to 100 other parties had registered as interveners in the proceedings. Jerome K. Kuykendall of Olympia, Washington, was there to represent the Washington Public Service Commission as its chairman. Before the hearings were over, Kuykendall would be appointed chairman of the FPC by President Eisenhower.

Tom J. McGrath, his son, Jerome McGrath, and Robert Lee Hall were there as counsel for the National Coal Association, the United Mine Workers of America, the Railway Labor Executives Association, and a dozen other coal and railway interests. The white-haired Tom McGrath had been opposing gas pipeline projects at FPC hearings for more than a decade in what appeared to be a vain struggle. But each day that he could delay a pipeline application meant more sales for the coal mines and more freight for the railways. Even if he had no chance of winning, just protracting the hearings was a victory for McGrath.

Trans-Canada Pipe Lines was there to do whatever it could to frustrate the plans of its rival, Western Pipe Lines. More than a score of municipalities were represented, from Soap Lake, Washington, to Melrose, Minnesota, while other interveners included the Quebec Hydro Commission, the New York Taxpayers Association, the Niagara Frontier State Park Commission (there to oppose the pipeline bridge across the Niagara River), and many more.

The first few days of the hearings were devoted to the opening statements of more than thirty lawyers, starting with Arthur Logan, counsel for Northwest Natural Gas. "I am convinced that if we didn't have the Canadian-United States boundary," Logan said, the line proposed by Northwest Natural since 1948, "would have been built and in operation at least two years ago." Logan attacked the all-Canadian argument of the Westcoast proposal, because it had been:

developed and advertised on the basis that it will develop the wastelands of northern British Columbia. I don't think this commission should be concerned with the development of the wastelands of northern British Columbia. I think they should consider only the welfare of the people who are going to buy 80 per cent of the gas who are residents south of the border.

The all-Canadian principle, so forcefully proclaimed in Canada, now found its counterpart, the all-American principle, proclaimed by Binford Arney, counsel for Pacific Northwest. Following the rebuff from Alberta, Arney said that Pacific Northwest did not "have any intention to further request or ask for one cubic foot of gas out of Canada." Instead, it would supply American consumers with American gas. "It is our firm belief," Arney argued, "that the market area desires to have a supply of gas that is not dependent upon future orders or conditions of administrative agencies of a foreign government."

Westcoast counsel Charles Shannon, by contrast, played on the theme of friendly Canadian-American relations. "This project," he claimed, "represents a co-operative joint venture of mutual aid and assistance to the United States and Canada and will be another example of the harmonious and co-operative relationships which have so long existed between the two countries."

The hearings on these applications lasted a little more than three weeks before they were indefinitely adjourned, in part as a result of a motion by Trans-Canada's counsel George Horning that all the applications should be dismissed.

In his opening statement, Horning made it clear that his purpose was to oppose all applications to import Canadian gas, because they would take gas that Trans-Canada wanted for its all-Canadian line from Alberta to Montreal. He failed to discern that the Peace River gas Westcoast proposed to export was not part of Trans-Canada's contemplated supply; that Westcoast had the political support of the governments of Alberta, British Columbia, and Canada, and, most importantly, C.D. Howe; that bucking Westcoast was not the way to win the political support that Trans-Canada would need. But worst of all, Horning argued that Canada would be completely unreliable as a source of gas for American consumers.

"If Canada desires to export its natural gas into the United

States, then there must be some basic change in the law of Canada," Horning observed,

> They have no concept of any rules, laws, orders in council, impairing the obligations of contracts. Every instrument and every exhibit which has been introduced in this proceeding can be varied, can be changed at any time in the future, can be wholly rescinded, without an opportunity for review. . . . How can it be said under that legal situation that any applicant can appear before this commission with a firm license not subject to being defeated at the will of an executive body of the government of our sister sovereignty?

Horning argued that without "legal authority" to "assure an uninterrupted and steady flow of gas," Canadian imports could result in "great public damage to the citizens of the United States."

By opposing any US imports of Canadian gas, Horning was unwittingly digging a pit for his own client. In seeking incorporation in Parliament, Trans-Canada had claimed that its project would "be an all-Canadian project, that it would be Canadian gas transported over an all-Canadian line, and that 100 per cent of the consumption would be in Canadian cities." But despite this claim, it soon became apparent that to pay for the world's longest gas pipeline would, in fact, require sales to the United States.

Finally, Horning's arguments were hardly in accord with the concerns of the US government. The Korean War was at its height, and fuel was needed in the Pacific Northwest for defence purposes. In May, 1951, a high-ranking official in the US Department of Defense had written to the Petroleum Administrator for Defense in the Department of the Interior:

> The proposed gas lines from Alberta would supply various United States and Canadian cities and strategic facilities along the route of the West Coast and would greatly increase the industrial mobilization potential of the area. From the viewpoint of this office, the export of natural gas from Alberta is essential to the defense preparedness of both the US and Canada. It is recommended, therefore, that, through appropriate channels, further representations be made to the Canadian government relative to the importance of our mutual

defense of permitting natural gas to be exported to the entire US Pacific Northwest.

It was not so much Horning's argument that Canada was unreliable that concerned FPC hearing examiner Glen Law, as the fact that none of the applicants yet had a complete case to present. None of them had firm and adequate supplies of gas, contracted sales, nor authority to export gas from Canada. Thus, in early July, the hearings were adjourned. They would not resume for another seven months, by which time those who wished to continue to pursue their proposals were required to have filed complete applications.

MURCHISON TO THE RESCUE

It did not take long for McMahon to point out to C.D. Howe that Horning's attack on Canada's credibility as an exporter was hardly the type of thing calculated to advance Canada's commercial interests, let alone Westcoast's. Howe, in turn, had only to drop a gentle hint in the ear of Trans-Canada promoter Clint Murchison.

Dallas-based Clinton W. Murchison, born in the tiny Texas town of Athens, was the prototypical Texas oil wheeler-dealer. A stocky, gregarious man, he started out in business in 1919, trading oil leases in West Texas. Six years later he sold out for a reported $5 million to retire at age thirty. Retirement soon bored Murchison, and he decided to try wildcatting for oil. Instead of finding oil, he struck natural gas, then as unwanted in Texas as the gas that had been flared at Turner Valley. While other wildcatters abandoned their gas leases, Murchison hung on to his, figuring that some day the stuff would be valuable. His Delhi Oil Corporation became one of the largest US gas producers.

Described as "a natural born horse trader," Murchison is quoted as having said that, "If you trade in peanuts, you can trade in watermelons, too. We buy anything that adds up." By the 1950s Murchison had bought substantial interests in more than fifty companies, including oil and gas producers, pipelines, an airline, banks, motels, drive-in theatres, a publishing house, a railway, insurance companies, a candy company, a steamship line, several bus and taxi firms, a supermarket chain, and several manufacturing firms. At a time when a millionaire was still a

151

wealthy man, Murchison was reported to be worth some $350 million.

Murchison had a 75,000-acre ranch in the Sierra Madre of Mexico where he liked to entertain such guests as the Duke and Duchess of Windsor and, on one occasion, C.D. Howe, much to Howe's latter political embarrassment. It was in the late 1940s, and Howe, then Minister of Transport, had been on a US tour with a group of other Canadians as guests of American Airlines, in which Murchison was a major shareholder. They had, Howe later said, stopped off for a couple of days at the Murchison ranch, "where we shot turkeys."

Murchison envisioned the Trans-Canada pipeline as the culmination of his business career, and by 1952 his Canadian subsidiary, Canadian Delhi Oil, had spent $6 million drilling for natural gas in southern Alberta. It did not take long for Murchison to figure out that bucking Canadian gas exports, and in particular the Westcoast project, was no way to win Howe's support for Trans-Canada. Thereafter, Murchison became an ally of Westcoast, using his behind-the-scenes influence to promote not only his own project, but also Frank McMahon's. Howe made this explicit in a telegram to McMahon:

> Murchison is here today and assures me that he has refused to have any share in the Fish pipeline project and has refused to release any part of his gas holdings to the line. He is undertaking to make Washington clear that he is supporting your project actively through his political connections. Am sure you can count on this. . . .

Murchison was as good as his word and may, in fact, have averted an early blow that threatened to kill Westcoast's hopes. The export permit Howe issued to Westcoast was good for only one year, Westcoast would have to seek annual renewals, and the FPC was not likely to look kindly on an application for a project predicated on a one-year permit.

McMahon brought the problem to Howe's attention in July, 1952, shortly after the FPC hearings had started. The Board of Transport Commissioners at this stage had still not given final approval for construction of the Westcoast line, but that did not stop Howe from taking prompt action. McMahon described what happened at his meeting with Howe in a letter to Senator Farris:

I told him what we were up against. He picked up the phone and called [Canadian Ambassador] Hume Wrong in Washington and told him to make a statement on behalf of the government in favour of our company. This was a grand situation for us, and Shannon and McDonald had the opportunity of helping them draft the statement in Washington before it was actually presented to the State Department and the Federal Power Commission.

Despite the fact that the transport board had yet to approve the Westcoast line, and despite the requirements of the Exportation of Electricity and Fluids Act, Howe had assured US authorities that it was the intention of the Government of Canada to authorize the exports and that the gas would continue to be available to US consumers. As far as Howe was concerned, that should have been that. After all, Canada had been exporting electricity to the United States under the same act for nearly half a century. American consumers had experienced no difficulty in relying on Canadian electricity, so there should be no problem in relying on Canadian gas.

The problem of the one-year permit continued to haunt Westcoast, despite Howe's communique. Ray Fish's Pacific Northwest Pipelines and every other interest opposed to US imports of Canadian gas used the one-year permit as a club to beat Westcoast at the FPC hearings, in public speeches, and in private politicking. McMahon brought the matter up again with Howe in the fall of 1952, and in a letter to Dal Grauer, president of the BC Electric Company, on October 30, McMahon noted that, "There is need of an exchange of the appropriate documents on the international level to assure complete continuity of supply to the American markets. I have taken this matter up with Mr Howe and have his assurance that whatever document is required in this connection to make the project work will be immediately forthcoming."

But nothing was forthcoming for another five months, until well after the FPC hearings had been recessed. On April 9, 1953, Clint Murchison wrote another of his innumerable "Dear C.D." letters to Howe, warning him of a serious situation:

This is extremely confidential, but they [the Federal Power Commission] propose at this present time to turn the Westcoast down altogether and to give Pacific Northwest a permit

153

with a lot of strings tied to it. It will probably be thirty days before they come with a definite ruling, so we should have ten or fifteen days in which to act. In my opinion, through your diplomatic sources you are going to have to go to the FPC and give them ample and absolute assurance that both the Parliament of the central government as well as the Parliament of British Columbia will be called for the purpose of enacting a law which would guarantee to that area a twenty-year gas supply.

Howe acted without delay. On April 14, he wrote to Murchison that the problem would be resolved by an order-in-council issued by the cabinet amending the regulations under the Electricity and Fluids Exportation Act so that Westcoast could be issued with a new permit authorizing exports for a firm period of twenty-two years. "Anything you can do to delay a ruling on the Westcoast Company application until the situation can be reviewed by the new members of the commission will be very helpful," Howe told Murchison. "The gas in the Peace River area should logically go to the West Coast. In fact it would be very difficult to find a way of using it anywhere else. Therefore, it is most important to Canada that the Westcoast application be approved."

The following day, Howe sent a telegram to McMahon in Calgary, informing him that the regulations had been amended and that a new Westcoast export permit was being airmailed to Canadian Ambassador Hume Wrong in Washington: "Please advise your representatives in Washington as I believe success of your application may depend upon placing this information before Federal Power Commission immediately."

In the United States, action of this nature would almost certainly have required legislation. In Ottawa, where the cabinet has sweeping powers to change legislation by the amendment of regulations, it was merely necessary for Howe to inform Parliament of what had been done. For a man like Howe, eager and impatient to see important things accomplished, it was so much more effective than a messy debate.

THE HEARING RESUMED

Murchison continued to drop Howe friendly little notes from time to time, offering his southern country-boy advice on how to

154

wheel and deal with Washington. A week after he had warned that the FPC was about to kill the Westcoast project, Murchison wrote Howe again concerning the recent appointment of Jerome Kuykendall as chairman of the FPC and the difficulties Ottawa was then experiencing in negotiating US participation in the planned St Lawrence Seaway and Power Project:

I think you should write Kuykendall and President Eisenhower and tell them that you have this Westcoast matter as well as the seaway on your mind and ask them for a contemporaneous date, because I know that you can use your sagacity and turn on your personal charm and get any damn thing you want out of either of them. While I have not met Mr Kuykendall personally . . . after checking very carefully on him and his past operations I have come to the firm conclusion that he is our sort of folks, and I know the President is.

The FPC hearings resumed on February 16, 1953, and the field had narrowed to two major contenders: Westcoast Transmission and Pacific Northwest Pipeline. The applications of Tennessee Gas and Niagara Gas Transmission to export US gas to Ontario and Quebec had been designated for separate hearings. Northwest Natural's application to ship Pincher Creek gas to Seattle was still active, but with the failure to obtain a permit from Alberta it was pretty much a dead letter. The application of Northern Natural to import gas into the US Midwest was in a similar position, with Western Pipe Lines still seeking Canadian authority for its line to Winnipeg and south to the Wisconsin border. Trans-Northwest was still there with its bid to import gas into the Inland Empire, but it was really an adjunct to the Westcoast application. Ray Fish and Frank McMahon were left as the principal adversaries.

Pacific Northwest, by this time, had a powerful ally in Phillips Petroleum Company of Bartlesville, Oklahoma, the largest natural gas producer in the United States. In a novel arrangement, Phillips contracted to sell to Pacific Northwest the gas reserves under its large holdings in the San Juan Basin. Phillips very much wanted the revenue from this sale, and in fact was counting on it to help pay off a $150 million loan.

There was a lot of gas in the San Juan Basin, but it was spread thinly over a large area, so that hundreds of wells would have to be drilled to produce it. The plans called for four wells per

155

square mile, compared to only one per square mile as in standard Canadian gas fields, and there was some question whether the price for San Jaun gas would cover the cost. According to the *Wall Street Journal*, the San Juan Basin was known as, "the largest non-commercial gas field in the world." The first production had started two years before, and El Paso Natural Gas Company had the best part of the San Juan reserves tied up under contracts (principally with Clint Murchison's Delhi Oil) for delivery to southern California. To make matters worse, Phillips Petroleum had just lost a historic contest in the US Supreme Court which required the FPC to regulate the wellhead prices of gas produced for shipment by inter-state pipelines. This development kept a firm lid on US gas prices for nearly a quarter of a century.

Pacific Northwest offered to buy gas in the San Juan Basin at twelve cents per thousand cubic feet, but there were no takers. It then made a deal whereby the oil companies were to drill some 600 wells, and instead of buying the gas, Pacific Northwest would buy the wells, at up to $80,000 each. In addition, Pacific would pay the oil companies royalties of five to nine cents for every thousand cubic feet of gas produced. Under this plan, the gas would cost twice as much as Pacific Northwest initially offered. But because it would be a regulated utility, Pacific Northwest expected to be allowed to pass the higher cost on to the ultimate consumers. In effect, it was a way to get around the FPC regulation of wellhead prices by having the wells operated as part of the pipeline system. On this basis, Pacific Northwest had contracted for the gas under some 300,000 acres in the San Juan Basin, including 180,000 acres controlled by Phillips.

The competition between Westcoast and Pacific Northwest touched off a bitter, personal feud between the heads of the two leading utilities supplying manufactured gas in the US Pacific Northwest, Henry Gellert of Seattle Gas Company and Charles Gueffroy of Portland Gas and Coke Company, in Portland, Oregon. The issue was whether or not Americans could depend on Canadian gas. Portland Gas was the largest utility in the region; Seattle Gas was the second largest. After failing to obtain natural gas from southern Alberta, Portland Gas looked to Westcoast, and Seattle Gas backed Pacific Northwest.

Gellert used full-page newspaper ads and radio broadcasts to campaign against importing Canadian gas. He accused Canada of denying the United States gas from nearby Pincher Creek so that it would be forced to buy gas from the more distant Peace River, in order to "aid in the development and exploitation of the gas and oil resources of British Columbia." This was done, he said, without any "consideration for the welfare" of US consumers who were expected to buy more than 80 per cent of the gas to be delivered by Westcoast. According to Gellert, over twenty years consumers south of the border would wind up paying as much as $200 million more than they would have had to pay for Pincher Creek gas. Even worse, US consumers would be at the mercy of foreign agencies and boards that could cut off supply or jack up prices at any time. The Westcoast line, said Gellert, "would serve Vancouver and all other Canadian markets first. The American market – our Pacific Northwest – would dangle at the end of the Canadian pipeline after all Canadian needs were satisfied. . . . We, an American utility, would actually become an economic vassal of a foreign power."

"Blatant nonsense," responded Gueffroy. "Are we economic vassals of Canada because we're dependent upon that thriving young nation for 90 per cent of our nickel, 75 per cent of our wood pulp, and 80 per cent of our newsprint . . .? If Mr Gellert wishes to expectorate in the eyes of America's best customer, so far as I'm concerned, he can spit alone."

Gueffroy and Gellert took their battle before the FPC, where Portland Gas intervened to support Westcoast. It had commissioned a study by Bechtel to evaluate the two competing proposals. The study estimated that Westcoast could deliver the gas at 20 per cent less cost than Pacific Northwest. That was not surprising, because the Westcoast line would be 1,000 miles long, compared to nearly 1,500 miles for Pacific Northwest. Initially, both lines were designed to deliver 200 million feet of gas per day. But the 24-inch Westcoast line could be expanded to deliver 400 million, while the small-diameter Pacific Northwest line could be expanded to only 300 million without laying additional pipe. Finally, the price that Westcoast proposed to pay at the wellhead for Peace River gas was less than half the price that Pacific Northwest had to pay for San Juan supplies.

Gueffroy's stand at the FPC initiated the intervention of six other gas distributors, including BC Electric, in support of Westcoast's application. These firms, together with Portland Gas, represented 70 per cent of the market and left Seattle Gas and

Spokane Gas and Fuel Company as the only potential customers opposing Westcoast. It looked as though Westcoast was, indeed, in the driver's seat.

In addition to supplying Portland and Seattle, Ray Fish's Pacific Northwest Pipeline also proposed to deliver gas to Denver, Colorado. The economics of its system depended on these sales. In February, 1954, Clint Murchison wrote Howe to report that Colorado Western Gas Pipe Line, of which two of his closest business associates were directors, had applied to build a direct pipeline from the San Juan Basin to Denver. Murchison wrote that this would provide cheaper gas for Denver than Fish's line, "which means the Denver market is going to be taken away from the Fish project, as politically they could not refuse" the Colorado application. "So you can tell Mr McMahon that Mr Fish is laid away in a barrel."

One cause of concern, however, was the new chairman of the Federal Power Commission, J.F. Kuykendall. A Spokane resident and former chairman of the Washington State Utilities Commission, Kuykendall was concerned about the price of gas in his home-town area, the Inland Empire. The combined proposals of Westcoast and Trans-Northwest Gas resulted in significantly higher prices for the Inland Empire than for Seattle and Portland, and considerably higher prices than for supplies delivered from Pincher Creek.

Although he lacked any authority to do so, Howe attempted to resolve this problem by promising a supply of southern Alberta gas for the Inland Empire. The offer was made during a meeting with Kuykendall in Washington, DC, on March 17, 1954, while the hearings were still underway. The following day, Howe wrote to Kuykendall:

> This will confirm my suggestion to you that provided part 1 of the application of Westcoast Transmission Company giving service to the West Coast is accepted, I am quite sure that within the next six months it will be possible to arrange a separate outlet for a gas line from southern Alberta to serve Spokane and the Inland Empire, thus bringing the cost of gas in the last mentioned area down at least to the price quoted for the coast cities. Permit for such an outlet would probably be given to Westcoast Transmission, although the question of who will obtain the permit will be a matter for the Province of Alberta to decide. As I told you, I am anxious to get on with

158

the pipeline from the Peace River field to Vancouver which is possible only if the decision on our application to serve the West Coast is favourable.

McMahon, meanwhile, was anxious to get on with an even bigger project, a pipeline from the Peace River all the way to San Francisco. Moving gas this extra distance would require a larger diameter pipe to move a greater volume and much larger reserves in the Peace River. A study by the Bechtel Corporation for West-coast concluded that a thirty-six-inch line, capable of moving more than twice as much gas as the planned twenty-four-inch line, could deliver Peace River gas to San Francisco for an economical price. All it would require would be an extra invest-ment of some $100 million and gas reserves in the Peace River of some 7 to 8 trillion cubic feet, three times the amount that had by then been found. The bigger the pipe, the lower the transporta-tion cost, and McMahon wanted to build the biggest line possi-ble. No one had yet built a long-distance pipeline as large as thirty-six inches. There was no doubt in McMahon's mind that the gas supply was there; it was just a matter of time to find it. But time was of the essence.

In February, 1954, McMahon appeared before the FPC for the final time, and he was questioned by FPC staff counsel Alvin Kurtz on the source of the $1 million that had by then been spent on studies and the hearings to advance the Westcoast project. McMahon was vague about where the money had come from. He said that the four sponsors (himself, Pacific, Sunray, and Eastman, Dillon) had originally committed to put up $75,000 each, or a total of $300,000, in what he described as "a pretty lax arrangement to start with." He thought that each of the sponsors had put up their share, "but I am not quite sure whether they have exactly." In any event, he said that he had advanced more than $200,000. "Now, the promotion . . . has gone along for several years, and instead of it costing $300,000 which we originally thought it might cost to start with, it has cost us a good deal over $1 million. So I cannot get into that particular part of it."

Pacific Northwest counsel Leon Payne grilled McMahon on earlier Westcoast literature that extolled the benefits of the pro-ject for Canada. Westcoast had intimated that Canadian cus-tomers would receive priority over American consumers, that Canada would benefit from large expenditures of American capital, and that "all questions of pipeline rates, safety regulations, and in fact all control would be under the provision of Canadian authorities." It was not exactly the type of evidence that Westcoast would chose to emphasize before the FPC.

"This was the propaganda that we put out" to thwart the plans of the Fish and Dixon proposals, McMahon candidly explained, ". . . it is straight propaganda, something of the type that Mr Gellert and other people have been writing, and that I read nearly every day in the newspapers."

Payne: "Well, in other words, what you are telling me, Mr McMahon, is that this is the propaganda you put out to the Canadians?"

McMahon: "That is exactly right. Just the same way that you have been putting it out to the Americans."

Payne continued to quote from the Westcoast propaganda: "Our minerals, our water power, our forests, and our oil and gas lands must be developed and utililized before we can reap the benefits they hold in store. We have everything to gain from the application of sound common sense in the development of all our natural resources."

Payne: "That statement would still be true, I take it."

McMahon: "Yes sir. I can hardly believe I wrote it, it's so good."

As the longest hearings in the history of the Federal Power Commission drew to a close, tempers were getting frayed. Jerome McGrath, counsel for the coal and railway interests, attempted to introduce last-minute evidence intended to show that the Peace River gas reserves were only half as great as Westcoast claimed. Westcoast counsel Charles Shannon protested that submitting evidence on such short notice, without the other parties being given the customary opportunity to examine the supporting exhibits in advance, was designed to prolong the hearings. "I think it's an outrage," Shannon said. "I have tried cases with Mr McGrath for many years, and I didn't think he would ever pull a stunt like this one."

"All these charges against my unfairness don't make any impression on me," McGrath blandly responded. "I try my lawsuits the way I want to. Now, he can protest from here to eternity, as far as I'm concerned . . . all this bellyaching about what I have done doesn't bother me a bit."

Four days later, on March 29, 1954, the argument turned on

160

how much time would be required to file briefs, supply reply briefs, and prepare final oral arguments before the full commission. Jerome McGrath asked for four months to prepare initial briefs, with more time for reply briefs and final arguments; altogether, at least another half year. "I know that people out there, the chambers of commerce, are wiring in, and citizens are wiring in, and they're criticizing the delay and all that sort of thing," McGrath said. But, "In the sort of hysteria that results from that kind of pressure, I'm afraid my clients won't get a square deal." He claimed that none of the applicants would fold their tents if a little extra time was taken. Phillips Petroleum "has been in and spent time and money, and with such an array of talent as I never saw before in a case. They have got by far the greatest amount of gas that Pacific Northwest expects to get. I don't think they're going to drop the bucket right in the middle of the fire here, as it were, and run out on Pacific Northwest."

Shannon argued that ten days was ample time to prepare the first briefs, and that McGrath's request was designed "to prevent the use of this year for construction. Now, that's what the four months would do."

Two days later, the commission ruled that, "prompt disposition of these matters is urgently required." The normal process involving findings and recommendations by the presiding examiner to the commission would be omitted. Twenty-five days were allowed to file briefs, another thirty days for reply briefs, and final argument by counsel before the full commission was set for June 1. The decision of the Federal Power Commission could be expected within two or three weeks after that.

INLAND NATURAL GAS

The focus of attention during the long years of the Westcoast regulatory hearings was on the large markets in Vancouver and the US Pacific Northwest where gas utilities were already supplying manufactured gas. Another market of critical importance, although much smaller in size, was the towns and villages in the interior of British Columbia, along the 700-mile Westcoast route from Fort St John to the US border. No utilities existed to supply these areas with manufactured gas, but something would have to be created if Westcoast's claim of providing a new source of energy throughout most of the province was to be achieved.

The cost of supplying gas to these locations could vary greatly, depending on the distance from the Peace River, the distance from the Westcoast mainline, and the amount of gas involved. The cost would be much less for a town like Prince George, close to the Peace River gas and right on the Westcoast route, than for a town such as Penticton, several hundred miles south and a considerable distance from the pipeline route. If the price were based on the individual costs to each town, a number would get very cheap gas, but others would not be able to afford it. The only way to serve the greatest number of communities was with a single, averaged price for each – in effect, a postage-stamp rate. It would mean that communities like Prince George would pay more, but communities like Penticton would pay less.

The simplest method to implement such a rate would be to establish one utility to service all BC interior towns. With this in mind, in late 1951 Westcoast provided John McMahon and Norman Whittall with a letter of intent granting them "the exclusive right to purchase gas from us" for the interior communities. John McMahon, a partner in the Vancouver investment firm of McMahon and Burns, had long experience in financing municipal and hospital bonds throughout BC and was well and favourably regarded throughout the province. John and Whittall formed Inland Natural Gas, aided by financial backing from Pacific Petroleums and engineering design from Westcoast and its contractor, Ford, Bacon & Davis.

Inland had no difficulty in negotiating utility franchises with the BC municipalities, except for Prince George, where local businessmen backed by the city council sought to form their own utility and purchase gas directly from Westcoast. Their hope was to get a cheaper supply of gas, but that would have played havoc with the concept of a postage-stamp rate and the goal of servicing the maximum number of communities. After a five-year battle, the BC Public Utilities Commission finally awarded the Prince George franchise to Inland.

In the mid-1950s, the largest potential market on the proposed Inland gas system was in the Okanagan Valley and on through the Kootenays to the mining area around Trail. But, at least initially, the economics would be marginal, and Westcoast agreed to pay a subsidy on the delivery of gas to that part of the system beyond Penticton. Inland experienced a decade of financial difficulty but emerged as a substantial and profitable utility that

162

serves most of the communities within the interior of British Columbia.

THE HOWARD HUGHES AND OTHER DEALS

In August, 1952, Whittall resigned as chairman of the board of Pacific Petroleums. He was succeeded by Frank McMahon, who is turn was succeeded as president by George McMahon, while Frank continued as president of Westcoast.

While Westcoast was fighting its regulatory battles, Pacific continued aggressive exploration work, drilling on its oil leases at Redwater, and searching for gas on its extensive holdings in the Peace River. By early 1954, Pacific and its partners had drilled more than 100 gas wells in the Peace River, mostly on the BC side. Although Pacific's revenues had increased spectacularly under McMahon's management, expenditures had risen even more rapidly. In 1953, the company wrote off dry-hole costs of $1.7 million and reported a loss of $600,000.

That, however, was no more than loose change compared to the amount of money that Howard Hughes was interested in spending on wildcat drilling through Pacific Petroleums in 1952. The recluse billionaire manufacturer of drilling bits, aviator, and motion-picture producer faced the prospect of either paying enormously increased taxes or increasing his investment spending substantially as a result of a change in US corporate income taxes. Hughes figured he might avoid the taxes by using more than $50 million a year on wildcat drilling, and he was interested in spending the money through Frank McMahon and his companies. It was an amount that even Pacific would be hard pressed to spend usefully.

While beating the bushes in Los Angeles for more capital, Frank McMahon had met Noah Dietrich, Hughes's chief lieutenant and financial advisor. It was Dietrich who first suggested the venture to Howard Hughes. McMahon was at the Santa Anita racetrack when Hughes contacted him by phone to suggest a meeting. They met in Hughes's antiseptic office in Los Angeles, with its bare walls, stainless-steel furniture, and a large bank of telephones. "Hughes was growing deaf but he wouldn't wear a hearing aid," McMahon later recalled. "You had to shout at him. He could hear better on the phone, so it was easier to do business with him by phone. He was constantly on the phone."

In July, 1952, a team of Pacific people – chief geologist Les Clark, landman Jim Statler, financial man Pat Bowsher, lawyer D.P. McDonald, and others – travelled to Los Angeles for a month of negotiations with Hughes and his staff. The Pacific team had worked up a series of wildcat ventures extending from off the Atlantic coast to western and northern Canada, with detailed geology, costs, and possible pay-outs for each prospect. In the end, the venture fell through after Hughes was unable to obtain assurance that he would be allowed to write off the expenditures for tax purposes, but a number of the wildcat proposals that Pacific had assembled were later put to good use.

In addition to wildcatting, McMahon plunged into another gambling business, horse racing. He bought his first race horse in 1952, when he formed Westmount Stock Farms. The following year he joined forces with partners Wilder Ripley (who later dropped out) and Calgary newspaper publisher and oil man Max Bell to form Alberta Ranches, later Golden West Farms. McMahon and Bell had a 640-acre thoroughbred ranch at Okotoks, near Calgary, but raced most of their horses in California. Their principal jockey was Johnny Longden, who claimed to be the youngest cowboy in history, rounding up neighbours' cows near Lethbridge at the age of ten, and later became the first jockey in history to ride more than 5,000 winners.

McMahon and Bell were soon hob-nobbing with the international horsey set. In London, Bell planned a party to celebrate their expected win of the Epsom Derby by Blue Sail in June, 1953. Blue Sail finished tenth, but 600 guests still turned up at the party in the posh Savoy Hotel to dance and drink champagne into the small hours of the day, according to a *Canadian Press* dispatch. The following month, the *Los Angeles Times* recorded that Frank and Isobel, "invited around 200 of the horsey set to drop in at the Beverly Hills Club for a victory celebration," after Royal Seranade won the $100,000 Gold Cup Classic at Hollywood.

Horse racing brought McMahon into contact with Chris Chenery, owner of a famous stallion, Hill Prince, and president of Southern Natural Gas Pipeline Company of Houston, Texas. One of the shareholders of this company was Charles Whittelsey, president of Ford, Bacon & Davis. McMahon sold Chenery on looking at the prospects of drilling in Canada. Pacific dusted off some of the proposals that had been prepared for Howard

164

Hughes, and in 1953 a subsidiary of Southern Natural, Southern Production Company, signed an agreement to spend $10 million exploring more than 3,000 acres of rights held by Pacific, Canadian Atlantic, Sunray, and Peace River Natural Gas. The following year, a similar farm-out was negotiated with Imperial Oil, which undertook to spend $9 million in exploratory drilling on properties held by the Pacific group.

No amount of business or social success can provide immunity to tragedy, and tragedy came to the family of Frank and Isobel McMahon on May 27, 1953, with the death of their eldest son, twenty-four-year-old Frank Grant McMahon, in a car cash. Both Frank and his younger brother Bill had worked in the oil fields, Frank with seismic crews and drilling rigs, and Bill with heavy equipment and oil-field supplies. At the time of his death, Frank was a geology student at Menlo College, Palo Alta, California. He was survived by his wife, Agnes, who later married Max Bell.

CLOSING ARGUMENTS

At the oral arguments presented to the Federal Power Commission on June 1 and 2, 1954, the counsel for each of the applicants, many of the interveners, and the FPC staff had their last say.

Arthur Logan for Northwest Natural Gas argued that his client's shorter line from Pincher Creek to Spokane, Seattle, Portland, and Vancouver could save US consumers $4 million a year compared to the Westcoast line, and he asked for a one-year reprieve. Logan claimed that the Northwest Natural line could be built in one year, instead of the two years required for either the Westcoast or Pacific Northwest line. Thus, "If one year from now we get this gas, we can meet the same delivery schedule" with a cheaper supply of gas. But every indication was that if the United States wanted Canadian gas, it would have to take it from the Peace River, not from Pincher Creek.

Leon Payne for Pacific Northwest described the Westcoast route as one, "where there is no access, no towns, no people;" it crossed the Coquihalla Pass where a pipeline break could be buried under 200 feet of snow and debris. The latter charge ignored the facts that the Trans-Mountain oil line had already been built through the Coquihalla Pass without any serious problems, the CPR had been running trains through the pass for decades with no great difficulties, and that at 3,600 feet it was half the maximum elevation of the Pacific Northwest route from San Juan.

Henry Gellert argued that the Westcoast line would subject "the financial integrity of the Seattle Gas Company and the industrial development of our city . . . to the control of a foreign power." But this view was opposed by the counsel for Portland Gas and Coke, who argued that the line from the San Juan Basin would cost US consumers $5 million a year more than the Westcoast line. California interests, including the City of San Francisco, Pacific Gas and Electric, Southern California Gas Company, and Southern Counties Gas Company, all opposed shipment of New Mexico gas to Seattle and favoured importation of Canadian gas from Westcoast. Their argument was that San Juan supplies were needed in California. "The Pacific northwest area and all of the west would be materially benefitted by a decision of this commission permitting the importation of natural gas from our friendly neighbor, Canada," according to Pacific Gas and Electric.

The State of New Mexico claimed that foreign imports had adversely affected the state's oil producing industry, "And we don't want to be confronted with the same situation in regard to gas. . . . We would not like to see gas imported from a foreign country."

Tom McGrath said that his clients "naturally" had "a little antipathy to a foreign fuel coming into this country and displacing, disrupting coal markets, putting miners and railroad men out of work, and taking our revenues away from us."

When the final word had been said, the transcript of the two years of hearings ran to 28,460 pages. In all the welter of words, most observers concluded that Westcoast had advanced the strongest case. It was now just a matter of waiting for the decision of the Federal Power Commission.

Frank and Isobel McMahon could now turn their attention to what promised to be the social event of the season in Calgary, the marriage of their daughter, Marion, on June 29. It was planned as the biggest wedding in Calgary's history. Invitations were sent out across the continent. Before the wedding, if all went well, Frank McMahon's twenty-year-old pipeline dream would become a reality.

CHAPTER ELEVEN

The FPC Battle: Round Two

For years to come in the offices of Pacific Petroleums on Calgary's Ninth Avenue it was known as "Black Friday"; June 18, 1954.

Pacific employees, waiting for word that day, knew that champagne had been stocked in the boardroom in anticipation of a victory celebration to which all were invited.

For weeks before, Frank McMahon had been offering $500 bets to his business associates that the Westcoast line would soon be approved by the Federal Power Commission, and there were no takers. But within the past week during telephone calls to Houston, the capital of the US gas pipeline business, he found a number of people now willing to take him up on the bet.

McMahon got the message on the 18th while he was sitting in the barber's chair in the Hotel Pierre in New York.

D.P. McDonald learned about it in a telephone call from Robert May of Wheat, May, and Shannon, Westcoast's Washington law firm.

The news was that the FPC had rejected the application of Westcoast Transmission Company to import Peace River natural gas into the US Pacific Northwest and had approved the proposed Pacific Northwest pipeline from the San Juan Basin in New Mexico.

May read McDonald the text of a brief news release issued by the FPC announcing the decision before the full text of the thirty-eight-page decision was available. McDonald's secretary recorded the conversation in shorthand. After May read the release, snippets from the conversation went like this:

McDonald: "It looks to me like a squeeze play to force us into providing them with the major portion of our gas to keep us as underdogs. We will just have to start on our other proposition, I presume."

May: "It was a good fight."

McDonald: "I just don't know – I didn't think they would go on that angle. They authorized Pacific Northwest? Did they find they had adequate reserves and everything?"

May: "I assume so."

McDonald: "Keep a stiff upper lip. I think we can get them ——it will take about a year or two, six months."

May: "It's a tough break. We will hold on. I am sure we haven't given up yet."

In New York, McMahon maintained his humour, telling his consoling friends a story in which he compared himself to a prairie farmer. On a bitterly cold winter night, the farmer resisted the call of nature as long as possible, rather than face the 150-foot dash through a blinding blizzard to the outhouse in the backyard. Once he could wait no longer, the farmer dashed for the outhouse, but on the way tripped and fell over the clothes line. By the time he picked himself up, the farmer found that he had already wet his pants. "Well," said the farmer, "I guess I just wasn't going to make it anyway." McMahon paused and repeated: "I guess I just wasn't going to make it anyway." The big pipe dream, it seemed, had just burst.

In approving the Pacific Northwest proposal, the Federal Power Commission found that its system, together with the related 300-mile line to Denver suggested by Colorado Interstate Gas Company, would supply more US communities with gas than the Westcoast project. "Moreover," the commissioners wrote, "the route of the proposed Pacific pipeline traverses at least three large undeveloped sedimentary basins in the states of Colorado, Utah, and Wyoming. Exploration and development of these production areas would be stimulated by providing an outlet for natural gas."

But the main reason for rejecting the Westcoast application was the commission's belief that no region of the United States should depend on a foreign country for its only source of natural gas. The report stressed that US consumers must be protected with secure supplies, while adding:

Such protection would not be afforded to any segment of the American people if its sole source of essential natural gas were

168

through importation from a foreign country without some intergovernmental agreement assuring the continued adequacy of its supply. Otherwise, all control over the production, allocation, and transportation to our border of such natural gas would be in the hands of agencies of foreign governments, whose primary interest would of necessity always be in the needs and advantages of their own people, and whose judgments and actions would be essentially dependent upon public opinion within that country, rather than upon the interests of American consumers. Regardless of any long and cherished friendly relations with any neighbor nation able to supply such areas with natural gas, it would not be in the public interest to permit the importation of its gas as the sole source for the consumers in need of an uninterruptible supply. . . .

The FPC report also observed that it was conceivable that imports could be authorized into a US market as "a supplementary supply of gas for its interruptible needs. We do not consider it to be in the public interest, however, to authorize a most important new project to serve a major area . . . which from the outset will be completely tied to and wholly dependent upon an exclusive source of supply entirely beyond the control of agencies of the United States."

FPC chairman Jerome Kuykendall issued a separate, brief decision, "dissenting in part" from the other four commissioners. Kuykendall still favoured the use of Pincher Creek gas, finding that, "The entire Pacific Northwest could be better and more cheaply served by natural gas transported from southern Alberta." His proposal was that the Pacific Northwest line from New Mexico should be approved within a stipulated time, "unless within such period the Canadian and appropriate provincial governments authorized the export of an adequate supply of gas from southern Alberta." That, however, was a step that Ottawa was not about to take.

Quickly recovering from the initial reaction that, "I wasn't going to make it, anyway," McMahon bounced back with his customary optimism. "It's been a setback," he conceded to reporters. "But we are not too concerned since we have worked on plans to export to California for some time."

Few were aware that Westcoast had, indeed, been studying the feasibility of supplying the California market, and fewer still were impressed by McMahon's display of confidence. During the final half hour of trading on the American Stock Exchange on Black Friday, shares of Pacific Petroleums fell from $12 to $6. On Monday, Canadian Atlantic fell from $7 to $3.50, while shares of Inland Natural Gas fell from $4 to fifty cents. "Many individuals and a few brokerage houses were wiped out," *Fortune* later reported.

McMahon now found himself bombarded with advice. Westcoast director George Martin wrote to express dismay at the idea that Westcoast might appeal the FPC decision: "It seems to me that such an appeal can only have a nuisance value at best and in the meantime would antagonize a number of people in Washington and elsewhere whom we will probably want to use in the near future. I think this is a case for us to show that we know how to lose in a gracious manner."

Others were more encouraging, and still others saw some glimmer of hope. George Hume, writing to McMahon from Ottawa three days after the decision, reflected the view of many informed observers that Pacific Northwest lacked an adequate supply of gas for its proposed line. Hume described it as "an uneconomic operation," adding:

> I presume there will now be an attempt to get gas from the Pincher Creek area to supplement that from the southwest United States. I hope that this will not be allowed as that would totally prejudice the development of the Peace River area. . . . Certainly we are not going to take a defeatist attitude towards the idea of getting gas out of the Peace River. It will be needed in California alright, but there may be some problems in getting it there.

Howe was upset by the FPC decision and wrote to Lester Pearson, then Secretary of State for External Affairs, that it was "tantamount to a complete embargo" and implied that "foreign relations are being handled by a commission of the United States government, rather than constituted US authorities." He recalled that during the Korean War Canada had approved gas export to the Anaconda Copper smelter in Montana as a defence measure which "certainly was not on an interruptible basis." Howe added:

> It may be well to remind the State Department that Canada has been exporting electrical energy to the US under firm contracts for the past forty years and that these contracts have

always been carried out regardless of the fact that power exported was from time to time urgently needed in Canada, particularly during two war periods. Our legislation governing the export of electrical energy is the same legislation that governs our export of gas. I do not know of any incident associated with the export of energy from Canada which would justify the finding of the FPC.

Kuykendall's dissenting opinion in the FPC breathed a brief flicker of life into the dying hopes for Faison Dixon's Northwest Natural pipeline. Three weeks after the FPC decision, a representative from the Morgan Stanley firm phoned Howe to enquire if there might now be a possibility of obtaining Pincher Creek gas for the West Coast market. "I told them that we would not consider any further export as long as the Federal Power Commission ruling is in effect that Canada can supply gas to the US only on an interruptible basis," Howe wrote to McMahon. "In other words, we will hold the status quo until you can explore the possibilities of disposing of the gas which you presently hold under export permit."

Marion McMahon's wedding to Dean Macdonald of Tacoma, Washington, went ahead as scheduled. It was Calgary's largest wedding. The former Calgary Stampede Queen was married at the Cathedral Church of the Redeemer, where thirty choir boys followed the couple down the aisle. A reception followed for some 500 guests at the Palliser Hotel. Hollywood designers were hired to produce the ladies' gowns and supervise the floral arrangements. Two Hollywood cameramen joined local photographers. McMahon's aircraft spent ten days flying guests to Calgary from across Canada and the United States. The father of the bride paid for 125 rooms at the Palliser, kept them stocked with liquor, picked up the tab for all meals, and provided twenty-four-hour taxi service for his guests. Extra supplies of champagne were flown in from Vancouver and Winnipeg, because Calgary's liquor stores had run out. If it were true that the McMahon empire was on the verge of crumbling after the FPC decision, none of the wedding guests appeared too concerned, least of all the father of the bride.

FREEZING FISH'S PIPELINE

The fact was, that despite his victory in the FPC battle, Ray Fish

171

had just about as much reason to worry as Frank McMahon. Few informed observers considered his pipeline an economical project, most thought that he did not have enough gas to fill the line, and there seemed little hope that he could obtain supplementary supplies from southern Alberta. *Business Week* had described his FPC certificate "as good as money in the bank." If that were so, he would have a hard time cashing in on it, because Westcoast and its allies did an effective job of freezing the account, as it were. At the same time, McMahon and his officials scampered around the United States for a series of negotiations aimed at a deal that would still see the line from the Peace River built. In the final half of 1954, actions to block Fish's plans included:

– Refusal of the Portland Gas and Coke Company to sign a gas purchase contract with Pacific Northwest. Although a temporary action, this left Fish without a sales contract with the largest utility in the market. Without it, financing the $160 million line would be almost impossible.

– Appeals by Westcoast and Trans-Northwest to the FPC to rehear their applications, another temporary measure.

– Court action seeking an order compelling the FPC to rehear the case.

– Negotiations by Westcoast with Pacific Gas and Electric to sell Peace River gas in San Francisco.

– Negotiations with El Paso Natural Gas Company, the only firm then supplying out-of-state gas (from New Mexico, Oklahoma, and Texas) to California.

– And finally, negotiations with Ray Fish and one of his strongest supporters, Phillips Petroleum.

In their applications to the FPC for a rehearing, both Westcoast and Trans-Northwest claimed that the commission had exceeded its authority by ruling that American consumers could not depend on gas imported from Canada. "The commission has assumed authority with respect to the conduct in international affairs which it has not been given and could not be given under the Constitution," the Trans-Northwest brief declared. For good measure, Trans-Northwest added that the decision was "an abuse of discretion, arbitrary, capricious, contrary to the weight of evidence adduced, and constitutes error in law." After due consideration, the FPC rejected the applications for rehearing, and Westcoast and Trans-Northwest then filed appeals in US federal courts against the FPC.

172

While pursuing these legal steps to block Pacific Northwest, Westcoast wasted no time in starting its round of negotiations. Discussions opened in San Francisco with Pacific Gas and Electric within three weeks of the FPC decision, and a few weeks later in El Paso, Texas, talks were underway with El Paso Natural Gas Company.

Based on studies by Bechtel, Westcoast proposed a $200 million, thirty-inch pipeline from the Peace River to the California-Oregon border, where up to half a billion cubic feet of gas per day would be available to Pacific Gas and Electric. The big San Francisco utility was interested in additional gas, because it supplied 2.5 million customers, and the demand was growing rapidly. One third of its gas came from California fields, where production was already declining, and two-thirds was supplied by El Paso, which PG&E felt could be hard-pressed to meet future demands. Despite this, Westcoast was unable to negotiate a satisfactory sales price with PG&E, whose officials suggested to McMahon that he should try to make a deal with Ray Fish.

One reason for PG&E's coolness was that, already relying on El Paso for two-thirds of its gas, it did not want to become increasingly dependent on pipeline systems over which it had no control. It was already thinking about building its own pipeline from Alberta to San Francisco, and as a company spokesman later testified, it wanted to control such a line "as distinguished from dealing with a pipeline company . . . which might have different interests from ours." Finally, PG&E was probably just a little leery that both Westcoast and Pacific Northwest would eventually wind up under the control of El Paso's dynamic president, Paul Kayser.

Kayser had formed the company in 1928 to build a 205-mile line to supply the town of El Paso. Nine years later it began delivering gas to California, which it virtually held as a captive market. Without a deal that gave El Paso a piece of the action, Kayser could not be expected to welcome intruders into his domain. Ray Fish and Frank McMahon both looked like intruders. In March, 1954, three months before the FPC decision, Kayser had approached both Fish and McMahon to sound out the possibilities of arranging a merger of the two competing projects, but only on a basis that would leave El Paso in control. Adding to El Paso's interest was the fact that, in 1950, it had picked up large oil and gas exploration permits in northern British Columbia

173

located north of Peace River in the Fort Nelson area and close to the borders of the Yukon and Northwest Territories. If Kayser could effect a suitable merger, he could control the whole gas transmission business west of the Rockies, from the Yukon to Mexico. McMahon and his partners, however, were confident they were going to win the FPC certificate and rejected Kayser's overtures. Kayser decided to bide his time.

After the cool reception in San Francisco, the Westcoast party pressed on to El Paso, where Paul Kayser was still patiently waiting for the universe to unfold as it should. Kayser allowed as how, yes, he was still interested. What he had in mind was that the Westcoast and Pacific Northwest pipelines should be integrated with El Paso's pipeline network to assure that the growing requirements for gas along the US West Coast would be met in the most efficient and economical manner. That would require further discussions with Pacific Gas and Electric and the opening of negotiations with Fish's group.

Before negotiations started with Ray Fish, a US federal court in Philadelphia handed Westcoast a lever that greatly strengthened its bargaining position, thanks to the legal efforts of Trans-Northwest. The Spokane firm was still determined to build its system to distribute gas throughout the Inland Empire. It would probably have been prepared to buy gas from Pacific Northwest, except that Pacific Northwest intended to build its own pipelines in the Inland Empire and had no intention of turning over the job to Trans-Northwest. Pacific Northwest had the FPC certificate to do just that, and no small-town outfit from the backwoods of Washington State was likely to stop them.

But Pacific Northwest failed to reckon with the acumen of the promoters of Trans-Northwest, Paul Graves and his legal partners in the Spokane firm of Graves, Kaizer, Greenough, and Company. The Graves firm launched an appeal seeking a court order requiring the FPC to rehear the entire case. Most appeals of this nature were heard by the Court of Appeal of the First District, in Washington, DC, where the judges were knowledgeable in the complex legal intricacies of pipeline issues. But Trans-Northwest had a novel argument to advance, and it was not interested in the pipeline expertise of the judges in Washington. It wanted a court that might be more sympathetic to its views and selected the Third Appelant District of the Federal Court in Philadelphia to file its appeal.

The basis of the Trans-Northwest appeal was the certificates it held from the Idaho Public Utilities Commission authorizing construction of its proposed system in seven counties and the gas franchises issued by the Board of County Commissioners of fourteen counties in the eastern part of the State of Washington. A Federal Power Commission certificate that sought to override these local authorities was an improper invasion of local rights and interests by a "foreign" agency, the Government of the United States in this case, Trans-Northwest argued. The Philadelphia court agreed and directed the FPC to rehear the Trans-Northwest case. In effect, this would reopen the entire proceedings.

The order from the Philadelphia court came just as Pacific Northwest was attempting to complete financing for its $160 million pipeline. Suddenly, the money for the first mortgage bonds from the big insurance companies, which was to account for three-quarters of the investment, was no longer available. The trouble stemmed from Algonquin Gas Transmission. This company had built a pipeline into New England under a similar legal cloud, only to have the line stand idle for more than a year, a very expensive white elephant. After the Algonquin case, money-lenders were not prepared to advance sums to build any further pipelines under such legal clouds. Pacific Northwest was stalemated.

It was K.S. "Boots" Adams, chairman of Phillips Petroleum, who got Ray Fish and Frank McMahon to sit at the same table. The reasons behind Adams' interest were complex, bound up as they were with the history of Phillips, and the negotiations were protracted.

Phillips Petroleum had been founded by "Uncle Frank" Phillips, who was born in Iowa and dressed in cowboy boots and wide brimmed hat. He moved to Oklahoma shortly after oil had been discovered in 1903 on land belonging to the Osage Indian Nation near Jake Bartle's trading post, the future site of Bartlesville. Phillips persuaded his two brothers to join him in a fling at wildcatting, leased lands from the Osage Nation, drilled two dry holes before finding oil, then brought in eighty producing wells without a miss. The Phillips brothers sold their oil wells and most of their leases, but Frank Phillips returned to the oil business to form Phillips Petroleum in 1917. Three years later, Boots Adams dropped out of college to work for the company as a warehouse clerk, and twelve years later he had worked his way up to become assistant to the man the company hands called "Uncle Frank." When Phillips retired in 1938, Boots Adams was named president and headed the company for the next twenty-six years. Led by Adams' shrewd gambles and wheeling-dealing, Phillips grew rapidly. By 1954, it was one of only eighteen US firms with assets of more than one billion dollars. A company vice-president later claimed that, "Frank Phillips built the foundation of this company, and Ken Adams put the building on it."

It was Adams who got Phillips Petroleum into the natural gas business and developed it into the largest gas producer in the United States, with large holdings in the San Juan Basin. But by 1954, *Fortune* magazine reported that Phillips was "quick to sell off moderately productive properties, like those at the San Juan field, and put the money to work in search of bigger if more hazardous earnings." The sale of its San Juan properties, however, depended on construction of the stalemated Pacific Northwest pipeline, and Phillips urgently wanted the sale to go through.

Boots Adams called his friend Clarence Wright of Sunray in Tulsa, a stone's throw from Bartlesville, and Wright set up a meeting in New York with Adams, McMahon, and Lloyd Gilmour of Eastman, Dillon. McMahon and Adams, cut from similar cloth, were soon to become fast friends and close business associates, but the bargaining was hard-nosed. Adams wanted McMahon and Fish to work out a market sharing deal which would allow both pipelines to be built and continually pressured Wright to induce McMahon to come to terms with Fish. McMahon and his group met with Fish and his group for two days of preliminary discussions in New York on October 11 and 12, 1954. Discussions were also continued with Paul Kayser, who played a key role in reaching an agreement.

The deal that was finally hammered out involved complex arrangements. It provided that Westcoast would build a thirty-inch line from the Peace River to Vancouver and the nearby US border point at Sumas, rather than the earlier proposed twenty-four-inch line. At Sumas, Pacific Northwest would buy 300 million cubic feet of gas from Westcoast: 50 million for the states of Washington and Oregon and 250 million to be delivered to El Paso at a point on the Pacific Northwest line in Idaho, called Mountainhome. From Mountainhome, El Paso would build a branch line through Nevada and then southwest to deliver most of this gas to Pacific Gas and Electric at San Francisco. Pacific Northwest would also have an option on a further 100 million cubic feet per day from Westcoast. Ray Fish's line would thus have gas pouring into it at both ends: BC gas moving south from Sumas, and New Mexico gas moving north from San Juan. Supplying Peace River gas in Washington and Oregon would also free an equivalent amount of San Juan gas, which El Paso would move to California through its existing lines.

These arrangements were agreed to at a meeting in Boots Adams' suite in the Drake Hotel in Chicago during the annual meeting of the American Petroleum Institute in late November, 1954. At the meeting were McMahon and D.P. McDonald for Westcoast; Clarence Wright and A.V. Smith for Sunray; Ray Fish and Dick Williams for Pacific Northwest; Lloyd Gilmour for Eastman, Dillon; and Charles Whittelsey for Ford, Bacon & Davis. An issue of hot debate was Ray Fish's demand to buy into the ownership of Westcoast as part of any deal. He asked for half interest. That would have all but squeezed out McMahon and his three major partners: Pacific, Sunray, and Eastman, Dillon. Wright finally said that he was tired of supporting Westcoast without a prospect for a market and that a market had to be found. To accommodate Fish, he agreed to give up Sunray's right to maintain up to a quarter interest in Westcoast. The matter was resolved by granting Adams an option to purchase one quarter of the Westcoast shares at the time of public financing and at the same price that the shares would be offered publicly. It was understood that Adams would make these shares available to Pacific Northwest.

The other matter was the price that Pacific Northwest would pay Westcoast for the gas delivered at Sumas. The determining factor was the amount it was considered could be charged for the sale of most of this gas by El Paso to Pacific Gas and Electric in San Francisco. After deducting the estimated transportation cost from Sumas to San Francisco, the result left Westcoast with a sales price of 22 cents per thousand cubic feet for both the initial 300 million cubic feet per day and the option on the further 100 million. It was not an attractive price for Westcoast, barely enough to cover its costs if everything went well. But it was the best that could be had, a case of take it or leave it, and leaving it meant that there would be no Westcoast pipeline. The important thing was to get the line built, because after that surely it would grow rapidly with the discovery of lots more gas in the Peace River.

The essential terms of the agreement were spelled out in three pages of hand-written notes, dated November 29, 1954, and initialled by McMahon and Fish. The lawyers then set to work to prepare more definitive documents. After the lawyers completed the paper work, the final papers were signed in Sunray's offices in Tulsa. A tongue-in-cheek news release issued by Sunray reported that Wright and Adams, "take pleasure in jointly announcing the wedding of their prodigal children, Pacific Northwest Pipeline Corporation, Houston, and Westcoast Transmission Company Limited, Calgary." The signing reportedly took place in Wright's office, number 1313, in the 13-storey Sunray Building, on December 13, at 9:13 am. "Thirteen has always been my lucky number," Wright said.

The Oil and Gas Journal described the arrangement as the "biggest gas deal in history;" it would "form a grid of transmission lines linking all major consuming areas west of the Rockies with all big gas-producing areas in the western half of the continent." In total, the agreement contemplated the construction of some 3,500 miles of pipelines, at a cost exceeding $500 million.

By the time the announcement was made, Westcoast had also completed one other step necessary for the arrangement. It had persuaded Trans-Northwest to drop the legal action that resulted in the court ordering the FPC to rehear its application and effectively stalemated Pacific Northwest long enough to allow negotiations. Paul Graves and his Spokane associates were rewarded for their efforts, and Trans-Northwest Inc faded from history.

As 1954 ended, everything seemed to be coming up a winner for McMahon. In California, his horses were running well. In New York, he had met theatrical producer Frederick Brisson (Rosalind Russell's husband) who was looking for backing for a Broadway musical. McMahon invested an initial $10,000 which had grown to $50,000 by the time the play opened on May 13. *Pajama Game* was greeted with rave reviews and became Broadway's most successful musical of the year.

Some formalities remained to complete "the biggest gas deal in history." In Canada, Westcoast still needed new export permits from the Alberta and federal governments and a new construction permit from the Board of Transport Commissioners for its

178

revised plan to build a thirty-inch line. These were obtained with little trouble. In the United States, Pacific Northwest and El Paso still had to obtain Federal Power Commission approval to import the gas from Westcoast before financing or construction of either line could start.

After the agreement had been reached, and because of the increased size of the project, the Westcoast board approved the sale of an additional 125,000 Westcoast shares at 5 cents each to the four original sponsors: Pacific Petroleums, Eastman, Dillon and Company, Sunray, and McMahon. That brought the total sale of 5-cent shares to 625,000. In addition, Eastman, Dillon and Mc-Mahon were given an option on a further 200,000 shares each, at a price 20 per cent greater than that to be set for the initial public offering.

The directors meeting at which these additional share sales were approved was held in Vancouver on January 28, 1955, and attended by George McMahon, Norman Whittall, Pat Bowsher, and D.P. McDonald. McDonald reported on the details of the agreement that had been reached after six months of negotiations. Because of the assistance rendered in these negotiations, it was agreed that the Bechtel Corporation of San Francisco would be retained as manager of engineering and construction. Ford, Bacon & Davis would handle the design of the compressor stations and act in a consulting role. Ford, Bacon & Davis had been working for Westcoast for five years without yet billing for its services. Now, payments amounting to $640,000 were authorized.

BACK TO THE FEDERAL POWER COMMISSION

The FPC hearings on the import applications by Pacific Northwest and El Paso opened in Washington on May 15, 1955, before examiner Glen Law, who had started off the first round of hearings three years earlier. The proceedings immediately ran into a road-block.

William Miller, counsel for Pacific Gas and Electric, said that the San Francisco utility would not take the Canadian gas that El Paso proposed to deliver through the spur line from Idaho to San Francisco. It would take an equivalent amount of San Juan gas delivered through El Paso's existing system to the Arizona border. But Miller said PG&E had made a "firm, final, and

179

definite conclusion that it would not accept delivery of the gas at any other point." He added that PG&E "does not object to the importation of this Canadian gas by Pacific Northwest."

"Provided that you don't have to use it, is that correct?" Glen Law asked.

Miller: "This is substantially correct, Mr Examiner."

Law: "That is what I wanted to get straightened out on, the sooner the quicker."

Leon Payne, however, declared that Pacific Northwest was "equally firm and definite" that it would not deliver its San Juan gas to El Paso for redelivery to PG&E.

This "is the first experience we have had where we couldn't get the market and the delivery point together," El Paso's counsel, A.R. Gambling, said. "We sincerely hope that some way will be worked out where this matter will be solved, and where a most worthwhile project will not be defeated by any misunderstandings."

Once more, it seemed, things had been stalemated.

Tom McGrath, still seeking delay for the benefit of the coal mines and railways, interjected to say that he had never seen a case "that presented such a maze of difficult, complex, and conflicting situations." He suggested the hearings be recessed until matters got straightened out, and he disputed the claims of the applicants that there was any need for a quick decision:

I don't know of anybody that wants Canadian gas that would suffer for the lack of it, because they haven't got any of it now anyway. . . . We don't want to be rushed in this thing. . . . I think perhaps the Westcoast Limited is to be commended for their daring. I know them pretty well, and, of course, they have been gambling an awful lot for several years, digging dry holes up in British Columbia. . . . But to come in here and say, "Mr Examiner, we have got to have a certificate in a hurry and therefore time is of the essence," is just so much ____ let me say, in more or less legal terms, I think it is frivolous.

Westcoast counsel Charles Shannon declared that he "sincerely did not think Mr McGrath would have the temerity to intervene in this case."

"Mr Shannon is surprised that I intervened in this case?" McGrath responded. "He would have been shocked to death if I hadn't."

180

Behind PG&E's refusal to take Canadian gas at San Francisco was the plan to build its own pipeline from southern Alberta to San Francisco, a scheme it had probably decided upon but not yet announced.

It took two months to resolve the impasse. In the end, it was agreed that virtually all the Canadian gas would be sold in the US northwest, rather than California. El Paso dropped its plans for a spur line to San Francisco, and Pacific Northwest agreed to deliver its San Juan gas to El Paso for the California market.

On November 25, 1955, the Federal Power Commission approved the importation of Canadian gas, ignoring the fact that the US Pacific Northwest still wound up depending on Canadian gas as virtually its sole source of supply. The approval was the green light for nearly $600 million in pipeline construction, including the $150 million Westcoast line, the $250 million Pacific Northwest line, and nearly $200 million by El Paso to expand its existing system to deliver more San Juan gas to California.

The final authorizations required by Westcoast had taken a record 357 days of public hearings before regulatory bodies, spread out over four years: 217 days before the Federal Power Commission in Washington, 136 days before the Alberta Oil and Gas Conservation Board in Calgary, and four days before the Board of Transport Commissioners in Ottawa. Before the final authorization was obtained, contractors had already started laying pipe on the Westcoast line, and Peace River gas was due to start flowing to Vancouver and the US northwest by the fall of 1957. After so many years as an idea in the mind of Frank McMahon, Westcoast Transmission was about to become a reality, an operating organization with a distinct corporate identity.

CHAPTER TWELVE

The Take-over Bid

After Westcoast had secured the necessary authorizations, all that was left were the details. Big details – like raising $150 million in financing and building Canada's first major natural gas pipeline.

McMahon was not one for details. A man of bold concepts and sweeping vision seldom is. He was, of course, vitally concerned that the line was properly financed and the construction job efficiently organized, but this was work mostly for those whose job it is to look after details. Besides, he had another deal to pursue. Even before all the arrangements were completed for financing construction of the Westcoast line in early 1956, McMahon envisioned rescuing the Trans-Canada Pipe Lines project from a financial and political quagmire and building the world's longest natural gas pipeline, from Alberta to Montreal, without government financial help. Except for the details, he had accomplished as much with the pipeline from the Peace River, so why not with this larger project?

From the time it was incorporated by the Parliament of Canada on April 30, 1949, seven years of tough fighting were necessary before Westcoast obtained all its permits in November, 1955, and its financing in early 1956. During that period, the promoters seeking to take Alberta gas eastward were engaged in an even longer battle, and they seemed to be losing.

Two main contenders had fought for the right to move Alberta gas eastward: Western Pipe Lines Limited, incorporated by a special act of Parliament on the same day as Westcoast, and Clint Murchison's Trans-Canada Pipe Lines.

The initial driving force behind Western Pipe Lines was Colonel Lionel D.M. Baxter, president of the Winnipeg investment firm of Osler, Hammond, and Nanton and one of the pioneers in prairie petroleum exploration. Baxter soon drew the support of other important backers: H. Ray Milner, president of the Calgary and Edmonton gas utilities, and two of Canada's largest investment houses, Wood Gundy of Toronto and Nesbitt, Thomson of Montreal. Alan Williamson of Vancouver, a vice-president of Wood Gundy, was a leading actor in the affairs of Western Pipe Lines, as was Dean Nesbitt of Nesbitt, Thomson.

Western proposed to build a line as far east as Winnipeg and then south to the Manitoba border town of Emerson, where after serving Canadian cities gas would be sold to American buyers. Baxter was convinced that it just would not make sense to move Alberta gas farther east across the Precambrian shield of northern Ontario to Toronto and Montreal. "I was asked over a year ago to look into the question of taking gas to Ontario, and I could not be convinced that it was economically feasible to take a line across a thousand miles of rock and muskeg and make it pay at the other end," Baxter told the Alberta Oil and Gas Conservation Board in 1950.

That was just exactly what Trans-Canada proposed to do. Application to remove gas from Alberta for this project was first made in September, 1950, by Canadian Delhi Oil, subsidiary of Murchison's Delhi Oil Corporation of Dallas. The following year, Trans-Canada Pipe Lines Limited was quickly incorporated by Parliament after Murchison agreed to a clause in its charter providing that its "main pipeline or lines . . . shall be located entirely within Canada," and Trans-Canada took over the application from Canadian Delhi.

By September, 1951, Western Pipe Lines had secured a contract to sell gas at Emerson to the Northern Natural Gas Company of Omaha, Nebraska. In a later "information letter" describing the project, Baxter claimed that, "The American deliveries are in the nature of a subsidy to Canadian users and have the effect of lowering the price and making an immediate project feasible." The best way to provide Ontario and Quebec with natural gas, Baxter wrote, would be by an equal "exchange arrangement between Canada and the United States. The supply of gas to the Pacific Northwest market and to the middle western United States would form a quid pro quo of American gas to eastern Canada." But just to be safe, Baxter went on to hedge his bets: "As an alternative, Western could extend its line to . . . eastern Canada if such a project could ever be demonstrated as economically possible."

Hearings on the competitive applications by Western and Trans-Canada continued before the Alberta board throughout 1951, 1952, and 1953. Evidence at the hearings clearly established that the oil companies would much prefer to sell their gas to the US Midwest than to Ontario and Quebec. Since the US market was closer, it would provide the producers with a higher price for the gas, after deducting the cost of transportation. Most of the producers also favoured an exchange arrangement to meet the requirements of eastern Canada. The Alberta government felt much the same way, for exactly the same reasons.

But in Ottawa, the uproar that had been raised over the proposals to ship Alberta gas to Vancouver over an American route apparently convinced the Liberal government that no matter what was most economically feasible, an all-Canadian route to the east was most politically feasible. On January 2, 1953, C.D. Howe wrote Alberta Premier Ernest Manning:

> Gas from Alberta must be available to potential customers in the provinces of Ontario and Quebec, and in the intervening provinces, before further export of gas could be authorized. I am aware that, for the period when natural gas is first made available in Ontario and Quebec, and until the load can be built up, such a pipeline is unlikely to be profitable, either for the producers of gas or for the owners of the pipeline. Nevertheless, there is evidence that a pipeline project for Ontario and Quebec can be worked out and that the project will be profitable over a period of years.

With that frank admission, it was easy to see why the Alberta government favoured the US market, concerned as it was about obtaining the highest price from the sale of its resources. But Howe said he thought it would be "helpful" for Manning to have the views of Ottawa "before any definite decisions are made by Alberta."

Six weeks later, Howe confirmed the all-Canadian principle as the firm policy of the government in a statement to the House of Commons on March 13, 1953. Howe noted that a recent FPC approval of a small volume of US gas exports to southwestern Ontario had stipulated that, "At all times, persons and municipalities in the United States are to receive preferential service over that given to the Union Gas Company of Canada." Under those conditions, Howe said, "There can be no possibility of obtaining a reliable source of supply for Canada in the United States," and the only reliable supply for Ontario and Quebec "must be from western Canada by means of an all-Canadian pipeline." Howe promised that no more gas exports would be approved until "we are convinced that there can be no economic use, present or future, for that natural gas within Canada."

This statement set the cornerstone of the government's natural gas policy. With the exception of the few Social Credit Members from Alberta, it was greeted with enthusiastic acclaim by the opposition parties, who quickly took the credit for having changed the government's course. "It was almost like the return of the Prodigal Son to hear him [Howe] saying these things," commented Conservative Member J.M. Macdonnell. "Some four years ago a few of us took a certain stand in connection with an all-Canadian route, and at first there was very little interest in it," recalled CCF Member Bert Herridge. "In fact, some people felt we were a bit dippy."

The whole country, it seemed, was united behind the all-Canadian pipeline principle. The public supported it. Every political party espoused it. The government endorsed it. But when it came time to put the principle into action, that support turned into bitter opposition.

Shortly after Howe's statement had cast the government's policy in concrete, an independent study conducted by the School of Business Administration at the University of Waterloo and Stanford University confirmed that Alberta offered the most economical and secure source of natural gas for Ontario and Quebec. But the study, paid for by Imperial Oil, also concluded that the best route to get that Alberta gas to eastern Canada was not by the all-Canadian route, but by a US route through Wisconsin and Michigan that returned to Canada in southwestern Ontario at Sarnia. This was the same route followed by the oil line. Such a route, claimed the study, would cut the cost of pipelining the gas by 20 per cent, as compared to the route across northern Ontario. The trouble was that a US route would leave northern Ontario without natural gas service, including Howe's hometown riding of Port Arthur (now Thunder Bay). Putting the oil line through the United States had caused enough of a storm.

A gas pipeline would be worse, because the US route for the oil line had not deprived northern Ontario of gasoline. But the only way that northern Ontario could get natural gas was with a pipeline through its territory.

The continued plans of The Consumers' Gas Company of Toronto to import US gas from Gardiner Symonds' Tennessee Gas Transmission was an obstacle for an all-Canadian pipeline. Consumers' represented the largest potential gas market in Canada, and it was vital to any pipeline plans to supply eastern Canada. Consumers' president Colonel Arthur Bishop and general manager Ed Tucker were crushed by Howe's aggressive opposition to their plans to use cheaper US gas supplies. They took out full-page newspaper ads in a campaign to win support for their plans but failed to budge Howe's opposition. Before the issue was resolved, Tucker had died unexpectedly.

On August 27, 1953, Murchison telegraphed Howe from Dallas, warning him that the FPC was about to approve 60 million cubic feet of US gas exports by Tennessee Gas for Consumers' Gas. "It is my understanding that the Federal Power Commission did not receive your letter concerning this contemplated action," Murchison wrote. "It is needless to tell you that Toronto market is vital in picture of Trans-Canada's all-Canadian pipeline. We are attempting to contact Washington people in authority to get this decision rescinded."

Murchison did not get the FPC decision rescinded, but Western Pipe Lines viewed this as more of an opportunity than a problem. On September 2, Alan Williamson wrote Howe from Vancouver outlining the deal that Western hoped to make with Tennessee Gas. Under this arrangement, Tennessee would supply the Toronto market for an interim period until the demand had built up to a level that would support a pipeline from Alberta. In the meantime, Western could construct its line to Winnipeg, exporting gas to Northern Natural Gas, later extending its line to Toronto and Montreal. Williamson claimed that, "Ultimately the consumers in Ontario would have cheaper gas quicker, and the producers in Alberta would have a better price and a market sooner than otherwise would be the case."

The scheme that Williamson described bore some resemblance to what eventually happened, but at the time Howe saw it only as a threat. There was no law, however, to prevent Consumers' from importing US gas, but Howe still found a way to stop it.

Until legislation could be prepared requiring a license to import gas, Howe applied the Navigable Waters Protection Act to prevent construction of the aerial pipeline crossing of the Niagara River downstream from the falls. The only ship navigating the waters thus protected was the *Maid of the Mist*. Possibly, it was in danger of being struck by a falling pipeline.

While the hearings on the applications of Western Pipe Lines and Trans-Canada to remove Alberta gas continued in Calgary during 1953, Howe approached Manning with the suggestion that it might be a good idea if these two projects were merged. The idea offered a compromise. It would satisfy Alberta's desire to sell gas into the US Midwest, while the export sales would also improve the economics of a line to eastern Canada, thus helping to achieve the desired all-Canadian pipeline.

The report of the Alberta Oil and Gas Conservation Board on the Western and Trans-Canada applications in November, 1953, paved the way for the merger. The board found at last that Alberta had enough surplus gas to allow some of it to be shipped to eastern Canada. It reported that Alberta's gas reserves had increased two-and-a-half times in a period of two-and-a-half years. But it said that it was "not fully satisfied" that either Western Pipe Lines or Trans-Canada could sell enough gas at prices that would make their pipelines economical.

The board also recommended the establishment of a "trunk line" system to collect all the export gas from the various Alberta fields and move it to the Alberta border where it could be picked up by any interprovincial or international pipeline authorized by Ottawa. This reflected Alberta's concern that if such pipelines extended into the province, then the federal government's control over them could lead to federal regulation of Alberta gas production and prices. That had already happened in the United States. The US Natural Gas Act of 1938 empowered the Federal Power Commission to regulate interstate gas pipelines, and in 1952 the Supreme Court ruled that this included not only the pipelines but the gas wells that supplied them. Alberta had no desire to see the same thing happen to its gas. As a result, the Alberta Gas Trunk Line Company was organized to build a gas grid throughout Alberta and stop Ottawa's authority at the border.

As soon as the board's report was out, Manning wrote to the two applicants, urging them to combine forces for "the construction at the earliest possible date of an all-Canadian pipeline from southern Alberta" to Quebec that would also export gas to the US Midwest. Manning said that he had "discussed this matter fully" with Prime Minister St Laurent and had "received assurance of his active co-operation in an effort to bring about the early completion of one sound, over-all economically feasible project."

The task of getting the two companies together was assigned to Howe, who called the sponsors to Ottawa for meetings during the first week of January, 1954. By January 12, Howe was able to announce that, following several days of discussion in which he had acted "as an honest broker," the two firms had agreed to merge. Trans-Canada was the continuing company, but ownership, pending public financing, was split fifty-fifty between the two sponsoring groups. Conservative Leader George Drew greeted the plan with approval and expressed the hope that, "we might proceed as rapidly as possible to do anything that might be necessary to expedite this important venture."

The next step was to find a president for Trans-Canada who would be acceptable to both sponsoring groups. The unanimous choice was Nathon Eldon Tanner, the Mormon schoolteacher who had served as Alberta Minister of Mines for eighteen years before leaving the government to establish Merrill Petroleums in 1952 with financial backing from the world's largest stock brokerage firm, Merrill, Lynch, Fenner, Pierce, and Beane. Tanner, a quiet and unassuming man, was the epitome of trust and confidence. Born in Salt Lake City, Utah, his parents had moved to a sod-roofed, dirt-floored shack on a farm near the Mormon community of Cardston in southern Alberta when Tanner was three months old. As a small-town teacher during the Depression, Tanner supplemented his meagre salary by selling suits and insurance and simultaneously became the high school principal at Cardston, a Bishop of the Mormon Church, a member of the town council, and a scoutmaster. Elected to the legislature in 1935 when Social Credit was swept to power in Alberta, Tanner was first named Speaker of the House and the following year appointed Minister of Mines. In the latter position, Tanner skilfully administered the province's oil and gas resources, brought hundreds of millions of dollars into the provincial coffers from royalties and the auctions of oil and gas leases, and helped transform Alberta from one of the most debt-ridden provincial governments in Canada to one of the most affluent.

Tanner did not want the Trans-Canada job. It was almost as political a job as that of a cabinet minister, and Tanner felt he had served his time in politics. What he wanted now, after making so much money for the government, was to make some for his family by taking advantage of the opportunity provided by Merrill Petroleums and to continue his church work. It took determined persuasion by Howe, Ray Milner, Manning, and others to convince Tanner that it was his duty to God and country to accept the Trans-Canada challenge.

With legislation that required a permit from the Department of Trade and Commerce (meaning C.D. Howe) to import gas, Howe seemed to have the problem of Consumers' Gas Company's planned US imports under control. Consumers' was granted a license to import gas under certain conditions. The eighty-mile, $5 million line to pick up the gas from Tennessee Gas at Niagara Falls and deliver it to Toronto was built by Trans-Canada Pipe Lines and leased to Consumers' subsidiary, Niagara Gas Transmission. The imports were to terminate after the line from Alberta had been built. Meanwhile, the US gas would help develop the market in Toronto, so that when completed the line from Alberta would have larger sales. The line from Niagara Falls was completed in December, 1954, and dramatically reduced fuel costs in Toronto. Within seven months, Consumers' Gas had made a second reduction in its rates, and the cost of heating a Toronto house with natural gas was estimated by the company at $175 a year, compared to $300 under the rates that had been charged for manufactured gas.

Trans-Canada successfully negotiated a new sales contract with Northern Natural Gas Company to replace the contract that had been held by Western Pipe Lines. Under the new agreement, Northern Natural would buy 100 million cubic feet of gas per day from Trans-Canada and hold an option on a further 100 million feet per day. The arrangement was conditional upon obtaining all necessary authorizations by the end of 1954, later extended to April 30, 1955.

In May, 1954, the Alberta Government granted Trans-Canada a permit to export 4.35 trillion cubic feet of gas from the province during a 27-year period. The authorization was conditional upon Trans-Canada obtaining approval from the Board of Transport Commissioners to build its line and approval from the FPC for the sales to Northern Natural. Manning announced that no difficulty was expected in meeting these conditions. On June 18, the Board of Transport Commissioners in Ottawa approved construction of Trans-Canada's line. It was the same day that the Federal Power Commission in Washington rejected the application of Westcoast Transmission and approved construction of the Pacific Northwest pipeline.

The Alberta and federal permits required Trans-Canada to complete financing for its $350 million line by the end of 1956. Construction was expected to start in the spring of 1955. It did not work out that way. The deadline for financing had to be extended half a dozen times and was not resolved until mid-1956, after it had become the epicentre of the storm in Parliament.

Trans-Canada's problems were manifold. The gas producers in Alberta were reluctant to sign gas sales contracts with Trans-Canada, because they considered it an uneconomical proposition. Consumers' Gas Company in Toronto, for the same reason, was unwilling to sign a purchase agreement. The Federal Power Commission was unwilling to authorize the import purchases by Northern Natural Gas from a system that had neither contracted supplies at one end, nor contracted sales at the other. Under these conditions, Trans-Canada was unable to sell the mortgage bonds that were to provide three-quarters of the funds to build the pipeline.

Refusal of the Alberta gas producers to sell their reserves to Trans-Canada contained some seeds of western alienation. Their first choice, particularly with respect to Gulf Oil and its crucial Pincher Creek gas, had been to sell to the nearest, highest-paying market, the US Pacific Northwest. That had been denied, and their second choice was the US Midwest. Finally, if it had to be sold to Ontario and Quebec, at least it ought to be shipped through the shortest, cheapest route, south from Winnipeg across the United States. Albertans had long felt that they had been unjustly forced to subsidize the tariffs that protected Ontario and Quebec manufacturers. Now, with the all-Canadian pipeline across northern Ontario, it seemed to some as though they were being called on to subsidize Ontario and Quebec consumers.

Howe first sought to resolve Trans-Canada's financing problems by having the federal government guarantee the interest payments on the company's bonds. In one of his few defeats, Howe's proposal was rejected by the cabinet.

A second effort to secure government financing help failed in

March, 1955, after weeks of intensive negotiations. This plan involved a loan of $55 million from the government's Industrial Development Bank, plus a $5 million investment in shares of Trans-Canada by the bank. Bank of Canada Governor James Coyne insisted that the loan be in the form of debentures that, at the option of the bank, could be converted into shares of Trans-Canada. Under this arrangement, the Government of Canada, instead of being simply a lender, could wind up as the major shareholder, owning more than half of the company. William Whiteford, president of Pittsburgh-based Gulf Oil Corporation, flatly refused to sell the Pincher Creek gas to a pipeline company that could wind up being controlled by the government. The deal broke down the day before the agreement was to be signed.

Chances of starting construction of the line in 1955 looked slim. Yet the pressures were great. Ontario, facing the prospect of critical shortages of electric power and fuel supplies, urgently wanted Alberta gas as fast as it could get it. And Alberta just as urgently wanted a market to avoid flaring and wasting the gas being produced in association with crude oil. To make matters worse, Trans-Canada's sales contract with Northern Natural had lapsed after April 30, and Northern had declined to grant Trans-Canada a second extension. Instead, Northern began negotiations to purchase Pincher Creek gas directly from Gulf, contemplating construction of its own pipeline on a direct route from southern Alberta to Minneapolis.

At this point, Howe weakened and seriously considered a line to Ontario across the shorter US route.

ANOTHER SYMONDS INVASION

Into the breach stepped Gardiner Symonds with a bold proposal. He would buy 200 million cubic feet of gas a day from Trans-Canada at Emerson and build a one thousand mile pipeline straight south to connect with Tennessee Gas Transmission's Texas to New England line at Nashville, Tennessee. The line from Emerson would be constructed by a new company, Midwest Gas Transmission, and it would allow Symonds to invade yet one more market area, the US Midwest. At the same time, Tennessee would ship more US gas into Canada, allowing Trans-Canada to extend the line from Niagara Falls as far as Montreal.

As soon as he heard what Symonds was up to, John Merriam,

president of Northern Natural, fired off a June 3, 1955, protest telegram to Eldon Tanner, with a copy to Howe. Merriam said he expected that,

Trans-Canada would not exercise any conditional right it had to cancel its contract with Northern for such period of time as was occasioned by Trans-Canada's own failure to perform. If the national Canadian policy is changed with respect to an all-Canadian route for delivery of natural gas to eastern Canada, we expect that if Trans-Canada Pipe Lines is involved in delivery of gas for such a United States route that Trans-Canada will live up to its obligation to Northern Natural Gas Company to offer such gas to Northern before offering it to anyone else. If Trans-Canada Pipe Lines continues its negotiations with other pipe lines in direct violation of its commitments to Northern Natural Gas Company we will be forced to take legal and other appropriate action.

From Edmonton, Ray Milner telegraphed back an angry response to Merriam: "What you say is a first class example of impudence, arrogance, and complete disregard for the facts." Milner accused Merriam of "endeavouring to arrogate to yourself the right to control any gas which Trans-Canada exports to the United States. In my opinion . . . Trans-Canada and its officers are under no obligation to you or Northern Natural, either moral or legal, and I personally am now opposed to any further negotiations with you."

The possibility that Ottawa might abandon the all-Canadian principle brought howls of protest from northern Ontario. "There was enough criticism of the oil pipeline going through the United States," the president of the Northwestern Ontario Liberal Association wrote Prime Minister St Laurent. "Any suggestion that the gas line would do the same would kill the prospect of ever electing another Liberal from Manitoba to Sudbury for a generation." The cabinet, having earlier refused to back the bonds for an all-Canadian pipeline, now refused to sanction anything other than an all-Canadian pipeline.

Howe was just as pleased. He did not really like the idea of either a gas swap or a pipeline route through the United States in any event. Besides, he was one of the Liberals between Manitoba and Sudbury who would soon have to seek re-election.

Reaffirmation of the all-Canadian principle brought some

revised ideas from Gardiner Symonds and from the three US Midwest gas distributors for short-term methods to supply eastern Canada while the Trans-Canada line was being built.

On July 21, 1955, John Merriam wrote to Tanner on behalf of Northern Natural; James Oates, chairman of Peoples Gas Light and Coke Company of Chicago; and Ralph T. McElvenny, president of American Natural Gas Company of Detroit. Merriam stated that the three gas distributors could provide Trans-Canada with a better deal than a new firm that would have to establish costly and duplicate facilities in the US Midwest. Moreover, the existing facilities could, with modest expansion, provide a connecting link to supply eastern Canada. "Our three companies are the only ones who can either build a major pipeline all the way from the Winnipeg border to eastern Canada for maximum volumes, or build piecemeal in small steps to handle existing volumes," Merriam wrote. "No one else can do this. We are prepared to extend to you and the Canadian authorities the full co-operation of our companies in working out a program of handling the gas supply question in the best possible manner for the public interest of our two countries."

Merriam sent a copy to Howe, who replied on July 26 that he had "had a talk with Mr Tanner and some of his associates this morning and understand that he will have a discussion with you shortly. I am hopeful that a program can be worked out with you and your group that will make it unnecessary to deal with others [i.e., Tennessee Gas] proposing to serve your territory." Three days later, Merriam wrote to Howe: "From the conversations with Mr Tanner it looks as if our companies would be able to work out a mutually satisfactory program that will fit the needs of the Canadian gas picture."

Symonds's invasion of the US Midwest market, however, was not eliminated that easily. Tennessee modified its plans to ship more US gas into eastern Canada to become an interim measure until the Trans-Canada line was completed. On July 5, Howe's assistant, Mitchell Sharp, advised Howe that the Tennessee proposal, "while interesting and ingenious, does not and cannot guarantee the eventual building of an all-Canadian pipeline." Sharp warned that the Tennessee proposal "will be fought vigorously . . . by competing pipelines whose territories would be invaded" and that, "It is likely to be years before the proposal obtains the necessary approvals, if it ever does."

But Symonds must have convinced Howe otherwise. On August 4, just nine days after he had written that he hoped the Northern group could make a deal with Trans-Canada, Howe advised Trans-Canada to make a deal with Tennessee. Following "a very satisfactory talk with Gardiner Symonds and his associates" the day before, Howe wrote to Tanner: "It would look as though Tennessee will have strong backing before the Federal Power Commission, and I am inclined to think that they can put the kind of support behind your project that their competitors are unwilling, and perhaps unable, to give . . . . On the strength of what I now know, if I were in your place I would be inclined to deal with Tennessee."

On August 15, Tanner wired Merriam that Trans-Canada had "executed a contract which meets its needs." The following day, Tennessee gas announced it had contracted to purchase gas from Trans-Canada at Emerson and provide Trans-Canada with additional interim US gas at Niagara Falls. In September, the Board of Transport Commissioners approved the extension of Trans-Canada's US-fed pipeline from Toronto to Montreal.

Following the deal with Tennessee, Trans-Canada was at last able to contract for the purchase of 315 million cubic feet of gas per day from southern Alberta, including 170 million feet of Pincher Creek gas from Gulf. The supply problem was finally resolved, the market demand in eastern Canada was being built up, and all that remained was to find the money to construct the line from Alberta.

Financing at this stage rested on two hopes. First was the establishment of a Crown corporation that would provide nearly one-third of the money needed for construction. Second was quick approval by the Federal Power Commission of the export sales from Emerson to Tennessee which would help assure Trans-Canada of enough revenues to borrow the remaining two-thirds.

The idea of the Crown corporation reflected the cost of the northern Ontario section of the all-Canadian route. The Ontario government described this section as "a prime national necessity," claiming it "would supplement power resources for the whole nation and would contribute to our economic self-sufficiency." The Ontario statement, however, also conceded that, "The span across northern Ontario presents an added difficulty which means that the line could become self-sustaining only after a number of years."

The plan worked out was that this 675-mile segment would be built by a Crown company, Northern Ontario Pipe Line Corporation, and leased to Trans-Canada. Trans-Canada, in turn, would operate it as part of its system and later purchase it. Estimated cost of the northern Ontario section was $118 million. The Ontario government agreed to contribute $35 million of the total, with the balance to be provided by Ottawa.

Howe wrote to Tanner on October 6, 1955, reporting that these arrangements had now been agreed upon. He added that he hoped "the application to the FPC can be filed shortly" (it was filed four days later) and that "Gardiner Symonds is meeting with success in cutting down the number of interventions in the proceedings. We must not fail to get the line financed this time."

The sequence of moves and counter-moves during this period strongly suggest that Symonds had persuaded Howe he could get quick approval from the FPC by making a deal with the three existing pipelines in the US Midwest to share the imported gas. To recapitulate these events: On July 5, Sharp says that opposition to the Tennessee proposal meant it would take years to get FPC approval. On July 26, Howe tells the three existing pipeline firms that he hopes Trans-Canada can work out a deal with them, rather than with Tennessee Gas. On August 3, Symonds visits Howe in Ottawa. On August 4, Howe advises Trans-Canada to make a deal with Tennessee Gas, rather than with the group of three. On October 6, Howe says he hopes that Symonds is succeeding in reducing opposition at the forthcoming FPC hearings.

In fact, Symonds was making little progress and seemed in no hurry to cut his opponents in on the gas supply he had arranged from Canada. For more than a year, a frustrated Howe kept berating Symonds for his failure to make a deal with his opponents, so that the gas export sales could be approved in time to help finance the Trans-Canada line. Symonds appeared as unwilling to share the gas supply he had lined up for the Midwest as he had earlier been unwilling to share the New England market with his rival in that battle.

In late 1955, however, there still seemed to be some hope that approval of export sales and government funds for the span across Ontario would permit construction of the Trans-Canada line to get underway the following summer. Attention turned to another problem: securing thirty-four-inch pipe for the section of the line from Alberta to Winnipeg. Steel pipe was in short supply, and if construction were to start in the summer of 1956, it would be necessary to order the pipe well in advance. Trans-Canada did not have the $40 million to buy the pipe and was unable to borrow it.

Gardiner Symonds arranged to provide the pipe, but he exacted a stiff price. In the deal that emerged after weeks of negotiations, Tennessee Gas, Gulf Oil, and Hudson's Bay Oil and Gas Company agreed to put up the money for the pipe, but in return each acquired a 17 per cent interest in Trans-Canada. That left the Murchison interests and the original sponsors of Western Pipe Lines sharing the remaining 49 per cent. Symonds emerged as the man in control of Trans-Canada Pipe Lines.

By the spring of 1956, the provinces were pressing for action on the line from Alberta. Manning had written to Prime Minister St Laurent to declare that, "Any further delay in commencing at least the western portion of the line may well prove disastrous to the entire project." Manitoba Premier Douglas Campbell wrote the Prime Minister that, "It is imperative that construction of the pipeline between Alberta and Winnipeg be completed this year." Ontario Provincial Treasurer Dana Porter wrote to Howe to state that, "Every day's delay invites the most serious consequences to the development of Ontario and to the national economy."

But hope for a quick FPC approval of the purchase of Trans-Canada gas at Emerson by Tennessee was fast fading, and with it was sinking any hope that Trans-Canada could raise the financing in time to start construction in 1956 without even more government help. And in Parliament, the opposition parties that had so vociferously demanded an all-Canadian pipeline now stood opposed to the government assistance that would make it possible. George Drew's earlier statement that the government ought to do "anything that might be necessary to expedite this important venture" apparently did not include the use of $118 million to aid a company that was then American controlled. John Diefenbaker warned that an earlier battle, which had defeated a government proposal to extend Howe's authority under the Defence Production Act, "will appear but a mere skirmish beside the battle we will wage when the bill regarding Trans-Canada Pipe Lines comes before Parliament." The way Diefenbaker saw it, Trans-Canada represented the first step toward Canada becoming "a virtual economic forty-ninth state." The argument that when the line was financed Canadian investors would be offered the opportunity to purchase more than half the ownership of Trans-Canada cut no ice.

McMAHON PLAYS HIS BID

This was the state of affairs when Frank McMahon walked into the office of C.D. Howe on Tuesday, March 27, 1956, with what looked like an offer that could not be refused. McMahon undertook to build by 1958 a gas pipeline from Alberta to Montreal, at least 70 per cent Canadian-owned, without any government financial assistance, other than the remission or deferral of import duties and sales taxes on the pipe. McMahon offered to "personally post with the government $500,000 performance cash to complete the project by 1958, subject only to being able to obtain necessary materials." He proposed to start construction of the section to Winnipeg that year, with completion no later than early 1957.

McMahon had been studying this plan for more than three months, and it was backed by the three US gas firms opposing Tennessee: Northern Natural Gas, Peoples Gas, and American Natural Gas. In fact, these firms approached McMahon with the idea after Trans-Canada had committed its gas to Tennessee.

McMahon's ability to finance the line without government help rested on two advantages claimed over the deal that Trans-Canada had made with Tennessee. The volume of export gas to be sold at Emerson would be 400 million cubic feet per day, twice the amount that Tennessee had contracted to purchase. And the price would be 20 per cent higher. That would provide nearly two-and-a-half times as much revenue from export sales to help pay for the cost of the line.

McMahon claimed that his three potential American customers could purchase more gas and pay a higher price than Tennessee, because they already had the market and pipelines supplying the Detroit-Chicago-Minneapolis-Milwaukee region, while Tennessee did not. According to McMahon, Trans-Canada was "dominated" by Tennessee, so that "the principal interest behind Trans-Canada's pipeline is dealing with itself as the principal purchaser in the United States." Tennessee's object, according to McMahon, was to get Canadian gas at a low price in order to invade the US Midwest market.

McMahon repeated Mitchell Sharp's earlier warning that Ten-

197

nessee faced a long battle in its bid to import gas from Trans-Canada. He wrote that his three "powerful" customers had:

> pledged to oppose with all their resources the invasion of their market areas by Tennessee or any other company. Nearly 100 companies have intervened before the Federal Power Commission in regard to the Tennessee Company proposal. As a result there is no hope that the Tennessee Company can obtain necessary Federal Power Commission authorization for many years to come, if indeed it can ever do so.

By contrast, McMahon implied that after working out an accommodation with Tennessee and his three customer companies, the required FPC authorization "can be obtained in the next few months."

In any event, McMahon said that the companies that he and his associates controlled were prepared to invest up to $45 million in equity capital to start construction that year, if necessary prior to the FPC authorization, which he said he had been "assured" could be obtained before the end of the year. In addition to Pacific Petroleums, Canadian Atlantic Oil, and Peace River Natural Gas, other backers of the McMahon plan included Calgary contractor Merv Dutton, Norman Whittall, and Calgary newspaper publisher and oil man Max Bell.

The McMahon group recognized that it could not start from scratch to acquire the Alberta export permit, the transport board's permit, the engineering studies, and the arrangements for pipe supply. Nor could it duplicate the work that Trans-Canada had accomplished to date. McMahon proposed to buy-out the interests of existing Trans-Canada shareholders if the company were unable to proceed immediately with its planned line. "The work already done by Trans-Canada is recognized, and we are prepared to take it over on an equitable basis," McMahon stated in the proposal he left with Howe on March 27. These and other details were outlined in the memorandum delivered to Howe at this initial meeting, followed by a series of letters and memos from McMahon on April 4, 13, 16, and 24.

While wrapping up the financing for the pipeline from the Peace River and attempting to engineer a take-over of the planned pipeline to Montreal, McMahon also found time for a second marriage. The year before, he and Isobel had divorced. On Tuesday, March 27, McMahon was in Ottawa meeting with

Howe to outline his proposal. The following Monday, April 2, he was back in the capital with the heads of Peoples Gas Light and Coke Company, American Natural Gas Company, and Northern Natural Gas Company to describe the same scheme to Mines Minister George Prudham and his Deputy Minister, George Hume. On Wednesday, he was at his residence at Palm Beach, Florida, to meet with thirteen representatives of these same firms. On Thursday, he was in New York, firing off a raft of letters and memoranda further describing his plan. On Saturday, he married Betty Betz, syndicated newspaper columnist and a fashion designer for teenagers.

Howe was skeptical of the McMahon proposal. Rather than taking it to cabinet, Howe simply sat on it. But Mines Minister George Prudham was equally skeptical of the deal that Trans-Canada had made with Tennessee Gas. As a result, a meeting was held in a small-town hotel outside Ottawa to explain the McMahon play to Prudham and George Hume. Accompanying McMahon at the meeting were Charles Hetherington and the heads of the three American gas companies: Ralph McElvenny of American Natural, John Merriam of Northern Natural, and Jim Oates of Peoples Gas. Prudham took the proposal to the Prime Minister.

According to McMahon, his correspondence to Howe on this matter had been marked "private and confidential," at Howe's insistence. One of McMahon's Westcoast officials mistakenly thought it would help apply pressure on Howe if copies of the documents were leaked to John Diefenbaker. Howe's doubts about the McMahon proposal "turned to anger when he learned that Prudham had gone over his head to the Prime Minister, and that McMahon's proposal had also been handed to his political opponents," Dale C. Thomson, St Laurent's administrative assistant, later wrote in his *Louis St Laurent: Canadian*.

Another proposal intended to achieve Canadian ownership of an all-Canadian pipeline had been advanced by the Toronto investment firm of Gairdner and Company. But the Gairdner plan required even more government support than Trans-Canada was to receive, so much that the government might as well have built the entire line. Howe was not adverse to government enterprises. He had fathered such government companies as Air Canada and the Canadian Broadcasting Corporation, and during the war he had created twenty-eight Crown corporations to cope with emergency demands. But Howe perceived that ownership of the pipe-line would trap the government into a regional conflict between the producer interests of Alberta and the consumer interests of Ontario and Quebec. The government preferred to see the pipeline resolve that conflict under private ownership.

Ignoring the McMahon proposal, and having committed the government to build the section across northern Ontario, Howe continued discussions with Trans-Canada and Gardiner Symonds on how to finance the 575-mile Alberta to Winnipeg section. On April 10, Symonds met with two of Howe's assistants, Mitchell Sharp and Doug Fraser, and offered to back out of the Trans-Canada deal. According to Sharp's memo on the meeting, the American companies were so "distressed and embarrassed by the 'gringo, go home' tone of the Parliamentary debates and press comments" that they were prepared to sell their 51 per cent of the Trans-Canada shares at cost to the government, or whoever else the government might approve. But that did not mean that Symonds would give up his battle to invade the US Midwest market. If he could not do it with Canadian gas, he would do it with Texas gas. Quoting Symonds at the meeting, Sharp wrote:

> The government must be under no illusion that his [Symonds's] departure from TCPL would enable it or any other company to sell gas to the companies presently operating in the midwest without as bitter a fight as Tennessee could put up before the FPC. He also emphasized repeatedly that he had every confidence that the FPC would approve his plans. The opponents described him as an invader; every market he had entered – West Virginia, the Mohawk Valley, New England, and New York City – had been previously served to some extent by other gas lines. In every case the FPC had approved his competitive plans, and in every market in which Tennessee operated there were from two to five alternative sources of supply. Chicago and San Francisco were the last two US metropolitan areas in which there was a gas service monopoly, and he was completely confident that he would be authorized to enter the Chicago area.

The next day, Symonds met with Howe. By this time, Trans-Canada favoured another year's delay, with construction to start in 1957. But Howe was determined that building should begin in

1956; it was bad enough missing out on the planned start in 1955, but a two-year delay would be intolerable. Howe proposed that Trans-Canada build the western section in 1956. It was thought that interim financing could be obtained if the government committed to purchase this part of the pipeline at 90 per cent of cost, and if final financing for the full line was not completed by November 1, 1957. In effect, the plan meant that if the imports at Emerson were not approved by the FPC within the next eighteen months, the Trans-Canada line would be taken over as a government enterprise. In that event, the banks would be protected on their loans to Trans-Canada, but the shareholders stood to lose half of their investment, or more. But even with this government purchase commitment, the deal fell through. Symonds reported later that he was unable to borrow the money from his bankers under this arrangement.

There now seemed only one way to get construction started in 1956. In addition to committing $118 million for the northern Ontario section, Howe proposed that the government lend Trans-Canada up to $80 million, covering as much as 90 per cent of the cost of the western line. If Trans-Canada failed to complete the section to Winnipeg in 1956, the government could take over, and the company shareholders could lose investments of up to $16 million. To allow Trans-Canada enough time to complete the western section that year, it was agreed that the deal would have to be approved by Parliament by June 7. After pleading by Howe, the cabinet accepted the proposal on May 7. That left exactly one month to get the legislation rammed through Parliament.

Diefenbaker, meanwhile, had been seeking to use the McMahon and Gairdner proposals as political clubs with which to hammer Howe and the government in the House. The opposition version was that the refusal to consider these alternatives demonstrated that Howe and the government were wedded to the American interests that dominated Trans-Canada and, supposedly, threatened to dominate Canada.

On April 13, Diefenbaker rose in the House and asked Howe to table the Gairdner and McMahon offers. Howe promised to table two documents from Gairdner, but said "I have no documents from the McMahon interests." On April 16, Howe repeated: "There were no McMahon documents."

Howe appears to have been stonewalling on the McMahon

proposal in the hope that McMahon would drop the plan. "The government has decided to extend further help to Trans-Canada, sufficient to enable the western section to be built this summer," Howe wrote to McMahon on April 30, although at this time the decision was still Howe's alone and as yet lacked approval by the cabinet. Howe continued: "We have reached the conclusion that Trans-Canada is the only agency in a position to commence immediate construction. Therefore, I suggest that it is useless for you to pursue this matter further at this time . . . . It seems to me that you will have your hands full for the next year or two without taking on added responsibilities."

On May 2, Conservative leader George Drew asked Howe in the House if he had "received a letter from Mr Frank McMahon in regard to the proposed pipeline." Howe responded: "I have no letter that I am free to table in this House."

Howe's defence had cracked, and it was apparent that the McMahon documents would soon have to come out into the open. The next day, before Parliament met, Howe phoned McMahon in New York and suggested more pointedly that McMahon should withdraw his proposal. Construction of the Westcoast line had barely started, and McMahon was concerned that if he became seriously cross-threaded with Howe, its completion could still face some problems. McMahon telegrammed Howe authorizing him to,

> remove the words private and confidential from my correspondence with you. With further reference to the correspondence I now find that my time is too seriously committed to the Westcoast Transmission project to further pursue the project of a gas pipeline eastward from Alberta, therefore I would ask you to consider the latter a closed subject as far as I am concerned.

When the House met at 2:30 that afternoon, George Drew wanted to know whether the government had "received assurance from Mr Frank McMahon that he has $50 million of equity capital now available to proceed with the pipeline to Montreal, and that he is prepared to deposit an adequate bond to guarantee the completion of the pipeline as far as Montreal by 1958."

Howe responded that he had "received no communication of the type indicated, but I have been in touch with Mr McMahon within the last few minutes, and he has agreed to allow me to remove the 'private and confidential' from his letters." Howe promised to table the correspondence as soon as copies could be made.

The McMahon proposal was at last out in the open. But it had been withdrawn, so it was a dead letter, except for the accusations of the opposition that Howe had misled Parliament by his earlier denials that he had received any "documents" from McMahon. "A letter addressed to me which I am not free to table is not a document of Parliament," Howe told the House the next day, May 4. He seemed to ignore the fact that Diefenbaker's motion on April 13 had specially requested not just "documents" but "a copy of all letters and other documents received by the government or any minister or official from Mr Frank McMahon. . . ." Howe continued: "I was asked for documents. The letter was marked private and when a letter is marked in that way, if you are going to respect a document at all, it must be private to you. . . . I get letters from my sister. I suppose I should announce in Parliament when I receive a letter from my sister?"

"About the pipeline?" asked Diefenbaker. "Is she advising you in regard to the pipeline?" Drew demanded.

Howe survived the attack on his handling of the matter and that same day wrote McMahon to express his appreciation of the withdrawal. Marking the letter "Secret, Private, Confidential, Personal, etc," Howe observed, "I am sure that in the long run your own interests will be advanced by your gracious withdrawal from what promised to be an impossible situation."

On May 8, Howe introduced in the House the bill authorizing the government to create the Northern Ontario Pipeline Corporation to build the $118 million span across northern Ontario and to loan Trans-Canada up to $80 million for construction of the Alberta to Winnipeg section. The methods by which the government applied the rules of closure to ram the legislation through in time to meet its contracted June 7 deadline with Trans-Canada, and the tumultuous uproar in Parliament, are well-recorded history. With closure cutting off debate, the bill obtained second reading at 1:47 AM on Saturday, June 2, third and final reading in the early hours of June 7, and Royal Assent on June 7, just hours before the agreement with Trans-Canada was due to expire. Construction was underway within a fortnight.

Senator Eugene Forsey later assessed the great pipeline debate.

"What the government did to Parliament a year ago on the pipeline bill was evil, unspeakably evil," Forsey wrote in the *Ottawa Journal* in May, 1957. "The great excuse, of course, is 'urgency.' It is no excuse at all. All the pipelines that ever were built or ever will be, are as dust in the balance beside our heritage of Parliamentary government." A lot of Canadians appeared to agree, and in the elections later that year the Liberal government was defeated after twenty-one years in office, ousted by the Conservatives, led by Diefenbaker. Among the defeated Liberals was Howe.

McMahon's withdrawal on May 3 did not completely end his hopes of taking over Trans-Canada. The proposal he offered Howe may have been dead, but there was nothing to stop him attempting to purchase Trans-Canada shares from American owners, such as Gulf, Hudson's Bay Oil and Gas, and others. He remained convinced that if he held control of Trans-Canada, he could sell gas at Emerson to the three Midwest pipeline companies at a higher price than Gardiner Symonds had offered to pay. On May 16, McMahon wrote to Senator Farris, saying that his group was still prepared to "return the control of Trans-Canada to Canadian investors by purchasing the stock of any American interest along with the remaining unissued treasury stock. A minimum of 70 per cent of the outstanding stock would be put into a voting trust controlled by Canadians." In December, Lloyd Gilmour of Eastman, Dillon wrote McMahon suggesting that, "Perhaps a deal might be made to take out part of Trans-Canada stockholders for an exchange with Westcoast." And by swapping Westcoast for Trans-Canada shares, McMahon "could probably, in due course, get control of it, or all of it." But by the end of 1956, McMahon appears to have given up, and in a letter to Boots Adams on December 21 he suggested that Phillips Petroleum might acquire control of Trans-Canada by purchasing the shares held by Clint Murchison and others. McMahon was not a gracious loser.

Howe had agreed to provide up to nearly $200 million of government funds for Trans-Canada. Gardiner Symonds had in turn undertaken to arrange a deal with the three US Midwest pipeline companies in order to secure US approval of gas imports from Trans-Canada. But Howe now found great difficulty in getting Symonds to perform.

On June 23, two weeks after the pipeline legislation had been approved, Howe wrote to Dean Nesbitt:

I had understood that Gardiner Symonds had promised to attempt a compromise with the Chicago people after the pipeline bill was passed. I have heard of no effort to that end. I sincerely hope that negotiations are progressing. I know that they will be well received by the FPC, and if successful, may well lead to a favourable decision in time to help financing. Please convey to Gardiner Symonds my insistence that something must be accomplished before November 1.

On November 29, Howe wrote to Symonds, describing the efforts to finance Trans-Canada as,

pretty much of a marginal performance, with some doubt as to whether it can be successfully completed in accordance with the undertaking given to the government by the Trans-Canada company. . . . We have been forced to note that your forecasts which induced Trans-Canada to enter into your contract, and induced the government to agree to the export, have so far not been justified. It seems to me that you have an obligation to use your best endeavour to break the deadlock without further delay and thus place Trans-Canada in a position where it can be financed to the extent first envisaged. . . . It would seem to me that the present is the time to approach the Chicago group for a compromise.

Symonds had been talking with the "Chicago group" – Northern Natural, American Natural, and Peoples Gas – but to little effect. The Chicago companies, among other things, wanted ownership of 75 per cent of the proposed line south of Emerson, but Symonds was prepared to offer them only a minority interest.

On December 15, Howe wrote to Canadian Ambassador Arnold Heeney in Washington:

Dean Acheson [former US Secretary of State and then a consulting lawyer for Tennessee Gas] must be told that Canada has reached the end of its patience, and that unless the Chicago talks lead to a settlement, action must be taken to end our promise to grant an export permit to Tennessee. Export of

205

gas at Winnipeg is helpful only at the time of financing the pipeline, and if it is not forthcoming in time we are better off without the export. . . . Tennessee would be very unwise to pass up any chance of settlement, even though some loss of prestige in the middle western situation is involved. We cannot concern ourselves about empire building by Tennessee in the middle west.

In the end, the export sales were "not forthcoming in time," and Trans-Canada had to finance without them. By early 1957, Trans-Canada had raised $264 million: $40 million from the sale of shares, $80 million from the sale of debentures, and $144 million in first mortgage bonds. Together with the $118 million that Ottawa spent to build the northern Ontario section, there was a total of $372 million to construct the entire line from Alberta to Montreal. Of the $80 million loan available for the western section, less than $50 million was actually borrowed, and by the end of February, 1957, it was paid back, together with nearly $1 million in interest. The final weld on the 2,230-mile line was made in October, 1958, the northern Ontario section was purchased from the government by Trans-Canada five years later, the American companies sold out their interests, and Trans-Canada became more than 90 per cent Canadian owned.

Given the chance, could Frank McMahon have built the line without financial assistance from the government? The question can probably never be answered. Certainly the larger volume and higher sales price that he arranged provided a much better chance of financing than the deal that Trans-Canada had arranged with Gardiner Symonds. Nor were all the reasons given about why the McMahon proposal would not work entirely valid. It was argued that the export volume of 400 million cubic feet of gas per day exceeded the amount available from Alberta. Yet many times this export volume was authorized within a few years. It was argued that McMahon did not have the purchase contracts or other permits. But right from the start McMahon had said that it was part of his plan that he would purchase Trans-Canada's undertakings and assets. It was argued that the only thirty-four-inch pipe available to start construction in 1956 was that which Tennessee had purchased for Trans-Canada. But it was difficult to see what Tennessee could have done with this pipe other than make it available for the line from Alberta to

Winnipeg, regardless of who built it. Tennessee had no other pipeline construction approved or even planned that required the use of such large-diameter pipe. In any event, two-thirds of the cost of buying this pipe had been paid for by Gulf and Hudson's Bay Oil and Gas, whose only interest was to get the pipeline built so that they could sell their gas.

To some extent, at least, McMahon's position appears to have been vindicated by subsequent developments. He had warned that the Symonds plan to invade the US Midwest would not be approved for many years. In fact, export sales to the US were not authorized until 1960, and then only on the basis that most of it went to the three companies to whom McMahon had proposed to sell. It was not until after the export sale had been achieved that the Trans-Canada line was able to operate on a sound financial basis and arrange for purchase of the northern Ontario section from the government.

A final footnote on Frank McMahon's bid to build the line to Montreal without government financial assistance was revealed on April 30, 1958, when US Attorney General William Rogers announced the return of a criminal indictment by a federal grand jury for violations of the Sherman Antitrust Act. Charged with having conspired to prevent the importation of Canadian gas by Tennessee were Northern Natural Gas Company, American Natural Gas Company, and Peoples Gas Light and Coke Company. Fines of $100,000 each were imposed on the three firms. Also named as a co-conspirator, although not a defendant in the case, was Frank McMahon.

While Frank McMahon had been chasing down this dead-end sideroad, Westcoast Transmission was gearing up to launch one of the largest construction projects that had then been undertaken in Canada.

CHAPTER THIRTEEN

Working on the Pipeline

When Frank McMahon told C.D. Howe in April, 1956, that he was ready to start building the Alberta to Winnipeg section of the all-Canadian pipeline to Montreal even before the FPC authorized the US gas purchases required to pay for it, it seemed like an audacious commitment. It was almost impossible to believe that anyone could manage to do that, except for the fact that it had been done once before, by Westcoast Transmission.

Westcoast was in a hurry to get its 650-mile pipeline from the Peace River built. It had a contract commitment to begin deliveries to Pacific Northwest Pipeline Corporation at Sumas, on the US border near Vancouver, by November 1, 1957. To meet that delivery date, it could not afford to be held up by the foot-dragging of any regulatory body.

The applications by Pacific Northwest and El Paso to import from Westcoast were filed with the FPC on May 23, 1955. On July 15, the hearings started, on September 30, they finished; on October 26, the final briefs were filed, and on November 25, the FPC approved the applications. But Westcoast, gambling on the outcome, had started buying pipe three months before the decision was made and started burying it more than a month before.

A management committee was formed to plan and supervise construction. It included members from Westcoast, from Bechtel as construction managers, and from Ford, Bacon & Davis as consulting engineers. Representing Westcoast were Frank McMahon, D.P. McDonald, Charles Hetherinton, Ted Megas (treasurer), and Lloyd Turner (public relations). Canadian Bechtel Limited was represented by Sid Bechtel Jr, R.L.

Hamilton, H.F. Waste, and J.V. Chambers. Ford, Bacon & Davis was represented by its president, Charles Whittelsey.

Steel mills were hard-pressed in 1955 to keep pace with orders from pipeline companies that were building at a hectic pace, and the management group concluded that Westcoast had better get its orders in early. No Canadian mills were then capable of producing thirty-inch diameter line pipe, and the bulk of it would have to come from US mills.

In August, Westcoast purchased its first 20 miles of 30-inch pipe from United States Steel Corporation; it amounted to some 5,000 tons and was to be delivered immediately. Purchase contracts for an additional 125,000 tons were placed with three other US mills in September. The largest single pipe purchase order was signed on October 17 for a further 75,000 tons from South Durham Steel and Iron Company in England. Except for the initial twenty miles, pipe deliveries under these contracts were to start in December and continue throughout 1956.

The total pipe orders amounted to 205,000 tons and a cost in excess of $50 million. Unless the FPC permit was obtained and financing subsequently arranged, there was no way that Westcoast would have the funds to pay for it, and the obligation would fall primarily on Pacific Petroleums. The magnitude of the gamble is suggested by the fact that, prior to a similar FPC decision on export sales, the only way the backers of Trans-Canada Pipelines were able to arrange orders for a $40 million supply of pipe was by selling 51 per cent interest in the company to Tennessee Gas Transmission and two oil companies.

At the same time that the pipe was being ordered by Westcoast, discussions were underway with contractors to install it. On September 21, Westcoast signed construction contracts with three firms that totalled $31.5 million. The contract for 120 miles of pipe at the south end of the system was awarded to Mannix Limited of Calgary; the middle 420 miles went to Canadian Bechtel and Conyes Construction Corporation of Los Angeles; and the most northerly 110 miles was awarded to Dutton-Williams Brothers Limited, a firm organized by Calgary contractor Merv Dutton, and Williams Brothers, a large pipeline construction firm of Tulsa, Oklahoma.

The first twenty miles of pipe was delivered at Vancouver in September, well before the FPC decision had been made, and thus long before Westcoast could arrange financing. To pay for the pipe, Pat Bowsher of Pacific Petroleums arranged a $2 million loan with Bill Hyndman, Calgary manager of the Royal Bank. Mannix Limited accepted responsibility for safe storage of the pipe.

But if the pipe could be installed before the oncoming winter rains, it would help avoid construction problems in the low-lying Fraser Valley. Bowsher again contacted Hyndman at the Royal Bank and suggested that the pipe might be stored "in the safest place there is." "Where is that?" Hyndman cautiously inquired. "Six feet under the ground," Bowsher replied.

The bank agreed that this was indeed the safest storage method. The Mannix crew immediately started clearing and grading the right-of-way in the Fraser Valley. A big bucket-wheel excavator dug a six-foot trench, and trucks arrived to string the thirty-foot sections of pipe along side the ditch. The first weld was made on October 21, and the first twenty miles of the Westcoast pipeline was soon coated, wrapped, and lowered in. The ditch was then backfilled, and the right-of-way cleaned up. All of this was finished well before the FPC permit was issued.

Hetherington recalls remarking to Hyndman, "Well, I guess that means that the Royal Bank is really in partnership with us now." It was, indeed. By the time Westcoast had obtained its first permanent financing, on May 1, 1956, the Royal Bank had advanced temporary loans amounting to $19 million. With that, the Royal Bank's chairman, James Muir, joined the Westcoast board of directors to keep a close Scottish eye on the company's financial affairs.

The day after the first weld had been made, the Westcoast board met in Calgary to officially authorize the pipe purchase orders and construction contracts. It was not a large meeting, just Frank and George McMahon, Pat Bowsher, and D.P. McDonald, enough to constitute a quorum. The directors also reviewed the plan of financing that had been drawn up, primarily by Eastman, Dillon in New York and by Wood Gundy in Toronto.

Total cost of the pipeline was estimated at $143 million, of which $78 million was to be provided by the large insurance companies in the form of first mortgage bonds. Three banks had tentatively agreed to provide $27 million in long-term loans, at an annual interest rate of 3.5 per cent, including $10 million each from the Royal Bank and the National City Bank of New York and $7 million from the Mellon Bank of Pittsburgh. Another $20 million was to be raised from the sale of twenty-five-subordinate debentures (convertible into common shares) and $17.4 million from the planned sale of common shares.

It was estimated that in its third year of operation, starting in the fall of 1960, Westcoast would be delivering gas at an average rate of some 350 million cubic feet per day. Some 50 million would be for BC consumers, and the balance would be exported to the United States. The initial capacity of the line would be 370 million feet per day, but this could be increased to 700 million by additional compressors to push the gas through faster.

Based on the fixed export price of 22 cents per thousand cubic feet, it was estimated that by its third year of operation Westcoast would be earning an after-tax profit of some 6 per cent on its total investment, provided that the line did not cost more than had been estimated. Because the debt would cost less than this, the shareholders could anticipate a return on their investment of possibly double or even triple the 6 per cent return. Well before the pipeline had been completed, however, it became clear that the cost would exceed the estimated $143 million and there would be little, if any, profit during the initial years of operation. But the pipeline had been designed to handle twice the initial throughput, and the prospect was that it would be only a matter of time before growing sales would put Westcoast in a solid profit position. All that was required was confidence.

Drawing up the deeds, trust agreements, and other documents required to execute the financing was a job handled by lawyers, with occasional advice from bewildered accountants trapped in a jungle of legal obfuscation. The formal financial documents were drawn up in New York with the aid of nine legal firms from New York, Vancouver, Calgary, Montreal, and Toronto. They represented the interests of US and Canadian bondholders, the banks, the underwriters for the sale of the debentures and shares, and Westcoast.

No Canadian project of this magnitude had ever been financed in the United States without the credit backing of government, or of large multinational corporations, such as Exxon, Gulf, Shell, and others in the case of the Interprovincial and Trans Mountain oil pipelines. The large sums involved, the lack of backing by

211

anyone with enough money to guarantee the debt, and subtle differences in American and Canadian laws and practices, made the money lenders very cautious and the negotiations difficult and protracted.

Ernie Bull of Senator Farris' Vancouver firm, later a Justice of the BC Supreme Court, was one of the lawyers representing Westcoast at the New York meetings. Bull had arrived in Calgary in January, 1956, to meet with D.P. McDonald, travelling with a small hand bag that contained one shirt, one pair of socks, a robe, and pyjamas. McDonald persuaded Bull to accompany him to the meetings in New York, and it was three months before Ernie Bull got back to Vancouver. In New York, Bull had one suit for every day of the week, the one that he wore. On the days that he sent the suit to the cleaners, he stayed in his room in the Ritz Towers working on revisions to the documents. Doug Owen, C.D. Howe's former executive assistant who went to work for McMahon in 1955, recalls the future Justice of the Supreme Court of BC working in his hotel room, dressed in socks, shorts, and a heavy bathrobe. Nearly one entire wall of the room was covered with drapes, and Bull stuck draft copies of the documents to them with straight pins, covering the wall with paper from floor to ceiling.

By the time the negotiations got underway in New York in January, 1956, revised cost estimates had increased the financing requirements by $15 million, to $158 million. The documents were all finally drawn up, and the closing of the offering of common shares and debentures provided Westcoast with funds of $39.1 million on May 1, while an additional $29.5 million was received the same day in long-term bank loans. The Royal Bank was paid back the $19 million it had provided in short-term loans, only to return $10.5 million of this in long-term loans. At the same time, arrangements had been completed for some $90 million in first mortgage bonds, funds that would be drawn on as required to meet construction costs during the following eighteen months. The major bond purchasers were the Metropolitan Life Insurance Company, New York Mutual Life Insurance Company, and Northwest Mutual Life Insurance Company. At the Hotel Pierre, McMahon threw another big party to celebrate the event.

With the completion of financing on May 1, Westcoast had 4,860,000 shares outstanding. Nearly one-quarter had been acquired by Pacific Northwest Pipeline at the offered price of $5 per share under the terms of the option granted to Boots Adams in the agreement of November, 1954. For a brief period Pacific Northwest was the largest shareholder of Westcoast, but it was never represented on the board, nor given any opportunity to control the management of the company.

Most of the money was borrowed from US investors, but most of the common shares were sold to Canadian investors, so that with its first public offering of shares Westcoast was some 55 per cent Canadian-owned. And a voting trust agreement was designed to ensure that control of Westcoast remained in Canada – in the hands of Frank McMahon and his associates. Under this arrangement most of the purchasers of common shares did not obtain voting rights, rather they were assigned to the voting trustees. The six trustees (four Canadians and two Americans) held the voting rights to 64 per cent of the shares. They were Frank and George McMahon, D.P. McDonald, Norman Whittall, Lloyd Gilmour, and E.T. Herndon, and later two from Eastman, Dillon and Company.

Including the shares purchased by Pacific Northwest, the underwriters, headed by Eastman, Dillon in the United States and Wood Gundy in Canada, offered some 3.9 million Westcoast shares in the initial public financing. They were immediately sold out, and within months Westcoast shares had risen from their offered price of $5 to a peak of $57. The 625,000 shares that the Westcoast sponsors had earlier purchased for $31,247 were, on paper, worth close to $40 million, although the market price was later to drop to less than half this peak level.

The sale of the five-cent shares was later sharply criticized, but not by the only people who could in any way be said to have suffered as a consequence, those who had paid $5 a share in the public offering. Any investor who had read the prospectus was well informed of this sale. In any event, the five-cent shares do not tell the full story. Close to 150,000 of them had been allocated to Frank McMahon. Half of these were for his associates, including George McMahon, Norman Whittall, D.P. McDonald, and others, so that Frank wound up with 74,188 shares in his own account. At the time of the first public offering on May 1, 1956, McMahon purchased a further quarter of a million shares at $5 each, and later another 200,000 shares at $6, under the option granted in January, 1955. In total, McMahon bought

213

500,000 Westcoast shares at an average price of $4.65. If he made a fortune out of this, those who paid $5 a share were hardly impoverished.

The initial financing for Westcoast had barely been completed before additional funds were required as a result not only of the steadily increasing cost estimates, but also because of a change in the arrangements under which Westcoast was to purchase Peace River gas from the oil companies. In 1955, Westcoast had signed contracts to buy gas at rates up to a maximum of 390 million cubic feet per day, 250 million to be supplied by Pacific, Sunray, Canadian Atlantic, Peace River Natural Gas, and their joint-venture partners. Under the terms of the contracts, the producers were to build the field gathering pipelines and the processing facilities required to remove the sulphur and liquids from the gas before it was shipped through the pipeline.

To handle the gas produced in the Fort St John and nearby fields in northeastern BC, construction was started in 1956 on a large processing complex at Taylor Flats, a few miles south of the town of Fort St John. The complex comprised three basic units: a plant being built by Jefferson Lake Sulphur Company to recover up to 600 tons of sulphur a day; a scrubbing plant owned by the producing companies which would remove condensate, propane, and butanes from the gas; and a refinery being built by Pacific Petroleums to produce gasoline, aviation fuel, and other products from the liquids supplied by the scrubbing plant.

The Pacific group of companies, however, found themselves hard pressed to finance these facilities, as well as the extensive drilling program required to produce the gas. The result was that the gas purchase contracts were re-negotiated, and Westcoast took over the $13 million gas scrubbing plant and the field gathering line. To handle this, Westcoast raised an additional $17.6 million in October, 1956, from the sale of additional first mortgage bonds, debentures, bank notes, and shares.

That, however, was still not the end of it. In July, 1957, Canadian Bechtel reported that a further $25 million would be required to complete the pipeline, and arrangements were made with Eastman, Dillon for the sale of $25 million in debentures, convertible into Westcoast shares. Financing for the pipeline had thus been increased from the original estimate of $143 million to $200 million (US funds), which netted Westcoast nearly $196 million after brokerage commissions and other financing costs.

214

Because there was no hope of recovering this added cost by increasing the price of the gas that had been contracted for, any profits that Westcoast might hope to earn would have to come from whatever additional sales it might be able to line up. Before the line was completed and thanks in part to arrangements with Phillips Petroleum, Westcoast had letters of intent from its US purchasers that would double its sales to some 700 million cubic feet per day. Despite the added costs, Westcoast would still be in good shape if the letters of intent could be converted into actual sales, if regulatory approvals were forthcoming, and if enough gas was available.

Phillips Petroleum became involved because it saw an opportunity to get into the natural gas liquids business in Canada by giving a helping hand to Pacific and Westcoast. In the United States, Phillips was the leading producer of natural gas, the leading marketer of propane and butanes recovered from its gas production, and the leading manufacturer of gasoline and other petroleum products refined from gas liquids. It was naturally interested in such an opportunity in Canada, and both Pacific and Westcoast could certainly use the help and expertise.

Charles Hetherington was the chief ramrod for both Westcoast and Pacific at this stage. As vice-president of Westcoast since 1952 and vice-president of Pacific since April, 1956, it was his job to make sure that all the work was finished and gas started flowing before November 1, 1957. This included completion of the pipeline, drilling the wells to produce the gas, construction of the gas processing and refining facilities at Taylor, and some means of marketing the gasoline and other products that would come pouring out of the Taylor complex.

Of several hundred oil companies active in Canada, only a handful are engaged in the manufacture and marketing of the end petroleum products. Most sell their crude oil to the big companies with the refineries and service stations and their natural gas to the pipeline companies. To many oil men, the refining and marketing end of the oil business is as foreign as selling advertising is to most newspaper reporters. Pacific was no exception. In 1956, it purchased, for shares and cash, X-L Refineries Limited which operated a small refinery at Dawson Creek and a few service stations along the Alaska Highway. Pacific bought X-L primarily for the service stations to provide an outlet for the products from the refinery being built at Taylor. The deal made

215

Pacific one of Canada's few "integrated" oil companies with oil wells, refineries, and service stations. (The Dawson Creek refinery was later converted into an asphalt plant and produced much of the material for paving the Alaska Highway.)

"Not knowing much about service stations, I was having a terrible time running this thing," Hetherington later recalled. "If a service station operator got angry and hung up his wrench, we'd wind up with an empty service station. Besides, we were having troubles enough building this gas plant and refinery at Taylor."

It was at this stage that Hetherington, at his Calgary office in the new Pacific Building, received a visitor from Tulsa. As Hetherington tells it, his guest walked in, put his feet on the desk, and the conversation went something like this:

> My name is George P. Bunn. I'm the executive assistant to Boots Adams, and I'm a man of few words. We've got three trillion cubic feet of gas up there in BC which we'd be glad to put behind the Westcoast line, but in return we'd like to join you in the gas liquids business. Phillips has made its way by being in the gas liquids business, and if you don't take us in as a partner, we'll just take our three trillion cubic feet and get into the gas liquids business in Canada on our own.

Hetherington thought it over for at least two seconds, then replied: "Well, Mr Bunn, we just might be able to fit you in here somewhere."

After negotiations in Tulsa, Pacific wound up with a new partner. Phillips purchased a half interest in the Dawson Creek refinery and X-L service stations for $855,000, took a half interest in the refinery being built at Taylor, agreed to look after the marketing end of the business, and contracted to sell Westcoast its gas reserves in both northeastern British Columbia and southwestern Alberta. Before long some forty service stations along the Alaska Highway had sprouted Phillips 66 signs, the first outside of the United States. Eventually, the marketing emblem was changed to Pacific 66.

From its exploration permits in northeastern British Columbia, Phillips agreed to sell 200 million feet of gas per day to Westcoast, while another 150 million feet per day was contracted to Westcoast from the Savanna Creek field, high on a ridge in the Alberta foothills, sixty miles southwest of Calgary. Savanna Creek, discovered by Phillips, Husky Oil, and Northern Natural

Gas Company, was thought to have 1.5 trillion cubic feet of gas, about half the amount that had been found in the Peace River country.

Based on the anticipated Peace River supplies from Phillips, Westcoast agreed to sell an additional 200 million feet per day to Pacific Northwest Pipeline, to be delivered as soon as the gas was available. Half of this was at the option price of twenty-two cents per thousand cubic feet, while the other half was to be at a price to be negotiated.

To deliver the gas from Savanna Creek, Westcoast proposed to build a new thirty-inch diameter pipeline, 174 miles from the foothills field, crossing the southeast corner of British Columbia to the Idaho border at Kingsgate. Pacific Northwest would extend its system northeast from Spokane to pick up the gas at Kingsgate. Westcoast would then have two pipelines feeding into the Pacific Northwest system: the Peace River pipeline delivering gas at Sumas and the Savanna Creek delivering gas at Kingsgate.

The new pipeline from Savanna Creek, combined with the required expansion of capacity to the Peace River line, would cost $100 million – half as much again as the cost of putting the original line into operation. By increasing its investment 50 per cent, Westcoast would be able to double its sales. This would be very profitable business, except for a couple of problems that soon emerged.

For one thing, of the 200 million feet per day that Phillips was to supply from northeastern British Columbia, 150 million was to come from fields that had yet to be discovered. Phillips never did discover them. Another problem involved Savanna Creek. Further drilling revealed that this field had far less gas than first estimated and would be able to provide only 50 million feet per day, rather than 150 million.

The plans that Pacific Northwest Pipeline had for selling the additional gas that it hoped to obtain from Westcoast led to another complication. Pacific Northwest planned to take this extra gas all the way through its system to southern California, where it had a very tentative sales arrangement with Pacific Gas Lighting of Los Angeles. This was not exactly welcomed by El Paso, with its monopoly on the supply of out-of-state gas to California. El Paso took care of that problem in late 1956 when it acquired Pacific Northwest in a swap of shares that reportedly gave Pacific Northwest shareholders a paper profit of $37 million, including $12 million for Ray Fish, the largest shareholder. The deal made El Paso the largest pipeline firm in the United States. It now had close to a hammerlock on the entire US gas market west of the Rocky Mountains, the most extensive pipeline grid in the United States, committed gas supplies from the Mexican border to northern British Columbia, and a 25 per cent interest in Westcoast Transmission. In addition, Paul Kayser and El Paso were busy exploring for their own gas reserves in northern BC.

To Kayser, El Paso's monopoly seemed justified on the basis that it would provide more efficient and lower cost gas service. Moreover, the charges and profits of inter-state pipelines like El Paso were fully regulated by the federal government, simply because they are, by their very nature, monopolies.

The US Department of Justice, however, held that by acquiring Pacific Northwest, El Paso had eliminated potential competition in supplying the California market, specifically the gas from Savanna Creek that Pacific Northwest had hoped to sell to Pacific Gas Lighting. These were supplies that largely did not exist. Six months after the merger, the Justice Department instigated court action under antitrust legislation, seeking to compel El Paso to divest its interest in Pacific Northwest. It took sixteen years of litigation, the longest antitrust case in US history, before El Paso finally disposed of its ownership in Pacific Northwest. During that period, El Paso was Westcoast's only export customer.

Another merger completed while the Westcoast line was being built experienced no similar difficulties. In 1957, Westcoast acquired Peace River Natural Gas Company, the firm established ten years earlier by McMahon, Whittall, George Martin, Victor Spencer, Frank Ross, and Pacific Petroleums to acquire the first BC oil and gas permits issued in the Peace River. Pacific owned more than half these shares, obtained in return for some $5 million in exploration and drilling advances. In the merger, Pacific acquired nearly 600,000 Westcoast shares, increasing its ownership of Westcoast from about 18 to 25 per cent. Pacific thus became the largest single owner of Westcoast, a position it maintained for the next two decades.

It was on Pacific and its drilling partners that Westcoast would have to rely for the bulk of its initial gas supplies when the pipeline was completed. To provide that gas required expenditures in excess of Pacific's revenues. Among other things, Pacific needed money for its share of a 70-well drilling program in the Fort St John area, half the cost of the refinery under construction at Taylor, and 190 houses to be built for Pacific and Westcoast employees at Fort St John.

Pacific planned to obtain the money with its first large debt financing: an issue of $15 million of debentures, convertible into Pacific shares, would be offered to US investors by a group of underwriters headed by its New York brokers, which by then had become Eastman Dillon, Union Securities & Company. Work on the detailed prospectus and registration statement required by the US Securities Exchange Commission started in August, 1956, under the supervision of Pat Bowsher and Len Youell in Pacific's finance department. Nearly six months later, on January 22, approval was granted by the SEC. At nine the following morning the debentures were offered by the underwriting group, and in less than half an hour they were all sold.

THE GREATEST EVENT FOR BRITISH COLUMBIA

Building the pipeline was a big job, but no bigger or tougher than other pipelines that had been laid in Canada by 1956. From the wheatlands of the Peace River, the route climbed through rolling foothills and crossed the Pine Pass, one of the lowest breaks through the Rocky Mountains, at an elevation of 3,300 feet. Then it turned south through heavy forest to the grasslands of the Cariboo country, crossed the Cascade Mountain Range by way of rugged Coquihalla Pass, then plunging down to the flat farmland of the Fraser Valley.

A seventy-five-foot swath was cleared through more than 500 miles of forest. Behind the loggers came a clanking army of machinery: graders, trenchers, welders, coat and wrap machines to swaddle the pipe with tar and asphalt, the big sideboom tractors that lower the pipe in the ditch, and the backfillers. Backhoes were used instead of trenchers in the foothills area of glacial boulders, while in the mountains the trench was blasted with dynamite. Concrete saddles were anchored over the pipe to keep it submerged in swamp and muskeg. At five major river crossings, the pipe emerged to cross the water in arching, aerial spans. Seven million tons of earth were moved, and into the trench went 230,000 tons of steel for 650 miles of 30-inch pipe, 83 miles of 26-inch and 68 miles of 4- to 6-inch gathering lines.

219

At the peak of construction in 1956, more than 2,200 men were working on the pipeline, and by early 1957 only 200 miles of pipe were left to be laid. Everything was on schedule, except for two problem areas.

In the southern 120 miles that embraced the Cascade Mountains and the flatlands of the Fraser Valley, Mannix Limited was having trouble keeping within the contracted price of $7.8 million and seemed in danger of falling behind schedule. In the Fraser Valley water flooded the ditch, and in the crossing of a mountain ridge near Hope, called Angel's Peak, Canadian Bechtel, as manager of construction, claimed that the Mannix crew had not blasted the ditch to the required depth.

In November, Mannix requested additional payment of several million dollars to cover these problems and complete its section of the line on time. Westcoast's position was that the problems had been created by Mannix, and the request was rejected. The possibility of cancelling the Mannix contract and calling in a new construction firm was examined, and it was estimated that this would cost an additional $800,000 to $1.7 million. After several weeks of negotiations, Fred Mannix and his lawyer, Peter Lougheed (later Alberta Premier), met for two days in New York with Frank McMahon, Charles Hetherington, D.P. McDonald, and H.F. Waste of Canadian Bechtel. The dispute was resolved after McMahon offered a bonus payment of $1 million over the contract price if Mannix completed the work on time. Mannix hired a new construction supervisor, finished laying the 120 miles of pipe in July, collected the extra $1 million, but still claimed to have lost more than $4 million on the job.

Another snag involved the shipment of faulty sections of thirty-inch pipe by the English firm of South Durham Steel and Iron. When the pipe was unloaded at the dock in Vancouver, defects were found in many of the thirty-foot lengths, and they were either repaired or shipped back to England. Some of the defective sections, however, found their way into the pipeline. As portions of the line were completed, they were filled with water and pressure-tested. Sixty-nine sections of South Durham pipe burst during these tests.

Westcoast submitted a claim for $3.7 million against South Durham for added expenses related to the faulty pipe, and the English firm responded with a cash offer of $500,000. The settlement finally reached provided payment of $600,000 by South Durham, plus a credit of $400,000 against orders for additional pipe.

As construction of the Westcoast line neared completion in 1957, McMahon was riding high, wide, and handsome. In New York, he had an elegant sixteenth-floor apartment on Park Avenue opposite the Waldorf Astoria which was decorated by Betty McMahon with delicate Japanese murals; a large house in Calgary; and a winter home in Palm Beach, Florida. On Calgary's Ninth Avenue, Pacific Petroleums moved into its new ten-storey Pacific Building in 1955, adjacent to the seven-storey Petroleum Building it had built in 1950. Adjoining McMahon's office on the top floor of the new building was a small apartment, as well as a huge lounge with chocolate and white rugs and a large stone fireplace for the entertainment of company guests.

Pilot Don Brady and co-pilot Gordon Davis shuttled McMahon around the continent in his flying office, the twin-engined Lockheed Lodestar. There McMahon worked at his desk, chain-smoked Black Cat cigarettes, and wore two grooves in the carpet, his pent-up energy released in the constant shuffling of his feet.

His interests flourished everywhere. In New York, his smash success with *Pajama Game*, in which he had already earned $200,000 on a $50,000 investment, was followed by more Broadway hits, such as *Damn Yankees*, *West Side Story*, *Fiorello*, and *Plain and Fancy*. In California, he went into partnership with Bill Gilmore of San Francisco, a wealthy steel producer, to purchase substantial interests in the Tanforan and Golden Gate race tracks.

One of his larger ventures was Alberta Phoenix Tube & Pipe Ltd, organized in 1955 to produce small-diameter pipe for oil and gas field gathering lines. In July, 1957, the $6.5 million plant in Edmonton was officially opened by Premier Manning. McMahon was president, and other backers were Bill Gilmore and half ownership by a large German steel firm, Phoenix-Rheinrohr of Düsseldorf.

Other interests, shared with brother George, included a stake in a fertilizer plant in Medicine Hat, Alberta (Northwest Nitro-Chemical Company), a gas exploration company in southern Alberta (New Gas Exploration Limited), and another new firm,

Charter Oil Company, organized to join the exploration play in the Peace River area and headed by McMahon's former drilling partner, Matt Newell. Although no longer president of Alberta Distillers, he remained on the board, and had reached the pinnacle of business recognition in Canada by joining the board of the Royal Bank. He roamed restlessly through a wide social circle that embraced bankers, jockeys, businessmen, actors, politicians, and drillers.

The only cloud on Westcoast's horizon on October 6, 1957, was a cold front that dumped an early snowfall on Fort St John and accumulated in eight-foot drifts. That could present a problem for the more than 300 guests who were due to arrive the following day for two days and $200,000 worth of official opening ceremonies of the Westcoast pipeline. As the snow fell on Fort St John that Sunday, the Westcoast guests were gathering from all across the continent at Calgary and Vancouver where Westcoast had provided overnight hotel accommodations. A Constellation aircraft chartered from Air Canada flew guests from New York to Calgary, while a DC6 chartered from Canadian Pacific Airlines brought more from Toronto. From Los Angeles and San Francisco, another DC6 chartered from CP Air brought even more to Vancouver. Two more DC6 aircraft were chartered for the people originating from Calgary. On Monday, the five chartered planes would fly to Fort St John, where the guests would inspect the large processing complex and a flaring gas well, returning to Vancouver that evening for more ceremonies at the Hotel Vancouver on Tuesday. Smaller corporate aircraft from Calgary, Tulsa, Houston, Bartlesville, and other points made up the rest of the armada.

In Calgary, Westcoast's Purchasing Manager, Sid Gray, spent the weekend collecting a great pile of topcoats and buying all the rubber boots and galoshes he could find in Calgary stores. In the waiting room of the Calgary airport Monday morning, the Westcoast guests were greeted by a grinning Frank McMahon, staggering under an arm-load of fleece-lined coats which he dispensed with the warning that, "It might be cold up there."

At Fort St John, Pacific had rounded up all the tractors it could locate to clear the snow off the airport runways. Several miles of corrugated cardboard were hastily spread over the snow and mud to form pathways. Eight chartered buses, driven up more than 400 miles from Edmonton, stood waiting at the airport. And a couple of hundred additional pairs of rubber boots had been assembled at the airport waiting room.

A champagne breakfast was served on the chartered flights to Fort St John, and by the time the aircraft arrived, the clouds had lifted on a brilliantly sunny but chilly day. With George McMahon acting as master of ceremonies, Alberta Mines Minister Ray Rierson spun a valve as big as a ship's wheel to symbolically start Alberta gas flowing through the pipe, while BC Mines Minister Ken Kiernan spun another valve to start the flow of BC gas.

From the ballroom of the Hotel Vancouver on Tuesday, following a luncheon for 500 guests, British Columbia Premier W.A.C. Bennett opened the valves at the Huntingdon meter station, seventy miles east. That started the first flow of gas from the Westcoast line into the system of the British Columbia Electric Company, serving the Vancouver area, and across the US border at Sumas to the Pacific Northwest system.

Standing in front of a control panel equipped with a large lever and a pair of red and green lights that looked like traffic signals, Bennett called the Huntingdon meter station over the radio network that had been set up.

"This is Vancouver calling Huntingdon meter station," his voice boomed over the amplifiers in the ballroom. "Can you hear me, Huntingdon?"

"This is Huntingdon. Go ahead Vancouver," came the response from Westcoast's division meter inspector Lin Bennett.

"Everything ready to turn the switch?" asked the Premier.

"All set."

"I am now going to turn on the gas," Bennett announced, and pulled the lever.

It had been planned that the sound of the gas roaring through the pipe would be picked up by the radio and broadcast over the amplifiers in the ballroom. The gas was flowing, but no noise was coming over the amplifiers. Behind the control panel, Westcoast technician Terry Lynch quickly turned up the "squelch" on the VHF radio creating a noise that, as far as anyone could tell, sounded like gas flowing through a pipeline.

"This is the greatest event for British Columbia since the completion of the Canadian Pacific Railway united the province with the rest of Canada," Bennett beamed. "All British Columbia will always be indebted to the McMahons."

Less than a week later, Westcoast was being accused in newspaper articles of charging excess prices to Canadian gas buyers, thereby subsidizing American consumers who were said to be paying 50 per cent less. In Parliament, McMahon was characterized by CCF leader M.J. Coldwell as one of the pipeline "robber barons," because of his profits on the five-cent shares of Westcoast. Harold Winch, veteran CCF member for Vancouver East, accused McMahon and other pipeline operators of "financial highway robbery."

Writing in the *Vancouver Sun* on October 12, five days after the official opening of the Westcoast line, Stanley Burke reported that the price paid by Pacific Northwest for gas picked up from Westcoast near the Huntingdon meter station was twenty-two cents per thousand cubic feet, while the price paid by BC Electric, calculated on the same demand factor of 90 per cent, amounted to thirty-two cents. Burke pointed out that the Exportation of Power and Fluids and Gas Importation Act, revised in 1955, contained this clause:

> The price charged by the licensee shall not be lower than the price at which power or gas, respectively, is supplied by him or his supplier in similar quantities under similar conditions of sale for consumption in Canada.

"These facts are certain to undergo some searching study by the new Conservative government in Ottawa, concerned as it is with 'Canadian resources for Canadians,' " Burke wrote.

That searching study was ordered three days later, on October 15, when John Diefenbaker's Conservative government appointed a Royal Commission to study such matters as the regulation of oil and gas pipelines, the export of oil and natural gas, the authority that might be granted to a proposed National Energy Board, the government's financing of Trans-Canada Pipe Lines, and other energy matters. The Borden Commission, as it became known, was headed by Henry Borden, QC, former chairman of the Brazilian Traction Light & Power Company. Other commissioners were J. Louis Levesque, president of Quebec Natural Gas Company; Dr George Britnell, an economist at the University of Saskatchewan; Dr R.M. Hardy, University of Alberta; Robert Howland, former deputy minister of the Nova Scotia Department of Trade and Industry (and later a chairman of the National Energy Board); and Vancouver lawyer Leon J. Ladner.

The Borden Commission hearings opened in Calgary on February 3, 1958, and first trained the searching light of its inquiry on the affairs of Trans-Canada Pipe Lines and the massive financial help it had received from the former Liberal government. The Conservatives had been elected in 1957 to form a minority government, and another election was expected soon. If the Conservatives hoped that the Borden Commission would come up with fresh revelations concerning Trans-Canada's financial affairs that would help them in the next election, they were doomed to disappointment. After all the thunder of the previous two years, the Borden Commission's examination of the witnesses for Trans-Canada was anti-climactic and a yawn for the news media.

On February 12, the spotlight turned on Westcoast, and commission counsel Arthur Pattillo focused it on the twenty-two-cent export sales price.

McMahon did not appear before the Borden Commission in Calgary; he was in a New York hospital, recuperating from an operation. Standing in the docket for the defence of Westcoast at Calgary, almost as though they were on trial, were D.P. McDonald, Charles Hetherington, and Westcoast's export customer, Paul Kayser, president of El Paso Natural Gas Company and chairman of its subsidiary, Pacific Northwest Pipelines. McMahon recuperated in time, however, to testify before the Borden hearings at Victoria in April and again at Toronto in July.

The investigation of Westcoast failed to prove that British Columbians were subsidizing American buyers of Canadian gas in Seattle and Portland. The American consumers, it turned out, were paying more than Canadian consumers, and it was the Americans, Westcoast argued, who were subsidizing the Canadians. But it did become clear that Westcoast had got stuck for twenty years with an export price that made it most unhappy, especially since its pipeline wound up costing some $50 million more than had been originally estimated. So the hearings focused on the circumstances that had compelled Westcoast to accept an export price of twenty-two cents as the only deal it could get. One of the reasons that emerged, at least by implication, was the

225

determination of Pacific Gas and Electric to obtain a supply of gas that it controlled.

PG&E had been distributing gas in San Francisco and northern California since 1929, initially gas produced in the state, but by 1958 two-thirds of its supplies came from El Paso. To break its dependency on El Paso, PG&E had by then applied for a 1,300-mile pipeline from Alberta to San Francisco. At thirty-six-inches in diameter, it would be the largest (but not the longest) pipeline in the world, and would cost $300 million. Vice-president James Moulton told the Borden Commission that "PG&E considers it most important" to obtain "a new source [of gas] by means of a pipeline which is independent of its principal supplier." PG&E had set up a series of companies to build the pipeline, "so that we have control of them from California to Canada. . . . There is a real value to having a direct contact with the producer through pipeline facilities that are under our control. We have found that can be very, very important."

So important that PG&E was prepared to pay a premium for the gas in order to control the pipeline. In 1954, it had rejected Westcoast's offer to deliver Peace River gas to San Francisco. Later, as we have seen, it squashed the alternative plan under which El Paso proposed to build the final leg for the movement of Peace River gas to the city. As Paul Kayser told the Borden hearings, "The completing of that line and the taking of the gas . . . down to San Francisco was not an easy thing to do."

"I guess it wasn't," Commission counsel Arthur Pattillo interjected. "You never did it."

"That is right," said Kayser. "That is exactly correct. . . . We were prevented from doing that because Pacific Gas and Electric Company had other plans."

The other plans were for the 1,300-mile pipeline that would deliver Alberta gas to San Francisco at an estimated price of forty-nine cents per thousand cubic feet. The Peace River gas that Westcoast had offered was priced at thirty-four cents, nearly one-third less. But then it did not provide PG&E with its own pipeline.

The proposed PG&E line from Alberta was in direct competition with the proposal of Westcoast and El Paso for the planned pipeline from Savanna Creek. More importantly, it raised the possibility that gas from southern and central Alberta might shut

Peace River gas out of the California market for decades, a real threat to Westcoast's future.

Pattillo also seemed concerned about El Paso's partial ownership of Westcoast. The inference was that El Paso somehow used this interest to influence the price or terms at which it obtained gas from Westcoast.

"As a 23 per cent shareholder [of Westcoast], you cannot tell us what the rate of return is on that twenty-two cent contract?" Pattillo asked.

Kayser: "I sure can't."

Pattillo: "You must have more than gas coming out of your ears."

The major question, though, was whether Westcoast was selling gas to an American buyer at a price less than it was charging its principal Canadian buyer under similar circumstances, which would violate Canadian law. Westcoast argued that the circumstances were not at all similar. Pacific Northwest bought 300 million cubic feet per day with a "take or pay" clause that required it to pay for any gas it did not take. BC Electric bought only one-fifth as much gas from Westcoast, with no minimum commitment volume, and no clause that would require it to pay for gas it did not take.

Who paid the most depended on where you measured it. At Westcoast's Huntingdon meter station, BC Electric paid thirty-two cents, while Pacific Northwest paid twenty-two cents. But BC Electric had to move the gas only forty miles to the Vancouver city gate, while Pacific Northwest had to deliver it nearly 300 miles to the city gates of Seattle and Portland. As a result, the city gate prices were actually higher for the American consumers.

McMahon said that the price structure reflected a commitment that Westcoast had made in 1952, under its original pipeline proposal, to supply gas to the principal West Coast utilities at the same price. "From the very start of negotiations the BC Electric Company joined with the Seattle Gas Company and the Portland Gas and Coke Company in requesting Westcoast to sell to Vancouver, Portland, and Seattle at the same price," McMahon said. "This whole thing was based on the economics to supply gas in Portland, Seattle, and Vancouver at a postage-stamp rate."

Nor did McMahon see that BC consumers were getting the short end of the stick. Because of the "facts which clearly show that British Columbia utility companies are receiving gas on more favourable terms than United States utilities, and in view of the fact that the BC consumers could not have obtained any gas at a reasonable price without the US market, it certainly cannot be true that the BC consumer is subsidizing the sale of gas to the United States," McMahon declared.

McMahon admitted that, "I am not happy with the contract. We should be getting more money because our costs were much higher than we expected." But he said it was the best price he was able to get at the time, it allowed the pipeline to be built, and he was hopeful of additional export sales at higher prices.

Unhappy though he was, McMahon rejected a suggestion by Pattillo that the government might intervene "to terminate this contract and get out of your commitment to Pacific Northwest." McMahon responded that he "would not want to be in a position of repudiation of a contract."

The commission ordered a study by the Boston consulting firm of Stone and Webster on the always highly complex matter of allocation of pipeline costs to indicate a fair division of charges between Westcoast's BC customers and its export customers. Stone and Webster concluded that Pacific Northwest, with its twenty-two-cent contract, was being under-charged and, in effect, subsidized by the BC utilities. Westcoast ordered similar cost studies by the firm of Sanderson and Porter of New York, R.A. Ransom of Washington, and Ford, Bacon & Davis, and they concluded that Pacific Northwest was subsidizing the BC customers.

In its interim report issued in October, the Borden Commission effectively admitted that it could not figure out who was subsidizing whom. It was, however, no happier than McMahon with the twenty-two-cent export price, but it did not suggest that the contract be torn up: "The Commission recognizes the sanctity of such a contract and does not consider that it would be wise or in the public interest to cancel or interfere with the existing export license with respect to the export of gas by Westcoast." Instead, it recommended that when Westcoast came to apply for additional export approval the government should make sure that the export gas "under the present contract and future contracts is being sold at average prices which are fair and reasonable and in the public interest of Canada."

The Borden Commission focused its wrath on the sale of 625,000 Westcoast shares at five cents each to the project sponsors: "We are of the view that the financing of Westcoast, in so far as the issuance of its common shares is concerned, was done in a manner which has resulted in those few who were associated in the venture receiving potential capital profits beyond any amount which, in our opinion, could be considered as reasonable or adequate compensation for the risks involved." Having stated that, the commissioners hastened to add that there was nothing illegal about the five-cent shares, that details of the deal were available to potential investors in the company prospectus, and that they did not add to the price of the gas.

If, as the political attacks alleged, Westcoast had raped the people of British Columbia, at least British Columbians seemed to enjoy it. The Westcoast pipeline meant more industry, more employment, more population, more opportunities, and lower energy costs. Production of the gas and operation of the pipeline, according to Westcoast, directly and indirectly provided 100,000 jobs in British Columbia. In the seven years since Pacific and its partners had started drilling in the Peace River, the population of Fort St John had increased from 800 to 4,000, Dawson Creek from 3,500 to 7,500, and Grande Prairie from 2,600 to 6,000. Virtually all the homes in these towns were by then heated with natural gas at half the cost that had earlier been paid for fuel oil.

In the greater Vancouver area, the advantages in cost and convenience of natural gas were attested to by the rate at which home owners were rushing to install gas furnaces. "Those who have ever tried to heat a home with wet cedar sawdust may have mercifully forgotten the soul searching experience," Cliff MacKay recalled in the *Vancouver Sun* in October, 1960. "But chances are they can still smell the fumes from the clogged hopper, gleaming evily in a damp basement." MacKay reported that before natural gas was available some 70,000 homes and buildings in the Vancouver area were heated with sawdust, while 2,300 furnaces were supplied with manufactured gas. By October, 1960, only 7,750 homes in the entire lower mainland of British Columbia were still heated with sawdust, while 67,000 were heated with natural gas.

The grime and soot that had blackened Vancouver were disappearing, and the dense killer fogs that had shrouded its streets were already lifting. An idea born a quarter of a century before was at last bearing benefits.

229

CHAPTER FOURTEEN

Pacific Prospers

Pacific Petroleums grew by running its business at a loss. Or at least, it seemed that way.

Before Frank McMahon assumed control of the company in 1948, Pacific had earned a very modest profit from its oil wells at Turner Valley. After McMahon took over, sales of oil and gas soared, with production from Leduc, Redwater, and elsewhere, but expenditures grew even faster. During the nine-year period to 1958, Pacific's sales had increased from $342,000 to $1.8 million a year, but its losses during the same period amounted to more than $2 million. With the start of gas production from the Peace River area, combined with a series of mergers, Pacific's sales grew even faster, and so did its losses. In the three years after 1958 Pacific's sales increased ten-fold to nearly $19 million per year, while losses totalled more than $11 million.

It was not as completely mad as it might seem. Pacific was operating at a loss, because it was spending more than it was earning to find and develop new reserves of oil and gas, raising money for this from loans and the issue of shares for cash or property. The losses were more than offset by growing assets, oil and gas in the ground, as good as money in the bank. Eventually they would generate profits. At least that was the theory, and it pretty well worked out that way.

Pacific was still very much a promotion. It was building for the future. It rested upon a promoter's ability to maintain the confidence of investors that something was being built that would someday be profitable, would generate earnings, would pay dividends. Asset growth is the object of promotion. Profit is the objective of investment. And it is the investment objective that must ultimately prevail.

Building for the future is fine. But sooner or later the future arrives. When it does, the successful promotional venture must undergo a metamorphosis. It must become a profit-earning enterprise, with growth based on today's profits rather than tomorrow's promise. It becomes a very different creature, and requires a different breed of people to run it.

Those who build the world's best ships seldom make the best sea captains. It is no different in the business world. Once built, to prosper the most successful promotional venture must be run by corporate administrators. They are seldom recruited from among promoters, any more than sea captains are recruited from the ranks of naval architects.

The metamorphosis of Pacific Petroleums began in 1957 with the establishment of its affiliate, Westcoast Transmission. The transformation proceeded with the start-up of production from the gas reserves that Pacific and its partners had found in the Peace River, a series of mergers that consolidated Pacific's position as a leading oil and gas producer, the transfer of management from promoters to administrators, and, finally, growing profits.

The period of transition, first at Pacific and later at Westcoast, did not always run as smoothly as a well-oiled machine. Frank and George McMahon, together with their chief lieutenants, Charles Hetherington, D.P. McDonald, Pat Bowsher, and Doug Owen, emerged as nonpareil promoters and corporate builders. They also demonstrated that the best corporate builders are seldom the best corporate administrators. Instead, it was a former roustabout from Oklahoma, Kelly Gibson, who became the key corporate administrator who would lead both Pacific and Westcoast during their most dynamic period of profit and growth.

Born in Broken Arrow, Oklahoma, the son of a farmer, Kelly Gibson completed his high school at the Oklahoma Military Academy and attended the Oklahoma Agriculture and Mechanical College at Stillwater for two years before dropping out in 1934 to marry, at age twenty-two, a cousin of Will Rogers, Juliette Robinson. A married man in the middle of the Depression felt lucky enough to take whatever job could be found, and

231

Kelly took temporary work as a roustabout for Gulf Oil, hand-digging ditches for oil field gathering lines in Kansas at fifty cents an hour. After nearly a year he managed to join Gulf's permanent work force, earning seventy-one cents an hour. During seven years in field producing operations and on drilling rigs, Gibson learned the oil business from the working end. He spent four wartime years as a training officer at a string of army training camps in the United States, then re-joined Gulf as a drilling foreman in Michigan.

In 1949, Gulf sent Gibson on a one-month assignment to Alberta to take charge of a fishing job that was holding up progress on an expensive wildcat test, its Pincher Creek gas discovery. Instead of one month, Gibson stayed in Alberta permanently and sixteen years later became a Canadian citizen. After the fishing was finished at Pincher Creek, Gibson was sent to look after drilling ten wells on leases that Gulf had acquired in the Redwater field. That was followed by the development of Gulf's oil discovery at Stettler, midway between Calgary and Edmonton, at the time Gulf's largest operation in Canada. Kelly was field superintendent in charge of drilling and getting the wells into production.

In 1956, Gulf merged its Canadian subsidiary with British American Oil Company of Toronto, and Gibson was transferred to Calgary as zone production manager responsible for supervision of drilling and producing operations throughout western Canada for the merged operation.

When Scotty Tosh retired as Pacific's drilling and production manager in 1957, he recommended that Kelly Gibson take over. McMahon offered Gibson the job of vice-president of production with Pacific at a salary of $30,000 a year, twice the amount that Gulf was paying, plus stock options.

Gibson joined Pacific in November, 1957, a month after the Westcoast pipeline was put on stream, just in time to be hit with the problems that Pacific would face in producing enough gas to keep the pipeline in business. "I was told I could run my side of the business the way I wanted," Gibson later recalled. "That was what was attractive to me, getting to put in some ideas I had in my mind about producing operations, things I was never able to do in Gulf. It was too big. I wasn't an engineer, and engineers were always trying to run the operations, and I never did let them do it. We were fussing and fighting all of the time." At

Pacific, one of the engineers that Gibson fussed with was Charles Hetherington.

Following incorporation in 1949, Westcoast was managed almost as a division of Pacific Petroleums for six years, during the long quest for the authorizations to build the pipeline. During the construction period, it was a creature of the builders: the engineers, contractors, pipe welders. Only after the gas was turned on did Westcoast begin to establish its own corporate identity. With the start of construction, Westcoast established its operating offices in Vancouver and later transferred its head office to the same city. Frank McMahon headed Westcoast's operations as president and chief executive officer. D.P. McDonald was appointed managing director in the fall of 1957, and Doug Owen was later named treasurer. McMahon moved to Vancouver in 1961.

In Calgary, "Mr Frank," as he was known to the staff, remained chairman and chief executive of Pacific, while "Mr George" was president. Charles Hetherington resigned as executive vice-president of Westcoast to become managing director of Pacific. Although he was seldom in Calgary after 1958, Frank kept in constant contact with Pacific's operations and was on the telephone almost daily with either George or Hetherington.

For George, the time had come to enjoy some of the rewards of success, and he was not as compelled by the relentless drive that consumed his elder brother. He valued time for a family life with his wife, Kay, and six children, and he was increasingly involved in community activities, particularly the Calgary Stampede Board, of which he was a director, and the Calgary Stampeder Football Club.

The community-owned football club was a special interest. George played football in college, coached a semi-professional team in New Westminster between 1939 and 1941, and in Calgary coached a junior team that included a young Peter Lougheed. He joined the board of the Stampeder Football Club in 1954 and became president in 1959. Frank had also been a director of the club before moving to Vancouver, but it was George that the Calgary press called "Mr Football." A job with an oil company was one of the lures used to attract professional players to Calgary in the 1950s and 1960s, and no company had more football players on its payroll than Pacific. Among them were Earl Lunsford, later general manager of the Winnipeg Blue

Bombers, and Jack Gotta, who later coached the Ottawa Rough Riders before becoming coach of the Calgary team.

At Calgary's Mewatta Stadium, the Stampeders enjoyed about the worst accommodation of any professional Canadian club in the late 1950s. *Calgary Herald* sports columnist Gordon Hunter described the Mewatta dressing rooms as "just this side of hovels," and George McMahon admitted, "I don't know how they were ever able to sign a player for a second season."

In 1960, the McMahon brothers led a community effort that resulted in the $1 million, 22,000-seat McMahon Stadium. The city gave the University of Calgary (then the Calgary branch of the University of Alberta) a 99-year lease on land for the new stadium, and Frank and George donated $300,000 cash. The balance of the money was raised by a bond issue indemnified by the McMahon brothers against any loss up to $625,000. Since expanded at a cost of several million dollars to more than 33,000 seats, McMahon Stadium is used by both the Stampeders and the University of Calgary.

With George running the football club and Frank heading Westcoast and still scouring North America in search of new deals, Hetherington and Gibson were left to operate Pacific Petroleums at the head office and Al McIntosh to run the wells in the Peace River area, where the problems lay.

GAS SUPPLY PROBLEMS

McIntosh started with Pacific in 1948, a university student working the summer months as a roustabout on a drilling rig. After graduation as a petroleum engineer in 1951, he joined Pacific's permanent staff and by 1957 was general manager of production at Fort St John.

One of the first problems encountered in producing gas for the pipeline was the formation of hydrates, a compound of frozen water and hydrocarbons that plugged well tubings. McIntosh experimented with the injection of glycol as an antifreeze. That kept the gas flowing long enough to warm up the wells and prevent further hydrate problems.

But the real difficulty was that there was less gas than Westcoast had counted on. In the Fort St John field, the two principal producing formations were a Triassic sandstone and a lower

Permo-Pennsylvanian limestone. The Permo-Penn reserves had been estimated at 400 billion cubic feet of gas, but development drilling revealed that the formation contained only 60 billion cubic feet. This not only cut back on the gas supply for the pipeline, but sadly affected the economics of the gas processing plant designed to recover large volumes of liquids from the Permo-Penn gas. On the Alberta side, the South Pouce field was produced at maximum rates. Within a few months the South Pouce wells were drawing water, and the field had to be shut down, cutting off another 60 million feet a day that Westcoast had counted on.

The immediate crisis was averted in 1958 when Westcoast's network of gathering pipelines was extended some ninety miles to hook up a number of small fields north of Fort St John. A further forty-mile extension of the gathering system was built in 1959. But supply problems were to continue to haunt Westcoast for years.

The big processing complex at Taylor was a headache. The scrubbing plant owned by Westcoast was designed to provide acid gas to the sulphur-recovery plant owned by Jefferson Lake and natural gas liquids to the petroleum products refinery owned jointly by Pacific and Phillips. Westcoast was to obtain a portion of the sales revenues in return for supplying the feedstock materials to these two facilities. But because the gas did not contain the proportions of liquids and sulphur the facilities had been designed to handle, things did not work out as planned. The sulphur plant produced only two-thirds of the anticipated volume of sulphur. The refinery was unable to produce high quality gasoline and could not handle all of the liquids supplied by the scrubbing plant. What the refinery could not use had to be flared.

"No one wanted the stuff that first came out of that refinery," recalls John Ballem. "We trucked some of it all the way to Edmonton where we sold it to Imperial Oil to put through their refinery. After paying the trucking costs to Edmonton, the price at the plant was about $1.35 a barrel, almost a give-away. It didn't matter, we had to get rid of it."

Ballem had joined Pacific in late 1956, following a law degree from Dalhousie University, a business degree from Harvard, and a short stint with Imperial Oil. He worked at Pacific first as Hetherington's executive assistant, later heading the legal

235

department and for awhile the marketing operation, before leaving for a law practice in partnership with Peter Lougheed.

Ballem had a lever to help persuade Imperial to buy the unloved material from the Taylor refinery. Pacific by this time had a small participation with Phillips, Sunray, and El Paso in a joint-venture exploration program in Venezuela. Pacific's share of the production was about 1,500 barrels a day. Imperial was buying Venezuelan oil for its Montreal refinery from parent Standard Oil of New Jersey at the posted field price of $2.50 a barrel, although it was being widely offered at a large discount. Ballem offered Imperial Pacific's Venezuelan oil at a price of $1.65 a barrel, but Imperial preferred to buy from its parent company at $2.50. Ballem's offer was an embarrassment that was withdrawn when Imperial agreed to buy the product from the Taylor plant for further refining.

Additional processing facilities had to be installed at the Taylor plant to use the liquids that were being flared and to produce an acceptable grade of gasoline. To pay for them, Phillips insisted that the contract with Westcoast be renegotiated. The final result was that, in March, 1959, Phillips took over operation of the jointly-owned refinery at Taylor, as well as the Dawson Creek refinery and the fifty service stations. The fifty-fifty ownership arrangement remained unchanged. But the new operating agreement, George McMahon said in making the announcement, would enable Pacific "to devote full attention to an exploration and development program on 4,747,226 acres in northeastern British Columbia." It also relieved Pacific of a substantial headache.

THE REVERSE ACQUISITION

The reputation of an oil company as a competent, efficient, and cost-conscious operator is a very valuable asset. Few exploration programs are conducted by oil companies in Canada except in partnership with other oil companies. One of the partners is normally selected to act as operator on behalf of all the participants in a particular venture. The role of operator can permit an independent oil company to build up more staff and technical resources than its own revenues might warrant. Confidence in the firm selected for this task is important. The confidence in Pacific as an operator was not enhanced by the initial gas production difficulties at Fort St John, nor by the start-up problems at the gas processing complex.

The whole tenor of the oil industry had changed by 1959. Gone was the gung-ho atmosphere of the early boom days. The oil companies had found so much oil in Alberta that they were able to sell only half of what they could produce. The emphasis had shifted to tight management control, cost-cutting, and technical expertise. Caution and conservatism had become the order of the day.

No one typified better than Hetherington the calculated risk-plunging type of attitude without which neither Pacific nor Westcoast could have succeeded. But the style that had built these companies was not the style that was now needed to run them. Hetherington was one of the first Pacific builders to leave; his terse, one-sentence letter of resignation was accepted by the Pacific board in January, 1959, and he set up shop as a petroleum consultant. Later, however, he was to re-join Westcoast.

In June, 1959, Hetherington was succeeded by Kelly Gibson, promoted from vice-president in charge of production to executive vice-president in charge of all of Pacific's day-to-day operations. Gibson had earned his spurs as a hard-working, no-frills administrator, ready to encourage those whom he thought met his exacting demands, and equally as ready to terminate the employment of those whom he thought did not. An associate recalls that Gibson worked late nearly every evening, "to approve every invoice, and sign every cheque. If you want to control what is really going on in an organization, that is the most effective way to do it." "I just worked country-boy style," Gibson later recalled. "We spent less money. Where we had three people, we used one." Out went the tenth floor executive apartment and the huge lounge with chocolate and white rugs and big stone fireplace.

Shortly after his new appointment, Gibson brought in Merrill Rasmussen from British American Oil (now Gulf Oil Canada) as vice-president of production. A Mormon from Cardston, Alberta, Rasmussen had been a schoolteacher before taking petroleum engineering at the University of Oklahoma, had worked with Gibson in Gulf's operations in the Stettler field, and was Edmonton-area production manager for British American at the time he joined Pacific.

Despite the start-up problems at Fort St John, Pacific continued to expand rapidly, in part by its continued aggressive exploration (in 1958 it found the first of the large gas fields in the Fort Nelson area, some 200 miles north of Fort St John), in part by additional financing (with a further $30 million debenture issue in 1958), but mostly by acquiring other companies in exchange for Pacific shares.

In 1958, Pacific issued more than 2.9 million shares, worth some $60 million at prevailing stock market prices, for separate acquisitions. The first and largest in 1958 was the acquisition of Merrill Petroleums for 1.5 million shares. The firm was founded by former Alberta Mines Minister Eldon Tanner, but by then it was headed by his son-in-law, Cliff Walker. The deal was negotiated in 1957 and completed early in 1958, following ratification by Merrill's shareholders. Merrill held substantial producing and prospective acreage in the Cardium sandstone play southwest of Edmonton that had produced Pembina, Canada's largest oil field, and a number of smaller pools.

Other acquisitions during 1958 included:

– Canadian Atlantic Oil Company, the launching-pad for McMahon's oil ventures in 1947, in which Pacific still held a substantial interest; the price: 1 million shares, worth about $20 million.

– Humber Oils Limited, with producing properties in the Pembina area; the price: 276,612 shares, worth about $5.5 million.

– Catalina Oils Limited; the price: 24,000 shares.

– Thirty-six oil wells at Pembina owned by a private syndicate headed by Max Bell; the price: 218,535 shares, worth more than $4 million. Other members of the Bell syndicate included *Vancouver Sun* editor Hal Straight, jockey Johnny Longden, former hockey star C.W. Conacher, Calgary contractor Fred Mannix, and Frank McMahon.

One person who did not prosper as a result of these transactions was Cliff Walker. Walker had started in the oil business as a drilling contractor with Cascade Drilling. When his father-in-law left Merrill Petroleums to head Trans-Canada Pipe Lines, Walker had stepped in as president of Merrill, which in turn purchased Cascade Drilling. In the merger with Pacific, Walker wound up with 85,000 Pacific shares, worth more than $2.5 million when the deal was negotiated in 1957. Walker subsequently bought back Cascade Drilling from Pacific, but these were difficult times in the drilling business. There was a large loan to be paid for the drilling rigs, and when the market price of Pacific shares plunged from a peak of $37 in 1957 to a low of $8 in 1960, Walker's business assets were wiped out.

The acquisitions, combined with the start of gas production from the Peace River, boosted Pacific's gross revenues from an annual rate of $1.3 million during the company's fiscal year ended February 28, 1957, to an annual rate of $10 million two year's later. But the company's losses during the same period increased from less than $640,000 to nearly $4.6 million per year.

Still, Pacific's twentieth annual report to its shareholders in 1959 was able to record a history of spectacular growth. In the two decades since Pacific had been founded, its properties had increased from eighty acres and two oil wells at Turner Valley to 9.3 million acres and interests in 1,700 oil and gas wells; its staff from a couple of employees to more than 400; its number of shareholders from a few score to more than 30,000.

But management's control of Pacific, always very tenuous, was further reduced by the 1958 transactions. By 1959, Pacific had 7.8 million shares outstanding, of which the McMahon brothers owned less than 3.5 percent, while the entire board of directors owned less than 5 per cent. Sunray had disposed of its holdings, and no single shareholder was in a position to control the company. That would soon change, however, due to yet another acquisition that Pacific was to make in 1960.

Pacific was, in effect, a Canadian company using American money. It was owned by 31,000 shareholders, of whom nearly 23,000 were Americans. But most of the owners were passive investors, so that in 1960 control was exercised by an eleven-man board, of whom nine were Canadians, and by the management and staff, virtually all Canadians. But the widely spread ownership made Pacific vulnerable to a take-over. It could be gobbled up at any time by a large international oil company and disappear from sight; and with it would go the effective control of Westcoast Transmission. A merger that would place a significant block of Pacific shares in the hands of a friendly investor might be one way to forestall a possible takeover and help ensure Pacific's continued survival.

Sunray (which by then had become Sunray-Midcontinent Oil Company) was a logical possibility. Most of Sunray's properties in Canada were owned in partnership with Pacific, and

McMahon and Sunray chairman Clarence Wright had several times discussed the possibility of merging their Canadian operations. During a trip to Tulsa for other business matters in mid-June, 1960, Frank called on his old friend, and the two once more discussed the advantages of merging their Canadian operations. It was agreed that it would be a good idea, but it would make even more sense to include the Canadian properties of Phillips. It was decided to sound out Boots Adams on the idea.

On July 7, McMahon returned to Tulsa, accompanied by Pat Bowsher and Les Clark, and on the following morning they met for breakfast with Clarence Wright and Sunray's senior vice-president, Hudson Harder, before driving to Bartlesville where a meeting had been arranged with Stanley Learned, chairman of Phillips' executive committee. Learned was interested in the idea, and in a one-hour discussion they concluded that the most logical procedure would be for Pacific to acquire the Canadian assets of Sunray and Phillips in exchange for Pacific shares. Wright, McMahon, and Learned agreed to sound out their respective boards and, if still interested, to meet for further talks.

On July 14, Sunray's Harder and Phillips vice-president John Houchin arrived in Calgary, where they met at the Palliser Hotel with George McMahon, Kelly Gibson, and Pat Bowsher to start negotiations. The following day, a letter of intent was signed that spelled out a formula under which they would seek to negotiate a merger. The number of shares issued by Pacific for the Canadian assets of Sunray and Phillips would be determined by detailed evaluation of Pacific and the properties it proposed to acquire.

The key to the deal lay in reaching unanimous agreement on the comparative value of assets worth more than $250 million. Without such agreement, the merger would not proceed. The letter of intent contained a "yard-stick" formula intended to ensure that all the assets would be evaluated on a comparative basis. Tangible assets, such as buildings, the gas processing and refining facilities, and service stations were to be evaluated at cost. Investments, such as Pacific's 26 per cent interest in Westcoast, would be valued at their quoted market prices on June 15.

It was agreed that estimating the comparative value of more than 5 million acres of unproven oil and gas rights held by the three companies in western Canada would be nearly impossible, so these holdings were excluded. The reserves of oil and gas, the principal assets, would be the toughest to judge. It was decided to use a yardstick of $1 per barrel of oil and four cents per thousand cubic feet of gas as the value of the reserves. The difficulty lay in estimating how much recoverable oil and gas lay under the proven leases held by each company. The only precise way the amount of producible oil or gas under a lease can be measured is after it has all been extracted. Before that time only estimates are available, based on interpretation of geological and engineering data. Yet it was these imprecise estimates that would largely determine how much Pacific would have to pay, in the way of shares, for the Sunray and Phillips properties.

The deal now hinged upon the ability of the technical experts to agree on the estimates of reserves under thousands of leases. The objective of each firm would be to establish the highest possible reserve estimates for its leases and minimize the reserves of other firms. The task was assigned to four engineers: Frank Ronaghan of Pacific, R.M. Archambeault of Phillips, D.E. Hall of Sunray, and John Maughan from the consulting firm of J.C. Sproule and Associates, who acted as an independent referee.

During three weeks of hard negotiations, the engineers met every day at Suite 909 in the Palliser Hotel in sessions that typically lasted from 8:30 in the morning until 11 at night. Surrounded by maps, calculators, well data, and engineering reports, they went painstakingly through a field-by-field study of the holdings of each company. Whenever an agreement could not be reached, Maughan was called in to help work out a compromise.

Secrecy was essential. If word got out prematurely that the three companies were negotiating a possible merger, it could lead to heavy stockmarket speculation that could jeopardize the prospects for a deal or lead to unfortunate consequences if no agreement were reached later. The negotiators were kept as isolated as a jury in a murder trial. Ronaghan had disappeared from his office the day before the negotiations began, and none of his associates, not even his secretary, knew where he had gone or when he would be back. To avoid being spotted by other Pacific staffers, Ronaghan was driven to the hotel by his wife every morning at 7:30 and picked up again after 11 PM. The negotiators ate most of their meals in the hotel room, and when they did eat in the dining room it was at separate tables. They came and went from the meetings at staggered intervals, got off the elevators at different floors, and either walked up or down to Room 909. From time to time, the engineers required maps or reports from their offices, and these were delivered by special messengers. Kelly Gibson was the messenger for Pacific, while the Canadian managers were the messengers for Phillips and Sunray. Like the four engineers, they made certain that they did not arrive at the hotel at the same time and got off the elevators on different floors. It was typical oil industry cloak and dagger stuff, involving what was up to then one of the largest mergers in the Canadian oil industry.

Based on the reserve estimates finally agreed to by the engineers, the combined assets of the three companies were valued at $294 million: $162 million for Pacific's holdings, $115 million for the Canadian properties of Phillips, and $17 million for Sunray's Canadian assets. Based on this valuation, the proposed merger contemplated that Pacific would issue 5,762,514 shares for the Phillips holdings and 861,310 for the Sunray properties, the Pacific shares valued at $19.91 each. The merger would increase Pacific's outstanding capital to nearly 14.8 million shares, of which 39 per cent would be owned by Phillips and 5.8 per cent by Sunray. It would be a "reverse" acquisition: Pacific would own the Phillips properties, but Phillips would own effective control of Pacific.

The merger was approved by the Pacific directors in Vancouver on August 30, and announced the same day, although subject to later ratification by the Pacific shareholders. Proof that the secret had been well kept was provided by the stockmarket. During the month since the first talks had been held, there had been no abnormal trading or price movement of Pacific shares. The announcement brought immediate heavy trading in Pacific shares on all North American exchanges, and the price jumped 30 per cent. The Pacific shareholders met in Calgary on December 20, 1960, to vote on the merger, and of the 31,020 registered shareholders only 147 disapproved.

Changes in management reflected the changes in ownership. Phillips elected three people on the twelve-man Pacific board: Learned, Houchin, and John Getgood, formerly manager of Phillips' international sales. Sunray named Hudson Harder. Frank and George remained on the board, Frank as chairman and George as vice-chairman, in advisory roles which they filled

242

for the next two years. Getgood was named president and chief executive, while a new executive committee consisted of Getgood as chairman, together with Frank, George, and Kelly Gibson. Following the merger, Frank was left to devote his attention to the problems of Westcoast, while George had more time for his community activities.

The deal with Phillips and Sunray did not complete Pacific's round of acquisitions. In 1962, it issued some 1.6 million shares with a market value of $28 million for the Canadian properties of Western Natural Gas Company of Houston, whose principal shareholders were Paul Kayser and El Paso. The major assets consisted of some 2 million acres of holdings and half a trillion cubic feet of gas in the Fort Nelson area, where Pacific was actively exploring, together with about 1 million acres of holdings and small oil reserves in Alberta. The Fort Nelson reserves were of great importance because of a planned 200-mile pipeline extension by Westcoast to add the gas in this region to its supplies. The following year, Pacific rounded out its holdings at Fort Nelson by purchasing El Paso's interest in 1.6 million acres (most of which had been held in partnership with Western) for $18.4 million. At about the same time, Pacific issued 2.4 million shares to acquire Bailey Selburn Oil and Gas, with an interest in nearly 2,000 Alberta oil and gas wells.

Phillips also increased its investment in Pacific, paying nearly $29 million for some 2.5 million Pacific shares, including the purchase of the shares that Pacific had issued to Western Natural Gas. The result of this was to increase Phillips' stake in Pacific from 39 per cent at the time of merger in 1960 to 45 per cent three years later.

In his first report to the shareholders as president of Pacific, for the company's fiscal year ended February 28, 1961, Getgood was able to announce that Pacific now ranked as the second largest gas producer and the eighth largest oil producer in Canada. Savings of $1 million a year had been achieved, "through reduction of administration and other expenses," Getgood reported, so that the company's losses had been cut to $2.9 million from $4.5 million two years earlier. The emphasis was on "a continuing effort during the past two years to reduce costs and increase efficiency." The result, he said, was that "Pacific's operations are now being conducted as efficiently and economically as any in the Canadian oil industry."

243

In 1961, Pacific changed its fiscal year to the calendar year. During the ten months of 1961, covered in the next shareholders report, Pacific finally broke the profit barrier, earning $1 million. Thereafter, Pacific's earnings increased every year for seventeen years in a row, climbing from $1 million or seven cents per share in 1961 to nearly $96 million or $4.44 per share in 1978. The machine that McMahon and his associates had built was being well managed.

John Getgood, an unassuming but dedicated worker with steel-grey hair chopped in a brush cut, had been a Phillips man for more than three decades before becoming president of Pacific for a period of a little more than three years. Under the Phillips style of management that Getgood brought from Bartlesville, Pacific was run by a team, with Getgood as leader, and other key members including Kelly Gibson (executive vice-president), Merrill Rasmussen (in charge of exploration and production), Pat Bowsher (in charge of finances until he retired in 1968 when he was succeeded by Bill Tye), and John Anderson (head of the legal department).

Getgood has described himself as an "oil peddler." Born in Northern Ireland, he arrived in Tulsa with his family as a teen-ager in 1923 and found work as an office boy for Marland Oil Company in Ponca City, Oklahoma. He later went to university intending to become a minister, but after two years he decided that it was not for him and went to work as an oil field scout, later as a refinery hand. Getgood joined the Phillips Petroleum sales force in 1929, and thirty years later he was in charge of the company's foreign sales, based in New York. Getgood was always ready to take on whatever task the company assigned him. Asked by Stanley Learned to take on the job at Pacific, his response was: "Of course. I'm a Phillips man and always have been."

His first job at Pacific, he later recalled, was to establish budgets for each of the departments. The only budget for the exploration department, Les Clark explained to him, had been whatever money Pacific had available. "If we needed more," Clark said, "Frank usually found it."

One of the big projects that Pacific undertook during Getgood's regime, with engineering help from Bartlesville, was construction of what was then the world's largest gas processing plant, together with a 586-mile pipeline to market the products. The project arose because of the bind Trans-Canada Pipe Lines had got caught in between its purchases and sales of natural gas. The energy value, or heat content, of natural gas can vary depending on the amount of liquids, such as propane, butanes, and condensates, contained in it. As a rule of thumb, one cubic foot of gas contains 1,000 British Thermal Units (or BTUs) but the more liquids contained in the gas the higher the BTU value. There is a limit to the amount of liquids that can be left in the gas, before it becomes too wet to handle in a pipeline. Under Trans-Canada's contracts with the gas producers, the price was based on 1,000 BTU per foot of gas, with proportionately higher prices for richer gas up to a maximum 1,150 BTU per foot. That meant that Trans-Canada paid up to 15 per cent more for gas with the maximum heat value.

Trans-Canada's problem was that while it was buying gas on a BTU basis, it was selling it on a volume basis. Under its long-term sales contracts, the utility companies in Ontario and Quebec paid stipulated prices per thousand cubic feet, regardless of whether the gas contained the minimum 950 BTU per foot or the maximum 1,150 BTU. Thus, Trans-Canada was forced to pay premiums of up to 15 per cent on the gas it purchased but was unable to recover this extra charge from its customers. By 1962, Trans-Canada was faced with a potential loss of as much as $1.5 million a year as a result, a figure that could climb higher as its sales volume increased.

The answer to the dilemma was the deal negotiated with Trans-Canada by Pacific in 1962 for construction of a large plant at Empress, Alberta, near the Saskatchewan border, where Trans-Canada took delivery of its gas from Alberta Gas Trunk Line. The plant to be built by Pacific would remove liquids from the gas, and the profits from the sale of these liquids would be split fifty-fifty by the two companies. The heat value of the gas delivered by Trans-Canada would be reduced to near the 950 BTU specified in the sales contracts. Consumers in Toronto would find that they would have to buy more gas to heat their homes.

Butanes and condensate removed from the gas at the Empress plant could be sold as feedstock for refineries and petrochemical plants. The main product, propane, would be marketed throughout western Canada by Pacific, primarily to farms and rural areas where small sales volumes made it uneconomical to provide natural gas by pipeline. The propane would be transported by a six-inch-diameter pipeline from Empress, 586 miles east to Winnipeg, and trucked to customers from distribution points along the pipeline.

The plant was designed to process 1 billion cubic feet of gas per day, nearly half of all the gas produced in Canada when it was completed in 1964. Up to 20,000 barrels a day of propane and other gas liquids could be extracted from it. The plant and pipeline cost $27 million, while a later $8 million expansion increased the processing capacity by 50 per cent to 1.5 billion cubic feet per day.

When the pipeline was put into operation, it was found that it contained a large number of sections of defective pipe. Propane escaped from the pipe through scores of tiny, pin-hole leaks, and migrated to the surface, where it killed the overlying vegetation. The leaky sections of pipe had to be dug up and repaired.

John Anderson recalls visiting one of the sites where the pipe was being repaired. The ditch had been excavated, exposing the pipe wrapped in its coating of yellow plastic in the general vicinity of the leak. One of the repair crew was in the ditch to locate the exact source of the leak. The method of detection consisted of playing a blow-torch across the top of the pipe, which would ignite a small flame of burning propane at the point of the leak. Horrified, Anderson envisioned an explosion about to happen, and his first thought was to turn and run like hell. The pipe, however, was eventually repaired without being blown up, and the Empress project was one of Pacific's most successful ventures. Launched at a time when there was little demand for propane and prices were depressed, it became a big money-maker as the market developed and prices increased.

In early 1964, John Getgood returned to Phillips as vice-president in charge of the company's sales department. To head Pacific for the next decade, Phillips Petroleum chose Kelly Gibson as company president, Pacific's fourth chief executive officer. Six years later, Gibson was the chief executive officer of both Pacific and Westcoast.

Pacific Petroleums had crossed a watershed. Following the acquisition of the Canadian properties of Phillips and Sunray it at last started earning profits. And during the next eighteen years it would be one of the fastest growing oil companies in Canada.

CHAPTER FIFTEEN

Westcoast Struggles

While Pacific prospered, Westcoast struggled.

The confident expectation before the pipeline was completed that booming sales and unlimited expansion would cure any difficulties created by the low sales price in the El Paso contract vanished after the gas started to flow. Westcoast found itself without enough revenues to meet the payments on its debts.

During the first three years the pipeline was in operation, Westcoast's losses amounted to $2.5 million. During the first twelve years, the profit on the investment of the shareholders averaged less than 5 per cent a year. The investment would have earned more money in a bank account or in government bonds. The earnings were not enough to pay for urgently needed new pipeline facilities, nor enough to allow Westcoast to borrow the required funds. Westcoast seemed to stagger from crisis to crisis, suffering from inadequate sales, inadequate gas supplies, and inadequate prices. It was kept alive by the faith of its principal shareholders – Pacific, Phillips, and El Paso – who helped provide the money Westcoast needed. They also spent enormous sums to find the necessary gas when few others were interested in developing BC reserves to sell at prices 25 to 50 per cent lower than the prices paid for Alberta gas.

The future had seemed bright when the pipeline was being built. In January, 1957, eight months before it was completed, a Westcoast memo outlined plans to nearly double the installed capacity, from 400 million to 750 million cubic feet per day, at an estimated cost of $100 million. This included additional compressor stations on the Peace River pipeline to push the gas through faster and a proposed pipeline from Savanna Creek in southwestern Alberta. The planned expansion would allow the pipeline to supply only a one-year increase in anticipated demand in California, Oregon, and Washington, and the memo suggested that, "United States sources can provide only a small portion of the required volume." There seemed to be every reason for optimism.

But Westcoast did not have enough revenues, and it did not have enough gas to fill its pipeline, and it did not have enough gas because it did not have enough revenue. It was a vicious circle.

A source of additional gas lay in the Nig Creek field, discovered in 1957 during a joint exploration program by Imperial, Gulf, Shell, and Texaco, referred to as the Northern Foothills Agreement (NFA) group. The Nig Creek discovery lay near the Alaska Highway, a short distance north of the Fort St John field, and could easily have been hooked into the Westcoast line. Westcoast could offer no more than six and a quarter cents per thousand cubic feet for Peace River gas, and the NFA group decided it would not be profitable to drill and produce the necessary wells at Nig Creek for a price of less than ten cents. It was not until the fall of 1960, three years after the line went on stream, that Westcoast was able to raise its price enough to sign up the NFA group for the purchase of this gas.

Had Nig Creek gas been available at the start, Westcoast's supply problems would have been much less difficult. Because it was not, and because there was less gas than anticipated at Fort St John, the supplies available from other wells were drawn down too hard. Before the Nig Creek gas was signed up, the South Pouce field in Alberta had been depleted, and the short length of pipeline to connect it was already abandoned.

In 1958 and 1959 Westcoast had been able to extend its gas gathering network to hook up some new, small pools northwest of Fort St John, but by 1960 it was strapped by lack of money. To meet Westcoast's debt payments, $2 million was provided by Pacific (50 per cent), El Paso, and Sunray (each 25 per cent) through the purchase of 117,500 Westcoast shares. To supply additional gas, Pacific also paid $1.4 million to build 25 miles of feeder pipelines which were leased to Westcoast. As more fields were found, more supply lines would be needed, and to finance them a new company was formed, Gas Trunk Line of British Columbia. It was hoped that most of the shares in Gas Trunk could be sold to the gas producing companies, with additional shares offered for public sale. There were plans that Gas Trunk would build not only the small pipelines to connect new fields in the Fort St John region, but also a major pipeline to what looked like a very promising new gas supply region centred on Fort Nelson, where the first gas had been found by Pacific in a Devonian reef.

With 1960 came further belt-tightening for Westcoast and grand, expansive plans for Gas Trunk. Ted Megas resigned at the beginning of the year, and McMahon's executive assistant, Doug Owen, moved from Calgary to Vancouver to succeed him as vice-president and treasurer. Before long, Owen was able to report that Westcoast's staff had been reduced by 42, or nearly 20 per cent, mostly at the head office. D.P. McDonald, managing director as well as general counsel, advised McMahon in April that Westcoast still faced "a very tight squeeze" to find enough gas to sell during the next two years, so that it could pay its debt charges without having to call on more funds from Pacific, El Paso, and Sunray.

Gas Trunk was intended to solve that problem by connecting the big reserves being developed at Fort Nelson. If a number of oil companies with gas reserves could be induced to participate, they could help guarantee the debt and make financing a snap. Gas Trunk "could be controlled and in a large measure owned by the producers in the field, thereby giving them an additional revenue from gas development," Westcoast claimed in a memo sent to the producing companies. One advantage pointed out was that because all its facilities would be in British Columbia, Gas Trunk would be regulated only by the BC government, "and could more readily meet the requirements of producers without the intervention of federal authorities represented by the National Energy Board." Obtaining BC permits for pipeline construction did not involve the long and expensive public hearings that the National Energy Board required.

But the only producers induced to join in Gas Trunk were Westcoast shareholders Pacific and El Paso, as well as El Paso's affiliate, Western Natural Gas. By mid-September, Gas Trunk had its permit, and McMahon announced that work would start right away on a big pipe-laying program: a 245-mile, 30-inch line from Fort Nelson to Westcoast's main line, costing $52 million; a $19 million processing plant at Fort Nelson to remove carbon dioxide contained in the gas from this region; and an $11 million program of additional gas-gathering lines in the Fort St John area. The gathering lines to connect new fields around Fort St John were built that year, but the line to Fort Nelson that McMahon had said would be on stream by the end of 1961 took a little longer.

Gas Trunk kicked off the interim financing in the form of a $6 million loan from the ever helpful Royal Bank. By late 1961, it had completed its first permanent financing of $15 million, of which $12 million represented various forms of debt with the remaining $3 million put up by the shareholders. Gas Trunk then became 70 per cent owned by Westcoast, Pacific, El Paso, and Western Natural, with 30 per cent of the shares sold publicly. It was a modest start, and Gas Trunk soon faced some challenges. For one thing, the National Energy Board was not that easily left out of the picture. Gas Trunk's system might be entirely within British Columbia, but for all practical purposes it was part and parcel of the Westcoast system, an interprovincial and international pipeline, subject to the regulation of the federal government.

The fact that Westcoast was in "a very tight squeeze" did nothing to slow down the rate at which deals were being put together: the Gas Trunk project, the Savanna Creek project, Pacific's string of acquisitions (culminating in the reverse takeover of Phillips and Sunray), and soon an oil pipeline project. McMahon, looking at the big picture, assembled the deals, and the staff ran after him to clean up the details. The projects did not always develop quite the way they were first planned.

The project to ship southern Alberta gas from Savanna Creek to El Paso for sale in California was one that came out differently. After it was found that the Savanna Creek field would not provide the required initial volumes of some 200 million feet per day, additional supply was found in a large field on the outskirts of Calgary. Saratoga Processing Company was organized to build field gathering facilities at Savanna Creek and a forty-three-mile pipeline along the high foothill-ridges to ship the sour gas, containing hydrogen sulphide, to a plant that Jefferson Lake would build in the Crowsnest Pass to remove the sulphur.

It was billed as another of those battles between pipeline titans: El Paso seeking Alberta gas in order to maintain its control

250

over the California market, and Pacific Gas and Electric seeking Alberta gas to escape its dependency on El Paso. Following public hearings, the Alberta Conservation Board ruled in 1958 that there was not enough surplus export gas available for both applicants and suggested that they get together on a single project. The result was that PG&E's big thirty-six-inch pipeline from Alberta to San Francisco was approved in 1960; El Paso's control of the California market was breached; Westcoast bought southern Alberta gas for sale to California, but wound up with little interest in the pipeline facilities that carried the gas. Westcoast had the major interest in the $10 million Saratoga undertaking and a one-third interest in 107 miles of the line to California, the section across the southeast corner of British Columbia. This portion of the system was built by Alberta Natural Gas Company, the firm originally chartered by a special act of Parliament for Faison Dixon's unsuccessful project, and in 1960 it was owned one-third each by Westcoast, a PG&E subsidiary, and the Canadian public. Westcoast's share cost it $2.84 million (again financed by a Royal Bank loan), but in 1965, still strapped for funds, Westcoast sold its interest in Alberta Natural Gas for $5.68 million. It was not a big deal, but Westcoast had at least doubled its investment in five years, as well as earning some dividends.

A PIPELINE FOR BENNETT

An even more profitable venture resulted from the permit that Westcoast won early in 1961 from W.A.C. Bennett's Social Credit government to build a pipeline to move crude oil from Fort St John to the refineries in Vancouver. But it brought down on the heads of McMahon and Bennett charges of a political pay-off.

From the time that he led his Social Credit band of political amateurs to power in 1952 as British Columbia's bulwark of free enterprise, William Andrew Cecil "Wacky" Bennett had strongly supported McMahon's endeavours to build the Westcoast line and develop the province's petroleum resources. He saw this development as essential to the prosperity of British Columbians. McMahon and Bennett came to be portrayed as "old buddies," and there were those who hinted that Bennett was McMahon's political puppet, flown around whenever he wished in West-coast's executive jet. In fact, Bennett flew aboard the Westcoast jet on only two occasions and was far from the puppet of any businessman.

But McMahon did little to dispel this image in a political statement published by the *Vancouver Province* in September, 1960, three days before a provincial election in which the socialist CCF party was the only alternative to Bennett. "A $450 million natural gas and oil development program, involving at least 10,000 permanent jobs for British Columbians and many hundreds more on immediate construction projects, could be wrecked by Monday's provincial election," McMahon declared. His statement continued:

I do not believe that the money for the natural gas and oil development program that is underway could be raised if the present stable government of British Columbia is displaced by a socialistic one. . . . I realize that the socialists and communists will no doubt say that I am attempting to intimidate the voters on the eve of an election, that I am involved in some sort of political conspiracy with the present government. Well, there has been so much wild talk from them already that I am ready to risk more of it if by doing so I am able to bring the facts into the open. . . . I know that it is unwise for a businessman to involve himself in politics. Probably I should not be doing it. But I consider the present political situation so potentially explosive for British Columbia and so dangerous for all of us that I feel I must speak now, not after the election.

There were, as McMahon had predicted, howls of protest over this alleged threat to the electorate, but in spite of McMahon's help Bennett still won the election. A later news item reported that fifty jobless people had picketed Westcoast's head office, carrying "placards demanding 10,000 jobs, which they said Westcoast president Frank McMahon said would be lost if the Social Credit government was not returned to power in the last provincial election. Mr McMahon was out to lunch."

Less than five months after the election, Bennett's government issued Westcoast Transmission a permit to lay an oil line beside the gas line, and Westcoast got nearly half the shares of a subsidiary set up to build the oil line in return for the use of the gas pipeline right-of-way. In the legislature in Victoria, the opposition parties were almost apoplectic in their attacks on the oil pipeline deal.

"We do not think this should have been handed over to Westcoast as just another profit-making venture," CCF member Alex MacDonald stated. Resuscitating the old issue of McMahon's five-cent shares of Westcoast, MacDonald charged that, "These stock options are risk-free, sure-fire, and largely tax-free capital gains. He's already too rich and has taken far too much wealth out of the province of BC." Randolph Harding, another CCF member, protested that, "This man threatened the voters. . . . This is a dangerous trend in a free society when tycoons with an almost monopolistic grip on the province come out with something like that." "How much did Frank McMahon and Westcoast Transmission pay to Social Credit campaign funds?" demanded Liberal leader Gordon Gibson. "How many millions will be made by McMahon and his friends this round out of the public business of the people of BC?"

But this time there were no options or five-cent shares. McMahon and his friends did make good profits on the shares that they bought in the oil pipeline company, but they paid $5 a share, exactly the same price as those sold publicly.

Nor did the image of a political payoff by Bennett to his old buddy Frank McMahon hold true. In any event, although they each admired the free enterprise spirit of the other, the hard-drinking Frank McMahon and teetotaller Bennett were not close social friends. Always deferential to those in authority in government, in correspondence and in person McMahon always very formally addressed Bennett as "Mr Premier" or "Mr Bennett." If anything, it was McMahon who was at the beck-and-call of Bennett, rather than the other way around.

Bennett was not the tool of any businessman. In *Bennett*, biographer Paddy Sherman reports that, "He thought nothing of dressing down business leaders who did not conform; of threatening an industry to get it to see things his way. . . . When businessmen came to protest one of his moves, he told them grimly he would save the province for free enterprise despite the free enterprisers. Then he lectured them that free enterprise would work only when they thought in terms of free enterprise for the working man." Frank McMahon was no exception.

McMahon got the permit to build the oil pipeline for only one reason: no one else was willing to undertake the job in the way that Bennett insisted it had to be done. And it took Bennett six years of badgering before McMahon, his hands full with other problems, agreed to undertake this "hardly-able deal."

It was not that McMahon was uninterested in building an oil pipeline, usually a far more profitable investment than a gas pipeline. McMahon had already expressed an interest in building an oil line from Alberta to Vancouver as early as 1949, and Westcoast had prepared an application to the Board of Transport Commissioners, but it was dropped when Pacific participated with a small interest in the construction of the Trans-Mountain line in 1951.

As soon as Pacific got a whiff of oil at Fort St John in late 1951, the idea of an oil line was revived. In July, 1952, McMahon had written to Sid Bechtel in San Francisco that, "We are going to have to think about putting in" a gas processing plant, a refinery, and an oil line "to hook into the Trans-Mountain system some two to three hundred miles south of where this development is taking place."

Bennett was just as eager to see construction of a line to take oil from the Peace River area of BC, but a hook-up with the Trans-Mountain line was not what he had in mind. An interprovincial carrier, Trans-Mountain was subject to regulation by the federal government. Bennett wanted an all-BC oil line to move BC oil, subject only to BC jurisdiction. A hook-up with Trans-Mountain would also involve building the connecting link from the Peace River area through Alberta to a point near Edson. Alberta's oil wells were producing at only half their capacity, and Bennett was concerned that this could lead to prorating any oil from the Peace River. He felt that Vancouver refineries should use BC oil to the full extent of its availability or their refinery capacity.

In December, 1954, Bennett first asked McMahon about the possibility of building an oil line alongside Westcoast's gas line, once the gas line was built. Bennett said he was sure that the search for gas in northeastern BC would also turn up large volumes of oil. McMahon promised to examine the possibilities and ordered a feasibility study by Ford, Bacon & Davis, completed the following March. The report concluded that an oil line along the gas route from Peace River to Vancouver would be feasible when enough oil had been found.

British Columbia's first significant oil find, in 1957, was the Boundary Lake field that straddled the Alberta-BC border east of Fort St John. But it was not exactly a giant. Asked by Bennett if Boundary Lake meant that there was enough oil for an all-BC line, McMahon replied that it was getting closer all the time and that studies were continuing. The following month, November, 1957, Bennett announced in a speech in Ottawa that the northern oil prospects looked so good that Westcoast "is now working on plans to build a parallel oil pipeline to the coast."

Nothing much seemed to happen to these plans during the next year and a half, and Bennett summoned McMahon from New York for a meeting in Victoria in May, 1959. A small amount of oil from some of the BC wells was being shipped by truck to the small refineries of Pacific and Phillips at Taylor and Dawson Creek. Hearings were expected to be held soon on applications for a local pipeline grid to replace these truck shipments. In addition, Peace River Oil Pipe Line Limited, owned by a group of major oil companies, was interested in moving the BC oil by pipeline some 250 miles southeast to join the Trans-Mountain line at Edson. Peace River would have to build a new pipeline only about half this distance, because it already had a line shipping oil from the Sturgeon Lake field in Alberta to the same destination. But Bennett was not happy with these ideas. He wanted to know how McMahon's plans for the oil line to Vancouver were coming along. McMahon said that it was still being studied; the discovered oil reserves were still not large enough. He further stated that his companies would not apply for the local oil grid, unless the other applicants failed to service the Dawson Creek and Taylor refineries. McMahon's group already had its hands full.

As it turned out, at least initially, Peace River Oil Pipe Line did propose to by-pass the Taylor and Dawson Creek refineries, so Pacific Petroleums joined the field as a last minute entry. Hearings were held in Victoria in June and July. There were four applicants: Pacific, Gibson Associated Oils, Trans-Prairie Pipelines, and Peace River. The first three proposed to connect the slowly growing number of small BC oil fields with the Taylor and Dawson Creek refineries and later, if enough oil were found, with the larger market in Vancouver. Only Peace River, with its proposed $10 million, eight-inch oil line, offered an immediate plan to ship the oil to the four Vancouver refineries.

Kelly Gibson, testifying for Pacific, said the logical route as soon as enough oil was found was an all-BC pipeline to Vancouver and the US Puget Sound. He said it would be "dangerous" to allow BC oil to be shipped on the round-about route through Alberta proposed by Peace River. It would subject BC oil to the control of both Alberta and the federal government and reduce the amount of production that would be available for a later all-BC pipeline.

But there was no other way to get BC oil to Vancouver, and so the Peace River company got the permit. Only there was a catch. A condition in the permit stipulated that the BC government could later order the flow of oil diverted from the Peace River pipeline to an all-BC pipeline. After mulling this over for more than half a year, the Peace River company decided that it could not finance the line under this condition, and in July, 1960, it gave the permit back to the government. Bennett was still no closer to getting the line that he envisioned would open the vast oil wealth of northern British Columbia.

A new permit was issued in August to Trans-Prairie Pipelines to construct 130 miles of small-diameter pipelines to connect the Beatton River, Milligan Creek, Doig River, and Boundary fields with the small refineries at Taylor and Dawson Creek. That would provide an outlet for less than a third of the oil that the BC wells were capable of producing. And it still left the problem of how to get the oil to Vancouver. Bennett proposed to haul it on the government-owned Pacific Great Eastern Railway that had been extended to Fort St John in order to move the sulphur recovered from the Westcoast gas.

If railways could move oil as cheaply as pipelines, there would be no pipelines. But by the time the gathering and railway charges were paid, BC producers would get at least $1 a barrel less than the price paid for Alberta oil. No one would rush to develop BC's oil supplies for $1.50 a barrel, and the railway idea was finally dropped as too costly.

Bennett was becoming increasingly frustrated. During the 1960 election campaign, he told an audience in Fort St John: "As soon as enough oil is developed here I give you my word that we will build or cause to be built an oil pipeline from the Peace River area to markets in Vancouver."

In the final six months of 1960, McMahon was beckoned four times to meet with the premier to talk about the oil line. He was still reluctant to build the all-BC line and suggested that Bennett take a second look at the Edson connection, an idea that was not well received. On December 13, Bennett summoned to Victoria the heads of the four oil companies with refineries at Vancouver: Bill Twaits of Imperial Oil, Ed Loughney of British American Oil, Ralph Baker of Standard Oil of BC, and W.M.V. Ash of Shell. Bennett accused the oil companies of holding back the development of BC oil in order to sell their Alberta oil. He said he suspected they were purposely drilling for gas and not for oil in British Columbia. "Mr Premier, you have a job waiting for you with Imperial whenever you retire from politics," Bill Twaits responded. "We need a man who can tell us whether we are going to find oil or gas. If you can do that, you can name your salary." The four companies still held out for the Edson connection. They agreed to meet again on January 5. Before then, on December 22, Bennett and McMahon again met at the Hotel Vancouver. Bennett said he did not like the offer by the oil companies and would ask all interested parties to once more submit plans for moving BC oil to Vancouver.

After the second meeting with the four major oil companies on January 5, Bennett announced that they had agreed to accept any BC oil delivered to their Vancouver refineries at competitive prices and that the government was inviting pipeline proposals. Proposals would have to be submitted by January 15, barely more than two weeks away.

Following his last meeting with Bennett on December 22, McMahon contacted Charles Hetherington, who was then operating a consulting business in Calgary, and asked him to check Westcoast's preliminary studies on the cost and feasibility of an oil line along the gas right-of-way. When Bennett announced that proposals were being invited, he was really looking at Westcoast. No one else had indicated any interest. With Hetherington's report in hand, McMahon phoned the premier to say that Westcoast was prepared to submit an application, but that it was a "hardly-able deal." Bennett replied that if Westcoast could not do it, the government would, and it would want to use Westcoast's right-of-way.

On Sunday, January 14, the day before the deadline, heavy rain driven by a southeast wind assaulted Vancouver from clouds so low that not even the seagulls were flying. Nothing was in the air, it seemed except Westcoast's Gulfstream jet on a flight to Victoria, where McMahon met once more with Bennett in the premier's office and submitted Westcoast's application for an oil line. Two weeks later, Mines and Petroleum Minister Ken Kiernan announced in the legislature that the government had approved construction of the Westcoast proposal.

It would be a 12-inch diameter pipeline following the Westcoast right-of-way 500 miles from Fort St John to Kamloops, where it would tie in with the Trans-Mountain line to move the oil the final 200 miles to Vancouver. The agreement with Westcoast provided that the government could later require the line to be extended directly to Vancouver; a lever that Bennett retained in the event that federal regulation of Trans-Mountain interfered with his control of BC oil. The pipeline would cost $35 million and was to be in operation that year. It would have an installed capacity to handle 27,000 barrels of oil per day, but pumping stations could boost this to the design capacity of 75,000 barrels per day, about the amount used by the four Vancouver refineries. There were then fewer than 100 oil wells in British Columbia, and they were capable of producing at a rate less than one-sixth the design capacity of the pipeline.

Success of the oil line would depend on whether or not increased drilling in northeastern BC resulted in the discovery and development of additional oil. E.C. Hurd, president of Trans-Mountain, was highly critical of the project, and at the company's annual meeting of shareholders he predicted that Peace River oil production would peak out within three to six years at a rate of 25,000 barrels per day – one-third of the proposed line's design capacity – and then start to decline. If Hurd was right, the pipeline would be a financial disaster.

Westcoast had an oil pipeline permit, but no money. A new company was formed to handle the project, Western Pacific Products & Crude Oil Pipelines Ltd, known more simply as Wespac. Pacific and El Paso covered the necessary debt. Forty-eight per cent of Wespac's issued shares were granted to Westcoast for use of the right-of-way and other facilities, with the balance sold for $4,625,000. Pacific and El Paso each purchased a 12 per cent interest, a public issue offered 10 per cent, and McMahon and his associates, including senior employees, purchased the remaining 18 per cent.

More oil was found in the Peace River, and Wespac was a smashing success. Within two years it started paying dividends of $1 per year on each share that had cost $5. By 1969, Wespac was

258

moving Peace River oil and gas liquids from the Taylor plant at a rate of 63,000 barrels per day, supplying more than two-thirds of the oil used by the four Vancouver refineries. In 1971, Westcoast Transmission merged its interests in Wespac and its producing subsidiary, originally the Peace River Natural Gas Company that had been formed in 1947 to develop gas supplies for Vancouver. The company formed by the merger of these two partially owned subsidiaries was Westcoast Petroleum Ltd.

THE SHORT HISTORY OF GAS TRUNK

Gas Trunk had a rougher time with its planned pipeline to the large Fort Nelson gas fields. Originally announced for completion before the end of 1961, the line was not completed until early 1965, and in the end it was built not by Gas Trunk, but by Westcoast itself.

One of the problems facing Gas Trunk lay in what some investors regarded as an act of outright socialism by the free enterprise government of W.A.C. Bennett that Frank McMahon had so ardently championed in the 1960 election. Less than a year later, two young legislative members of the New Democratic Party (by then successor to the CCF), Dave Barrett and Jim Rhodes, smuggled a caged crow into the legislature to send across the aisle to the premier. They were rubbing in the fact that by calling a special session of the legislature to expropriate BC Electric, Bennett, the free enterprise champion, was about to do what the NDP and CCF had long advocated.

BC Electric became the government-owned BC Hydro and Power Authority. One of the effects of the take-over was to make investors nervous about putting money into other BC utilities, like Gas Trunk Line of British Columbia. Westcoast, federally incorporated and regulated, was considered a safer refuge from such excursions into the realms of socialism.

But there were more difficult problems facing construction of the Fort Nelson line: inadequate reserves and inadequate markets. El Paso, Westcoast's principal customer, had envisioned the promising gas reserves of Fort Nelson as a perfect supply to help meet the growing requirements of California. But El Paso's monopoly as California's only gas supplier was crumbling, partly as a result of the large PG&E line from Alberta to San Francisco,

259

and also as a result of another competing line from Texas to southern California. Therefore, it would be a few years before El Paso had any need of Fort Nelson gas.

The supply aspect was mostly a matter of time. Half a dozen gas fields found in Devonian reefs in the Fort Nelson region were undeniably large discoveries, but even so it would still require a few years of further drilling to prove up enough reserves to support the pipeline. In early 1961, the year the line was to have been built, my article in *Oilweek* quoted an admission by Westcoast's gas supply manager, Peter Kutney, that the line might have to be delayed a couple of years pending the development of more reserves. That was not exactly the type of optimistic assessment that McMahon had issued a few months before. "You better not let Frank see that *Oilweek* article," Doug Owen warned Kutney. "You might get fired." That particular issue did not pass across McMahon's desk.

Westcoast was in a peculiar bind. It needed additional gas just to meet its existing sales contracts. But a line from Fort Nelson would not pay unless it moved a lot of gas. Thus, even though it could not meet its existing sales commitments, Westcoast had to find still more sales in order to get the Fort Nelson gas. By mid-1963, the anticipated Fort Nelson reserves had been proven up, and more sales had been found through a short-term arrangement to provide gas for BC Hydro's thermal-electric power plant near Vancouver and a small increase in sales to El Paso. It looked as though it might be just barely feasible to go ahead with the Fort Nelson project.

For a variety of reasons, it was decided that this should not, after all, be an undertaking by Gas Trunk: the economics looked thin, investors were wary because of the provincial take-over of BC Electric, and the National Energy Board had started to grumble that the extension to Fort Nelson should be part of the Westcoast system and thus subject to federal regulation. It was agreed that Westcoast would offer 40,000 of its shares in exchange for the same number of outstanding shares of Gas Trunk, an offer which eventually saw Gas Trunk absorbed by Westcoast.

This meant that Westcoast would clearly have to get approval for the Fort Nelson extension from the National Energy Board. Meanwhile, why not at least get a start on construction under the permit that the BC government had issued to Gas Trunk? Acting as an "agent" for Gas Trunk, Westcoast began preliminary construction of the line in the winter of 1963-64. Then it applied to the National Energy Board for its permission. The federal agency held three days of public hearing in Vancouver during May, 1964, by which time $10 million had already been spent on the line.

Two months later, the board issued its decision. Once again, Westcoast had started construction before it had full authorization, and the board was not pleased. "The board cannot escape the impression that the applicant, in setting its course of action, was consciously circumventing the intent if not the letter of the National Energy Board Act," the report stated. The board said it would have preferred only a twenty-six-inch line, which in its view was large enough to handle the anticipated gas volumes from Fort Nelson, but it was stuck with the fact that Westcoast had already started building a thirty-inch line. "After weighing all considerations, the board concludes that it is in the public interest, in order to provide the additional gas necessary to supply the future needs of BC consumers and authorized exports that the thirty-inch line be completed," the decision stated.

The next problem was how to raise the money to complete the $57 million pipeline, as well as the gas processing plant at Fort Nelson. McMahon and Doug Owen met to discuss the matter with Art Mayne, executive vice-president of the Royal Bank and a director of Westcoast. They were in Mayne's office at the Royal Bank's headquarters in Montreal, Mayne with his feet propped up on his desk, and they were debating whether it would be best to try and borrow the money in the form of first mortgage bonds, or whether they should try to raise some equity capital by selling more Westcoast shares. "Why can't we have both?" McMahon asked. "Is there any reason we can't have convertible first mortgage bonds?"

No one had ever heard of a mortgage on a pipeline that was convertible into common shares. It would be something like a mortgage on a house that could, at the lender's discretion, be converted into part ownership of the house. No one had ever thought of doing anything quite like that. But it worked. More than $17 million in convertible first mortgage bonds were successfully offered for public sale in Canada by a group of underwriters headed by Wood Gundy, while an additional $40 million was sold to a group of large Canadian institutional investors.

Until the sale of these bonds could be completed, the Royal Bank stepped in with another short-term loan amounting to $35 million.

The line from Fort Nelson was on stream by February, 1965, flowing gas from the nearby Clarke Lake field. It would require several years and several hundred miles of additional lateral lines to connect the other gas fields that lay in a fan-shaped area stretching 100 miles across the stunted forest and muskeg from Fort Nelson into the Yukon and Northwest Territories, fields with fascinating names like Kotcho Lake, Petitot River, Klua, Beaver River, Celibeta Lake, and Yoyo. And some devastating surprises lay in store by the time they were all connected to the grid.

SOME CHANGES AT THE HELM

Surely, the worst of Westcoast's problems were now over. For the first time, it had a seemingly abundant supply of gas at one end of its pipeline, and who could doubt that in the long-run the market at the other end was insatiable.

There were a series of management changes at Westcoast. In 1956, George Hume, McMahon's civil-servant ally from the time of the Flathead venture in 1932, had retired as Federal Director General of Scientific Surveys. Hume stepped down with full honours that included an Order of the British Empire after thirty-five years of government service, and he joined Westcoast as chief geologist. Westcoast was not an active operator in the search for oil and gas, and it was not a demanding post. Hume retired from the company in 1964.

As had been the case with Pacific, the time was coming – possibly even overdue – to acknowledge that it was not the builders but administrators who were required to help run Westcoast effectively. Boots Adams agreed. Phillips Petroleum, through Pacific and through its own holdings, had the biggest stake in Westcoast. Adams had just the man to help his friend McMahon. He was Bob Stewart, a methodical engineer and a twenty-six year veteran of Phillips who had risen to become vice-president in charge of the gas department.

Stewart joined Westcoast in 1963 as president and chief executive. McMahon became chairman of the board. Doug Owen moved from vice-president to executive vice-president, and D.P.

McDonald was appointed senior vice-president, as well as general manager.

Stewart brought with him from Phillips the organizational charts and procedures to run a tight ship. Westcoast sprouted new committees and a "Policy and Procedures Manual" that covered everything from how to release information to the press to the use of company vehicles. A new operating committee examined every budget item in detail, and nothing was too small to escape its attention. While McMahon and Owen wrestled with how to raise $55 million in convertible bonds, an item in the minutes of the operating committee noted that Peter Kutney needed a metal bookcase to store "valuable documents" transferred from his former office in Calgary: "This item was not included in his 1965 capital budget, and the committee approved an expenditure request for a steel bookcase costing $75.00."

Stewart's idea of running a tight ship did not include the corporate jet aircraft that McMahon used as Westcoast's chief deal maker. Stewart insisted that the aircraft had to go. McMahon suggested that Stewart might have to go. Two years after he had joined Westcoast, Stewart stepped down as chief executive, and McMahon once more assumed the title (he had never considered that he had relinquished the role) of head man.

Seven months after Stewart stepped down, Westcoast did sell the Gulfstream aircraft, only to replace it with a $1.35 million Falcon jet. For his part, Stewart later became vice-president of Westcoast, president of its oil subsidiary, Wespac, and president of another subsidiary, Pacific Northern Gas.

Doug Owen became the new Westcoast president. D.P. McDonald was still general manager. Charles Hetherington left his consulting business in Calgary to re-join Westcoast as vice-president and McMahon's executive assistant after Art Allyne died of a sudden heart attack in December, 1966. Allyne, who had been chief engineer in charge of construction of El Paso's Pacific Northwest pipeline from New Mexico, had joined Westcoast in 1960 and was vice-president in charge of engineering at the time of his death. The builders were back in charge at Westcoast.

It was probably just as well. There was still one more pipeline to build. It was a branch line from Westcoast's main system, from Prince George west to the port city of Prince Rupert. Crossing 430 miles of rugged mountains and heavy forest at a cost of

$30 million to serve an area with a population of only 50,000, it was a typical McMahon pipeline, financially precarious and funded on faith in BC growth and development. The first report that Westcoast was considering a branch line to Prince Rupert was revealed by Art Allyne during testimony before a National Energy Board hearing in March, 1965. He intimated that it would not be an easy venture and that Westcoast would require a partner before proceeding. Shortly after, Great Northern Gas Utilities Limited joined Westcoast as the co-sponsor of a new firm that would build the line, Pacific Northern Gas Ltd. Great Northern, in turn backed by the Tulsa-based pipeline engineers and builders Williams Brothers, operated propane and natural gas distribution systems in a number of small communities in Alberta and British Columbia.

There was much delay in getting the project underway. A permit was not obtained from the BC Public Utilities Commission until December, 1966, when it was announced that the mainline would be completed by the fall of 1967. In fact, it was not completed until more than a year after that, in late 1968. By that time, Great Northern had taken a second look at the economics and decided it wanted out. Westcoast agreed to take over its interest and reimburse Great Northern for its expenditures. Most of the equity capital was raised by a public sale of shares, and the money was borrowed from the Equitable Life Insurance Company of New York. Equitable Life agreed to lend the money only on the condition that the pipeline was operated in the fashion of a wholly-owned subsidiary. Thus, even though Westcoast owned only a minority of the Pacific Northern shares, it owned all the voting shares. Pacific Northern operated at a loss for several years before it finally achieved a modest profit position.

It was the last McMahon pipeline. Like all the others – the gas pipeline from the Peace River, the extension to Fort Nelson, the oil pipeline, the Inland system built by John McMahon and Norman Whittall to distribute gas throughout the interior of British Columbia – it would not have been built, at least not for many years, if it had been left to the more cautious businessmen. And British Columbia would have been the poorer for the lack of it.

Construction also started in 1968 on Westcoast's new head office building on Georgia Street, the unique twelve-storey structure whose cantilevered floors hang suspended by a dozen steel cables from the central support-core of reinforced concrete.

264

Westcoast had started life in cramped quarters in Calgary's Toronto General Trust Building, later moving to the Petroleum and Pacific Buildings on Ninth Avenue. A temporary office had been opened on Burrard Street in 1956, and the following year operating offices were established on the top three-and-a-half floors of an eight-storey building on Georgia Street. The head office, as well as the operating offices, were transferred from Calgary to Vancouver in 1960, and the move to Westcoast's first permanent home was completed in 1970.

From his office on the top floor of the new building, McMahon commanded a magnificent view of Vancouver harbour, the water alive with the traffic of big ships and small pleasure craft and framed by the forest of Stanley Park and the background of mountains. On the North Shore he could see, too, the bright yellow mound of a stockpile of sulphur, some of it stripped from the Peace River gas and hauled here by rail for shipment to the markets of the world. Before the Westcoast line was built, all the sulphur used by BC pulp mills and other industries was imported, but now sulphur was a substantial source of BC export revenues.

The prospects for Westcoast had never looked better than in early 1968 as construction got underway on the new head office building. Inadequate supplies seemed only a horror of the past, as new discoveries in the Fort Nelson area made it one of the hottest gas-hunting regions on the continent. The two most recent finds had been made by Amoco Canada Limited, a subsidiary of Standard Oil Company of Indiana, at Beaver River, just south of the Yukon border, and at Pointed Mountain, some thirty miles northeast in the Northwest Territories. The reserves at these two fields were estimated at 2.5 trillion to 3.5 trillion cubic feet. Westcoast had contracted to buy this gas from Amoco and planned a 110-mile line from Fort Nelson to tie in these fields. Meanwhile, some seventy miles of lines had already been laid out of Fort Nelson to connect the Yoyo, Kotcho Lake, and Sierra fields. The capacity of Westcoast's mainline south of Fort St John had been increased by nearly 50 per cent by the installation of additional compressor horsepower and the first looping with 36-inch diameter pipe. It was planned that this would lead in stages, as supply and demand grew, to two parallel lines from Fort St John to the US border: the original thirty-inch line and a parallel thirty-six-inch line. Westcoast's expenditures to extend and expand its system in 1966 and 1967 had totalled some $90 million.

All this had been made possible by the continued growth of gas sales in British Columbia and, more importantly, by the breakthrough in export sales to El Paso. For nearly a decade after the Westcoast line had been completed, the anticipated growth in export sales had not materialized. El Paso faced increased competition from Alberta and southwest US gas, and Westcoast had been stuck with the original sales of 300 million feet per day at the price of 22 cents set in 1954. In early 1968, Westcoast won approval to double its export sales at an appreciably higher price.

THE WASHINGTON-OTTAWA SQUEEZE

It took a two-year battle that sandwiched Westcoast between the conflicting regulatory demands of the US Federal Power Commission in Washington and the National Energy Board in Ottawa to win the approval of larger export sales at higher prices. The approval promised at last to put the pipeline on a solid financial footing.

On February 28, 1966, McMahon had signed a contract with El Paso to double Westcoast's export sales, with the daily volume increasing by 100 million feet each year for three years starting in late 1966. The contract increased the 1954 price from twenty-two to twenty-seven cents for the total volume of export sales. But it was subject to the approval of both the Federal Power Commission and the National Energy Board, and that is where the battle was fought.

Following hearings before the NEB, Prime Minister Lester Pearson announced in April, 1967, that the federal cabinet had approved the additional exports, more than a year after the contract had been signed. Four months later, the FPC turned down the deal. In a four-to-one decision, the US commissioners ruled that El Paso could import additional gas from Westcoast at a price of twenty-nine and a half cents, but the old twenty-two-cent contract, that still had ten years to run, could not be disturbed, and no escalation provision would be permitted. "It is only fair to alert both the United States and Canadian interests at an early time that gas imports into the United States will not be approved at unjustifiably high prices," the FPC report declared.

266

The lone dissenting commissioner, John Carver, warned that his colleagues were provoking a "high noon" confrontation with Canada.

Back to the Energy Board went Westcoast to seek Canadian approval to sell on the terms laid down by the US authorities. No way, said the National Energy Board. The FPC's insistence that Westcoast could not charge its export customer more than it charged its BC customers would mean selling Canadian gas in the US for less than it is worth, the Energy Board ruled. "In the case of a company whose Canadian customers have for a decade been subziding the existing export, this is not an attractive prospect," it added.

While the two governments waged their war of words, there was some relief for Westcoast. It was allowed to export an additional 100 million cubic feet per day under a temporary month-to-month license, but it was clear that this was no effective solution to the impasse.

After an eyeball-to-eyeball confrontation, it was the FPC that blinked first. In February, 1968 – two years after the contract had been signed – it ruled that El Paso could step up its purchases from Westcoast from 300 million to 500 million cubic feet per day. The 22 cents for the original 300 million was left unchanged, but the price for the additional 200 million was set at 32 cents, bringing the average to about 26 cents. This the NEB and the federal cabinet accepted, and the impasse was finally resolved.

Two years had been spent in haggling over pennies. Within a few more years the prices were to soar, not by cents per thousand cubic feet, but by dollars. But that was down the road.

Edwin C. Phillips had a hankering in 1968 to return west. Born in Saskatoon, he had been raised and educated in Alberta before moving to Toronto to start his business career, first with Loblaw Groceteria Company, then Dominion Sugar Company. In 1947, he joined The Consumers' Gas Company as assistant to general manager Ed Tucker. Phillips was involved in studying the feasibility of bringing in natural gas from Lousiana to replace the high-cost manufactured gas, with which Consumers' was losing both money and customers. Phillips left Consumers' in 1952, and by the time he decided to move west he was president of Trane Company of Canada, a manufacturer of air conditioning equipment owned by a US parent. He and his wife had decided that Vancouver was where they wanted to live, and Westcoast looked like the company for him.

After several letters and telephone calls, Phillips finally obtained an appointment with McMahon, and they met for lunch at Trader Vic's in Vancouver's Bayshore Inn. McMahon talked about horse racing and about his plans for a gas pipeline that would be the grand-daddy of them all, the biggest ever. Oil had been found the year before at Prudhoe Bay on the Arctic coast of Alaska, the largest oil field in North America, as large as all the oil fields of Canada put together. And the reserves of natural gas were almost as great. What was needed to make use of this gas was a pipeline stretching across the length of North America, with Westcoast's line right in the middle of the route, at least the route that McMahon envisioned. "We're going to run that pipeline right through British Columbia," McMahon told Phillips. "We're on the flyway."

After lunch, they walked back to the Westcoast offices and into Doug Owen's office, where D.P. McDonald was visiting from Calgary. "This is Ed Phillips," McMahon said. "He comes from Toronto, he's moving out here, and I've told him we've some things to do and we'd put him to work." With that, McMahon left. "Do you know anything about cutting costs?" Owen asked. "I think so," said Phillips. "That's what manufacturing is really about." "Good," said Owen, "That's where we'll put you to work."

By the time Ed Phillips joined Westcoast in August as vice-president, cutting costs had become a matter of survival for the company. The prospects that had glowed so brightly at the start of the year had blown up with a ruptured pipeline at Fort Nelson. Blown up forty-six times, in fact. The fault lay with some forty-eight miles of twenty-four-inch-diameter pipe laid in late 1967 to connect the Kotcho Lake and Yoyo fields with the gas plant at Fort Nelson. The line had cost $6.5 million, and a year after it had gone into operation nearly another million dollars had been spent trying to patch forty-six separate breaks. The repair work had been a nightmare for Ray Mordan, manager of engineering and operations, and his field crews. In the quagmire of summer muskeg, tractors could sink out of sight; they had to be chained together like a string of elephants to pull one another out of trouble. When the ditch was opened to repair the pipe, it immediately filled with water. Helicopters were used to fly in large pumps. In the winter, the ground was firm, but temperatures dropped to −60 C, with strong winds. As soon as one section was fixed, another broke.

The repair costs, combined with the loss of gas supplies and revenues, slashed Westcoast's profits from nearly $9 million in 1976 to $2.4 million in 1968, and the return on the shareholders' investment was a scant 2.7 per cent. A corporation must grow or die; its thermometer of health is its profits, and earnings less than the rate of inflation are really a loss. Westcoast was still financially ill.

By the end of 1968, it was clear that the Yoyo lateral would have to be replaced entirely. Ironically, the faulty pipe had come from the Calgary mill of Canadian Phoenix Steel & Pipe, successor to Alberta Phoenix, the firm that McMahon had founded a decade earlier to build a small-diameter pipe mill at Edmonton. Westcoast sued Canadian Phoenix for more than $13 million, but the company eventually accepted an out-of-court settlement for $6.8 million.

McMahon was now sixty-seven. His friend and loyal ally, Boots Adams, the man who could control the largest block of Westcoast stock, had retired from Phillips Petroleum the year before. Frank, Betty, and their two daughters, Francine and Bettina, spent increasing time at their home in Palm Beach. He was absorbed in horse racing.

For a hard-working, two-fisted diamond driller it had been a long road from the roaring mining camps of the British Columbia frontier to the posh society of Palm Beach. But there were at least some similarities, according to former Bulgarian Olympic coach Dimiter Spassoff, who had worked in Palm Beach as a physical therapist since 1937. His clients had included Al Capone, Dwight Eisenhower, Carry Grant, Harry Truman, Richard Nixon, Barbara Hutton, Douglas Fairbanks, and Frank McMahon. "In Palm Beach, so the legend goes, they shoot off a cannon at 5 PM to signal the start of the martini waterfalls," Dimiter writes in his 1979 autobiography, *My Fabulous Life*. "Frank habitually beat the gun."

In 1969 McMahon, with his beautiful horse Majestic Prince, bid for the most coveted award in racing, the Triple Crown. No

269

longer in partnership with Max Bell, he had been racing under his own colours – black and gold – since 1966. His trainer was Johnny Longden.

In 1966, at Santa Anita, Longden had booted in his 6,032nd winner to end one of the all-time great jockey careers. He had ridden in 32,406 races during thirty-nine years, and the horses he rode had earned more than $24 million. But Longden had paid a price. He had broken both arms, both collarbones, both legs (one of them five times), both feet, his back, and most of his ribs. After one accident, he was paralyzed from the waist down and told he would never ride again. But he had recovered to ride in thousands more races.

With Longden as trainer, McMahon's horses were tearing up the tracks. In 1966, they won the Will Rogers Stakes at Hollywood Park with Aqua Vite, and again in 1967 with Jungle Road. In 1968, they took the Canadian Queen's Plate with Merger, while Baffle set a track record at Tanforan for the 1-1/16th mile. But the big challenge was the Triple Crown.

The Triple Crown events in 1969 were set in the following order: May 3, the Kentucky Derby at Churchill Downs; May 17, the Preakness at Pimlico; and June 7, the Belmont Stakes at New York. In nearly a century, only eight horses had won the Triple Crown. One of them was Count Fleet, ridden by Johnny Longden in 1943. Majestic Prince, ridden by Bill Hartack, was favoured to become the ninth Triple Crown winner. He had been purchased by McMahon as a yearling in 1967 from Leslie Coombs of Spendthrift Farms, Kentucky, at the annual Kentucky Keeneland sale for a record $250,000. As a two-year-old and a three-year-old, the Prince had won eight races in a row, including the $100,000 purse at the Santa Anita Derby that March.

It was a grand day at Churchill Downs. In the box behind the McMahon party sat a man whom Frank had known as a California Senator and a golfing partner, Richard Nixon, first US President to attend the Kentucky Derby, together with Pat and Ronald Reagan and a clutch of cabinet ministers. Majestic Prince beat Paul Mellon's Arts and Letters by a neck to win the Kentucky Derby. At Pimlico, Majestic Prince again beat Arts and Letters in another neck-and-neck thriller to win the Preakness. After the race, Longden announced that Majestic Prince would take a rest and miss the Belmont Stakes. Two-thirds of the way to a Triple Crown, and the trainer had dropped him from the big race. McMahon thought that over for forty-eight hours and then had the Prince shipped to New York. *Sports Illustrated* ran a four-page feature on McMahon's decision to overrule his trainer and take his horse to the 101st running of the Belmont Stakes. "If Majestic Prince is ready for the race, he will run," McMahon announced. "If he's not, he won't."

On the eve of the race, Longden announced that the Prince was fit. The atmosphere at the New York track, reported *Sports Illustrated*, was extraordinary. "Raquel Welch tripping lightly down the geranium-lined Victory Lane on her way to a skinny-dipping exercise in one of the infields would not have raised more eyebrows" than the presence of the Prince. "The moment he arrived from Pimlico he became the most famous and admired transient ever to park his feed tub at America's finest horse park." Fans waited as long as four hours to catch a fleeting glimpse of the Prince. More than 200 out-of-town reporters came to New York to cover the race. The paddock was jammed with McMahon's friends, including such celebrities as former movie stars Jane Russell and Joan Fontaine. "Hundreds of fans elbowed their way into the amphitheater paddock stands and burst into spontaneous applause when Majestic Prince appeared. When the small field paraded under the stands on its way to the track, hundreds more whooped and hollered and beat their fists on the windows."

Arts and Letters trounced Majestic Prince, winning by five-and-a-half lengths. Hartack "gave his horse an astonishingly bad ride," *Sports Illustrated* later commented. It was Hartack's last ride for McMahon.

After the Belmont Stakes, Majestic Prince was retired to stud and was syndicated by Leslie Coombs for $1,960,000, a record for that time.

On October 21, 1969, McMahon submitted to the Westcoast directors his letter of resignation as chairman of the board, chief executive officer, and chairman of the executive committee. It was accepted by the board the same day, and a resolution was passed declaring that the establishment of BC's oil and gas producing industry was "in large measure" due to "the pioneer spirit, enthusiasm, resourcefulness, and imagination displayed by Mr McMahon over several decades," while the success of Westcoast and its affiliates was a result of his "earnest efforts and untiring devotion."

Doug Owen was named chief operating officer as well as president. D.P. McDonald was appointed chairman of the board and chairman of the executive committee. Two new directors were appointed to the board, Pacific president Kelly Gibson and Ed Phillips, by then Westcoast vice-president, administration, with special responsibilities for operations, engineering, comptrolling, and industrial relations. Charles Hetherington was appointed vice-president in charge of corporate development. A new executive committee was struck: Owen; McDonald; John Houchin, vice-president of Phillips; Art Mayne, now retired from the Royal Bank and a financial consultant; and Gibson.

McMahon's role in the management of Westcoast was not yet completely severed. He remained on the board. He still held more shares than any other individual, more, in fact, than the personal holdings of all the other directors combined. And under the terms of a contract signed the previous year, he was to continue to be employed by the company as a consultant until he died, resigned, or was unable to perform the duties of a consultant because of permanent sickness or disability. The contract specified that he was to be provided with an office, a secretary (his long-time secretary, Mrs Edna Stahl), a car, driver, and the use of the company aircraft for company business.

But shortly after McMahon retired, so did the aircraft. Owen reported to the executive committee that the Falcon jet had been evaluated at $1.3 million. When no buyer could be found, it was put in storage, and later sold for $600,000.

Owen and D.P. were now in charge, but they had lots of help from McMahon. In his letter of resignation, McMahon had written:

> Once free from the executive and administrative responsibilities, I will be in a good position to concentrate my efforts on the development of new ventures and the extension of the company's current undertakings. My services should be of considerable value to the company in addition to the assistance I may render to the executive and administrative heads of the company from time to time.

Owen and D.P. both felt a great sense of loyalty to McMahon. Owen had worked for him for fifteen years, D.P. for twenty. It was difficult for them to disregard any advice that McMahon might offer from time to time, and it was still not entirely clear who was running the company. The man Phillips Petroleum decided ought run it was Kelly Gibson. He had gained their complete confidence with his administration of Pacific, and they wanted him to manage Westcoast as well.

In mid-1970, McMahon retired from the Westcoast board, remaining director emeritus, but otherwise ending his active association with the company he had founded twenty-one years earlier. Under an arrangement agreed to at this time, McMahon swapped his 338,682 Westcoast shares for 270,946 shares of Pacific, and then swapped the Pacific shares for an equal number of Phillips Petroleum. The Pacific and Phillips stocks were both trading at close to the same price, but Pacific shares paid an annual dividend of twenty-five cents, while Phillips paid $1.30. At the time of the transaction, McMahon's holdings in Westcoast were worth more than $6 million.

By mid-1970, Gibson was chairman and chief executive officer of Westcoast, as well as president and CEO of Pacific. Gibson made it clear that those who wanted to run with him would have to run his way, and they would have to run hard and fast. He asked Ed Phillips if he was "hungry enough" for the job as president. "I'll have you flying so fast that your coat-tails won't touch the seat of your trousers," Gibson warned. The change-over was effected within a year. Hetherington left to become president of Panarctic Oils Limited, the government-industry consortium exploring for oil and gas in the Arctic Islands. Doug Owen left to head a mining venture and work as McMahon's personal financial advisor. Peter Kutney, vice-president of sales and supply, left to form another mining and oil venture and met with spectacular success as head of Coseka Resources. Ray Mordan, vice-president of engineering and operations, left to join Arctic Gas, the ill-fated consortium that proposed to transport natural gas from both Prudhoe Bay and the Mackenzie Delta through a single pipeline. Len Youell, company secretary who had worked for Pacific and Westcoast since 1945, accepted early retirement and shortly after joined Petro-Canada. After his seven-month tenure as chairman, D.P. again became senior vice-president and general counsel, retiring from the company in 1977 after twenty-eight years of active association. Too active to stay retired, D.P., then aged seventy-two, resumed his private law practice in Calgary.

Progression in the new regime was orderly. Gibson remained

273

CEO for nearly seven years before retiring. Ed Phillips moved up from vice-president, to president, to chairman. John Anderson followed up the ladder from treasurer, to vice-president, to president.

HOW THE NDP RESCUED WESTCOAST

The problems that haunted Westcoast did not vanish with the changing of the guard. They reached their climax in 1973. Three significant events set the stage: construction of 110 miles of pipeline to connect the big gas reserves of Amoco at Beaver River and Pointed Mountain, new sales contract arrangements negotiated with El Paso, and the election in 1972 of David Barrett's New Democratic Party that ended W.A.C. Bennett's twenty-year rule in British Columbia.

In 1970, the National Energy Board noted that the United States faced "a gas shortage, perhaps even an energy shortage," and that Canadian gas exporters enjoyed "something like a seller's market." These new conditions were reflected in the next deal that Westcoast negotiated with El Paso, providing for the second increase in both the volume and price of exports. The volume was increased from a maximum rate of 500 million to 800 million feet per day. The old twenty-two-cent contract was at last scrapped, and Westcoast's export price was increased from an average of twenty-six to thirty-three cents, with provision for further escalation.

Following hearings before the Energy Board, the federal government approved the increased sales to El Paso but added another condition. The price that Westcoast charged El Paso at the US border at Sumas would have to be 5 per cent more than the price charged to BC Hydro at the same delivery point. This, together with a few other changes, would require some more negotiations, and minutes of the executive committee noted that a revised contract "will be presented to El Paso on a take it or leave it basis." El Paso took it, and the additional sales to El Paso were planned to start in November, 1971, building up to the full 800 million feet per day over two years.

To deliver the increased volumes to El Paso would require the largest expansion in Westcoast's history. To finance this, Westcoast raised $235 million in a little more than two years, including $200 million in long-term debt from Canadian lenders, and $35 million for shares sold to existing shareholders.

Still another increase in the export volume and price – the third since Westcoast began business – was announced in March, 1973. Subject to Canadian and US approvals, the exports would be increased more than 50 per cent by 1977, at a price still to be determined. The new contract offered other features. The price of the existing sales was immediately boosted from thirty-three to thirty-eight cents to reflect increased prices paid to BC gas producers. To help find the gas needed for the additional exports, El Paso agreed to pay a further 1.5-cent incentive bonus and to fund $80 million in advances to the oil companies for exploration expenditures, the advances to be recovered from later sales of gas.

This latest contract with El Paso, however, was soon overshadowed by other events. The election of Dave Barrett's NDP government in August, 1972, following years of bitter political attack on Westcoast by the NDP and its predecessor, the CCF, cast a shadow of apprehension. Barrett talked about expropriating Westcoast, and in the nine months after the election the price of Westcoast shares steadily declined from $31 to $18. The NDP had not forgotten McMahon's intervention in the 1960 election. "Westcoast is paying a high price for that," Barrett declared.

By May, 1973, despite the new contracts with El Paso, Westcoast was once again in a bind. Higher prices paid to gas producers at Fort St John as a result of an award by an arbitration panel had added $13 million a year to costs. About $10 million of this was passed on to El Paso and $3 million swallowed by Westcoast because it was unable to increase prices to BC buyers. A new tax applied by the provincial government that month on gas used by Westcoast as fuel at its compressor stations amounted to another $5 million a year. In 1972, Westcoast had reported its best earnings ever, providing a return of 8.2 per cent on its investment. With these and other added costs, it looked as though the best that Westcoast could expect in 1973 would be a return in the order of 4 per cent.

Westcoast's earnings had never been regulated. It had operated in the classical manner of business, buying and selling and keeping what was left in between as profit. The National Energy Board had the authority to regulate Westcoast's earnings but never had any reason to exercise that authority. Westcoast's earnings had always been less than any regulatory body would set. Within weeks after the BC government had announced the new

275

tax on compressor fuel, Westcoast applied to the NEB to have its earnings regulated. That would involve some added, and perhaps unwelcome, government intervention, but it would also provide Westcoast with assured and higher profits than it had ever enjoyed before. Westcoast could not unilaterally change its sales contract in order to charge more, but the National Energy Board could. Before the year was out, Westcoast was rescued by regulatory control of its earnings, but not by the NEB. The help came from Dave Barrett's NDP government.

Shortly after the election, Barrett turned to his old friend Jim Rhodes for a study of energy policy matters. Barrett and Rhodes had first been elected to the legislature in 1960 and had been roommates when the legislature was in session in Victoria. Rhodes dropped out of politics after serving one term to become a businessman with a printing plant in his home town of Surrey. He called himself a "red capitalist." On the day that Barrett's government was elected he sold his printing business and later told Barrett that he was "the first free enterpriser in BC to sell out when the socialists arrived."

Rhodes and Vancouver lawyer Martin Taylor took a two-month crash course in energy politics, talking to government and oil company officials from Alberta, Saskatchewan, Ottawa, England, and Norway. In June, a newly appointed BC Energy Commission, with Rhodes as chairman and Martin as counsel, started hearings in Vancouver, and the focus of its interest was Westcoast Transmission. Taylor zeroed in on Westcoast's monopolistic position as the sole buyer, transporter, and wholesale seller of BC gas and its contract arrangements with its largest customer, El Paso.

Ed Phillips, testifying before the hearings, offered a "simple remedy" to anyone concerned about the fact that Westcoast was the only buyer of gas from BC producers. If the gas utilities that Westcoast supplied "have the slightest dissatisfaction with the buying function that Westcoast has performed for them, we will abdicate," Phillips said. "And let them do that."

For a quarter of a century, Westcoast had been squeezed between the buying and the selling functions. If someone else wanted to do the buying, Westcoast would be glad to haul the gas under contract arrangements that would provide it with a reasonable profit on its investment. Phillips had started the ball rolling down the right path.

Before the ball was played, another disaster struck Westcoast. Amoco's giant gas fields at Beaver River and Pointed Mountain, the main supply for Westcoast's additional sales to El Paso and the backbone for an expansion investment of some $200 million, had turned out to be more like two pygmies. Amoco had advised Westcoast in August of some production difficulties, but the full extent was not known until mid-September. The wells started sucking up water with the gas, and the production rate from the two fields had to be slashed by two-thirds. Westcoast suddenly lost nearly 20 per cent of its gas supplies. For the next half dozen years, Westcoast was unable to provide all the gas it had contracted to sell. Combined with the added cost of the new field tax, the higher prices paid to the Fort St John producers, and other cost increases, Westcoast was confronted with the severest financial crisis in its corporate history.

Gibson contacted all of Westcoast's customers – BC Hydro, Inland Natural Gas, Pacific Northern Gas, and El Paso – advising them that the shortfall would be shared proportionately by each of them. Barrett's government was up in arms. No reduction in supplies to BC customers would be permitted; US buyers would have to suffer the shortfall. The government declared an Emergency Measures Act that would allow it to take over the province's entire gas industry. Westcoast found some additional gas that helped to alleviate the shortage that winter and undertook not to cut-back its BC customers.

While this crisis was just beginning to gather steam, Jim Rhodes's Energy Commission had issued an interim report in September. It found that BC natural gas was being sold in both British Columbia and the US Northwest at 40 to 50 per cent less than the price of alternative energy, resulting in a loss of more than $100 million a year to BC producers and to the provincial government as the owner of the resource. And because El Paso bought 70 per cent of the gas, it was the United States that reaped most of the benefit of the low prices. The commission recommended "immediate steps" to raise the price of BC gas to its competitive value and the establishment of a "provincial Crown agency empowered to engage in production, processing, transmission, and marketing of natural gas." The provincial agency would be the BC Petroleum Corporation, and its first chairman would be Jim Rhodes.

Westcoast issued a statement saying that it agreed with the

commission's "main thrust that the basic problem is that the province's valuable natural resource is being sold at artifically low prices, both in British Columbia and in the export market."

After the report was out, Rhodes met with Gibson and Phillips at the Timber Club in the Hotel Vancouver to discuss arrangements that would achieve the immediate price increase. The bill to establish the Petroleum Corporation had already been introduced, and Rhodes suggested that the government corporation take over Westcoast's gas purchase and sales contracts, leaving Westcoast to operate as a shipping company, like a railway, that would earn a regulated profit on its investment.

In two weeks of intensive negotiations, Westcoast and the BCPC, as it became known familiarly, hammered out an agreement. The government corporation would take over Westcoast's 120 purchaser contracts with 80 producers but not the sales contracts. BCPC would buy the gas from the producers, then Westcoast would buy it from BCPC and sell it to the utilities and El Paso. The prices would be set to allow Westcoast to earn, initially, 9.5 per cent on its investment. For Westcoast, the deal meant that instead of facing the worst financial crisis in its history, it would be assured of larger profits than it had ever made before.

The other aspect of the arrangement involved the "immediate steps" to increase the price of gas to a level that matched the price of other fuels. The key lay in obtaining the agreement of the BC Hydro Authority to accept prices nearly double those stipulated in its contract with Westcoast. Under the contract with El Paso, the export price would automatically increase to 5 per cent more than whatever BC Hydro paid.

On Sunday, November 11, Rhodes met with the board of BC Hydro to outline the arrangement that they were asked to accept. David Cass-Beggs, the recently appointed chairman of BC Hydro, did not like it. He had a contract to buy gas from Westcoast for thirty-one cents, and now he was being asked to sign a letter of agreement with Westcoast that would set the price at fifty-eight cents.

Tuesday, November 13, was the red letter day. On that day, Jim Rhodes turned forty-two, the BC Power Petroleum Corporation came into being, the directors of Westcoast met to officially authorize the agreement assigning the gas purchase contracts to BCPC, and David Cass-Beggs balked at signing the letter that would trigger a $100 million a year increase in the price of BC gas.

Pacific Petroleums' jet was standing ready at the airport, scheduled to take off at 5 PM that evening on a flight to Ottawa. It was to carry Kelly Gibson, Ed Phillips, John Anderson, Jim Rhodes, and BCPC lawyer Joe Pelrine, together with copies of Westcoast's agreements with BCPC and with BC Hydro. The group was to meet the next day with Energy Minister Donald Macdonald and National Energy Board chairman Marshall Crowe. Ottawa's approval of the arrangement was required because Westcoast was a federally regulated pipeline, even if its earnings were not.

But without the letter signed by Cass-Beggs there was no deal, and Cass-Beggs had declined to see anyone from Westcoast. From the BC Hydro building, Westcoast vice-president Ron Rutherford, armed with the letter for Cass-Beggs to sign, phoned Gibson at the Westcoast building to report that, "Cass-Beggs won't see me." Jim Rhodes phoned at 2 PM and was told that Cass-Beggs was unavailable, and no one else was authorized to act in this matter. Rhodes phoned Barrett in Victoria, then demanded an interview with Cass-Beggs at which he relayed a message from the premier. Exactly what was said has not been disclosed, but Cass-Beggs agreed to see Rutherford and signed the letter without reading it. By 6 PM the Pacific aircraft was flying to Ottawa. On Wednesday, the Westcoast group met with Donald Macdonald and Marshall Crowe. The deal was publicly announced on Thursday.

El Paso was simultaneously hit with a cut-back in its contracted gas supplies from Westcoast and a $70 million a year increase in the purchase price. The extra revenues were split three ways, Westcoast, the gas producers, and the provincial government each receiving a share of the pie. The prices paid to the gas producers were doubled. Within two years, the government's revenues from gas sales jumped from $5 million to $90 million a year. It was barely a start, as energy prices skyrocketted in the next eight years, triggered by the 1973 oil embargo of the Organization of Petroleum Exporting Countries. But it was a good start.

A sequel to the NDP rescue of Westcoast was the government's purchase, two months later, of a large block of Westcoast shares.

After sixteen years of legal battles, El Paso Natural Gas Company was finally ordered by the US Supreme Court to get rid of the pipeline from New Mexico to Seattle that it had acquired from Ray Fish and the other shareholders of Pacific Northwest Pipeline in 1956. The line was being turned over to a new firm, Northwest Pipeline Corporation, headquartered in Salt Lake City, Utah. The court's divestiture order also required El Paso to dispose of its holdings of 1,157,125 shares of Westcoast, then representing 13.5 per cent of the ownership of the company, the second largest block after that controlled by Pacific and Phillips.

Early in January, Rhodes received a phone call at his new office with the BC Petroleum Corporation from Toronto investment dealer Gary Van Nest of Wisener and Partners Co Ltd. Van Nest said he could arrange for the purchase of the Westcoast shares held by El Paso for about $25 million, the current market price, and wondered if BCPC would be interested in buying them. Rhodes said there would be a conflict of interest if BCPC were to hold an interest in Westcoast Transmission. But perhaps the government would be interested. Why not phone the premier and ask him? "In fact," said Rodes, "if you were to phone the premier at, say, 10 tomorrow morning, I just might happen to be in the premier's office."

Rhodes was in Barrett's office the next morning when the call came through from Van Nest. After listening for awhile, Barrett cupped his hand over the receiver and spoke to Rhodes: "There's a young broker on the phone, brash as hell. Wants to know if we would like to buy a piece of Westcoast. Is it a good buy?"

Of course it was a good buy. Had not Jim Rhodes just arranged that Westcoast would earn a guaranteed profit of 9.5 per cent on its total pipeline investment, and probably more than that on the shareholders' investment? Rhodes said that at about $22 a share, it would be an excellent investment. Barrett asked the broker to hold on a little longer, while on another telephone he called Deputy Finance Minister Gerry Bryson. "Have we got $25 million dollars to buy some Westcoast shares?" Barrett asked. Bryson allowed as how the money could be made available. "Yes, we'll take it," Barrett told Van Nest. The purchase was confirmed later that day. The price came to $25,456,750. It did turn out to be a profitable investment.

CHAPTER SIXTEEN

The New Era

The year 1973 ushered in a new era, not only for Westcoast Transmission, but also for the entire petroleum and natural gas industry; not only in Canada but throughout the world.

In September, 1973, the BC Energy Commission found that the province's natural gas was being sold for little more than half the comparable price of fuel oil. Oil prices, in Canada and elsewhere, had already been edging up in the past year. One month after the report of the BC Energy Commission, they exploded. In October of that year, Egyptian and Syrian forces attacked Israeli-held territory on the Golan Heights and the East Bank of the Suez Canal. In the wake of this latest Middle East war, Arab members of the Organization of Petroleum Exporting Countries embargoed shipments of their oil to the United States and a number of other nations. Within four months, the price of oil had quadrupled. In the next five years, it tripled. In the next two years, it doubled. Within seven years, the world price of crude oil – the largest single commodity in international trade – had increased twenty-five fold.

As with other fuels, the price of natural gas increased in tandem with oil, especially gas from Canada sold to the United States. It had taken Westcoast sixteen years to increase its export sales price from twenty-two cents to about sixty-three cents per thousand cubic feet. During the next eight years, the government of Canada increased the export price to $4.94 in US funds, or about $6.00 Canadian.

In the process, Westcoast's gas purchase prices, sales prices, and profits had all ceased to be determined by market competition and were set by government regulation. And government regulation left Westcoast with more profits than a competitive market ever had. Before its earnings were regulated, the best profit that Westcoast had ever made was less than $21 million in 1972. In 1981, its regulated profits amounted to nearly $69 million. But the provincial government, through BCPC, had done even better. In 1972, the government collected some $5 million in royalties on natural gas production. In 1980, it collected $235 million on BCPC's operations. Additional revenues from natural gas by-products, crude oil production, and lease payments brought the government's total oil and gas revenues for its 1981 fiscal year to $447 million.

In March, 1977, Kelly Gibson retired from Westcoast after seven years as chief executive officer. At the end of 1974, he had retired from Pacific Petroleums after seventeen years of employment, ten as CEO. He had seen both companies transformed from small, precarious ventures into large, profitable corporations. During his tenure years with Pacific, the company's revenues had grown from $1.3 million a year to $230 million a year from an annual loss approaching $2 million a year to a net profit of $45 million a year. Most of the growth had taken place under his direction as chief executive officer.

The man from Broken Arrow had come a long way since starting out as a roustabout at fify cents an hour, and so had the companies he managed. One reason that they got there was that Gibson drove himself mercilessly and demanded almost as much from those with whom he worked. No toolpusher had been tougher than Gibson, and he could be as tough in the boardroom as he had been on the drilling floor. He was respected, and even admired, by those who stood up to and stayed with him. Many of those who jumped ship, or were pushed overboard – and their number was great – have a different assessment. But Gibson made the bottom line count. His school had been on the floor of the drilling rigs, and he never managed to completely hide his disdain for engineers. But he was the engineer who ran the machines that Frank McMahon had built. And they ran like express trains with the throttles open wide.

TAKE-OVER WARS

After he retired as an officer and employee of Pacific, Gibson remained a director for a further four years. He had one more link to forge, a connecting link in the final transformation of the company.

That transformation was no less than the disappearance of Pacific; it became a vital part of Canada's national oil company, Petro-Canada, and the star prize in one of the most dramatic acquisition rivalries in Canadian corporate history.

By the 1970s, Phillips Petroleum had come to look upon its ownership of nearly a half interest in Pacific almost as a passive investment. Phillips had only two directors on the Pacific board. If Pacific wanted any engineering or other technical help from Phillips, it asked for it, and it paid a fee for the service. Under Gibson's management, Pacific was generating steadily growing revenues and earnings, so there was little need for Bartlesville to interfere.

Like any investment, Phillips' stake in Pacific was always for sale if the price was right and the money could be put to better use elsewhere. By 1973, Phillips decided that its investment in Pacific might, indeed, be put to better use elsewhere. Phillips had just discovered its big Ekofisk oil field under the waters of the North Sea, offshore from Norway. It would soon prove to be the most profitable discovery in the company's history, but first a very large investment had to be made to bring the giant oil field into production. Faced with this need for capital, Phillips decided that its stake in Pacific might be more profitably invested in the development of the Ekofisk field.

Phillips offered its Pacific shares to the Canada Development Corporation, the investment firm primarily owned by the Government of Canada, for $300 million. At the request of Phillips chairman Bill Martin, Gibson approached CDC chairman marshall Crowe (later chairman of the National Energy Board) to make the offer. The CDC was then in the midst of a court battle over its offer to buy the mining company, Texas Gulf. Phillips thought that if CDC lost out on its bid for Texas Gulf, it might be interested in looking at Pacific. But the CDC did get Texas Gulf, and the matter was not pursued.

The possibility of a Pacific sale next came up in the fall of 1977 when Gibson, then retired from Pacific but still on the board, and Petro-Canada president Wilbert Hopper met at a social function in Calgary. The controversial national oil company was then less than two years old, and its main assets consisted of the

283

former Canadian properties of Atlantic Richfield Oil Company which it had acquired for some $350 million. It still had a long way to go to become a big player in the oil league. Bill Hopper, a chubby ball of explosive energy, wanted to see Petro-Canada get there in a hurry. Hopper asked Gibson if he thought there was any chance that Phillips might be interested in selling its Pacific shares. Gibson said Phillips had been interested in selling at one time and offered to enquire whether it still was. Gibson suggested that it might also be well to discuss the matter with Pacific president Merrill Rasmussen.

During the next few weeks, Hopper met with Rasmussen to explore the possibility of an acquisition in general terms, Petro-Canada vice-president Joel Bell obtained some non-confidential information on Pacific's operations from vice-president Bill Tye, and Gibson reported to Hopper on the reaction from Bartlesville. Phillips had managed to raise the money to develop its Ekofisk field (a task made much easier after OPEC had kicked off the explosion in oil prices in late 1973) and no longer had the same interest in selling its Pacific shares. But it would be willing to discuss the matter. Hopper, however, had decided not to pursue the matter further at that time.

By the following June, Hopper was engaged in an intense corporate battle to acquire Husky Oil Company for $500 million. He lost. Before long, that loss would prove to be one of the best things that ever happened to Bill Hopper and Petro-Canada.

Husky Oil had been founded in 1938 with the purchase of four oil wells and a small shut-down refinery at Cody, Wyoming, by Glenn Nielson, a former Alberta sheep rancher. Forty years later, Husky and Glenn Nielson were both still headquartered in the small cowtown of Cody, where Husky occupied a converted railway hotel. Husky's operations, however, were fairly evenly spread across Canada and the United States. In Canada, Husky pioneered in the task of coaxing out of the ground the heavy, viscous oil that lays in blanket sands straddling the Alberta-Saskatchewan border near Lloydminster. The heavy oil is a thick, molasses-like guck that few others were interested in until OPEC created the oil supply crisis in 1974. Suddenly, a lot of people were interested in Husky's former orphan oil, including Petro-Canada.

A rumour that Husky was the object of a planned take-over bumped the price of its shares by $4.75 to $35.75 on the Toronto

Stock Exchange during the early hours of Thursday, June 8, 1978. Trading in the Husky shares was suspended by exchange authorities until the cause of the sudden price jump was made known. The reason was Petro-Canada's planned offer to purchase Husky shares at $45 each, or a total of $490 million for the 10.9 million outstanding shares. Details of the offer were first outlined to Husky chairman Glenn Nielson, then seventy-six, and his son, Jim, president of the company, at a meeting in Calgary that Saturday with Bill Hopper and his financial advisors.

The Nielson family stood to collect $90 million for their 18 per cent interest in Husky. But they were not happy. Glenn Nielson's pain at the prospect of losing control of the company he had spent four decades building was intensified by the thought of paying some $30 million in US taxes under the cash offer proposed by Petro-Canada. In a weekend of fast-paced negotiations, Nielson raised a counter offer from eighty-year-old Dr Armand Hammer of the Occidental Petroleum Corporation in Los Angeles. Because it involved a swap of stock rather than a cash payment, the Occidental proposal would save the Nielsons and other Husky shareholders large tax payments.

Trading in Husky shares remained suspended for four days, from Thursday morning, June 8, until noon the following Tuesday. By then, the proposed offers of both Petro-Canada and Occidental had been made public, and the price of Husky shares had jumped more than 50 per cent, from $31 to $47. For the next couple of weeks, Petro-Canada and Occidental waged a bidding war for Husky. Petro-Canada upped its offer from $47 to $52 a share. Occidental revised its first offer to a share swap worth about $54 per Husky share. But when the battle was all over, control of Husky had been captured in a lightning raid by beetle-browed Robert Blair of Alberta Gas Trunk Line. Blair's manoeuvre left regulatory authorities less than pleased.

Alberta Gas Trunk Line, later renamed Nova Corporation, had been buying Husky shares on the open market for nearly six months by the time the bidding war between Petro-Canada and Occidental broke out. It had acquired nearly 5 per cent of Husky, the maximum amount it could hold without having to publicly disclose its interest. Blair faced two choices: sell the Husky shares at a healthy profit, or shoot for control of the company. On Thursday, June 22, Blair made the decision to go for control of Husky. By the following Tuesday, Alberta Gas Trunk had spent some $160 million to increase its interest in Husky to more than one-third.

Blair's raid was made possible by a group of New York arbitrageurs, investment specialists who plunge millions of dollars to seek quick profits based on price discrepancies in stock market situations. A take-over often offers a ripe opportunity for such specialists, because the trading price of the target company is often less than the offered price, reflecting an element of risk that the proposed take-over might fall through. If there is a bidding war that could escalate the price, all the better, as far as the arbitrageurs are concerned. Husky was an ideal situation. Within a period of two weeks, arbitrageurs for a small number of large investment houses had purchased Husky shares representing more than one-quarter of the ownership. It was the existence of this block of shares held by a small number of investors that enabled Blair to conduct his lightning raid by means of purchases on the open market.

Alberta Gas Trunk Line's entry into the middle of the bidding war between Petro-Canada and Occidental helped push the price of Husky shares to more than $52, up $21 or nearly 70 per cent in less than three weeks. But when on June 27 Blair had secured 35 per cent of the Husky shares, enough to effectively exercise control, he suddenly stopped buying. The next day, the price of Husky shares fell by $10. The Ontario Securities Commission and the Toronto Stock Exchange both frowned on Blair's raid, because Alberta Gas Trunk had not disclosed its interest in Husky until its buying spree was over, and because it had not made an open offer to all shareholders. Alberta Gas Trunk did, however, later make an offer to the other shareholders to complete its purchase of Husky. It turned out to be a costly offer.

Hopper and Petro-Canada were widely portrayed as the inept losers in the battle for Husky. But within a few weeks, Bill Hopper was out shopping again, this time for a far larger and much more profitable purchase, Pacific Petroleums. Once more he would face competition from the ever aggressive Bob Blair for the largest corporate acquisition in Canada's history.

One evening shortly after the Husky battle, Gibson was in the lobby of the Royal York Hotel in Toronto buying a newspaper, when he ran into Bill Hopper, who invited him to the bar for a drink. "I'd sure like to reopen talks with Phillips," Hopper said. Gibson suggested that he phone Phillips senior vice-president

R.A. Roberts, who was also one of the two Phillips directors on the Pacific board, and arrange a meeting with the Phillips management.

Negotiations to hammer out a deal for the purchase of the 48 per cent Phillips interest in Pacific began on August 17, when Hopper first met with Phillips chairman Bill Martin. The talks continued in great secrecy for nearly three months. It was in part because of the rumours of a take-over bid that Petro-Canada had lost out in its efforts to acquire Husky Oil, and this time Hopper was determined that there would be no leak. Only a very small team at Petro-Canada was aware of what was happening. Hopper's first meeting with Martin was held in Kansas City, while subsequent meetings were held in Washington and other cities. Not once during these discussions did the Petro-Canada team travel to Phillips' head office; merely being observed travelling to Bartlesville could have been enough to trip the rumour mill. So secret were the discussions that not even Pacific president Merrill Rasmussen was aware of what was happening, until it was all over.

Less cautious was Bob Blair, eager to add Pacific Petroleums to his string of corporate conquests. Effectively an instrument of the Alberta government, Alberta Gas Trunk Line had been organized in the mid-1950s under a mandate that restricted its activities to the operation of a natural gas pipeline grid within Alberta. But under Blair's direction, AGTL had spread its wings far and wide. In the 1970s, it became heavily involved in the development of Alberta's petrochemical industry, based on the use of natural gas and gas liquids. Acquisition of Pacific, with its large production of gas and gas liquids, together with its interest in Westcoast, would have made Alberta Gas Trunk Line the dominant factor in the Canadian gas industry.

Blair first approached Rasmussen about the possibility of buying the Phillips interest in Pacific, and Rasmussen arranged a meeting for Blair in Bartlesville. After a luncheon with Phillips chairman Bill Martin, president Bill Douce, and other key officials, Blair announced that he was prepared to pay $48 each for the Pacific shares and then flew back to Calgary.

A rumour that a take-over bid for Pacific was in the offing did, indeed, leak out. Possibly, Blair and his party had been noticed travelling to Bartlesville. In any event, on September 28, 1978, Pacific shares jumped from $41 to $48. Rasmussen issued a statement that he was "unaware of any circumstance or information that would be responsible for the increased activity that has occurred in the trading of the company's shares."

Apparently, Blair's offer of $48 a share for Pacific was intended as his opening bid. But back in Calgary, he decided to delay pressing negotiations for the time being. At that moment, Alberta Gas Trunk was preparing a large offering of preferred shares. If it were actively engaged in negotiations to acquire the Pacific shares, it would have to disclose that fact in the prospectus. Blair decided to wait a couple of months, until after the sale of the preferred shares had been completed, before resuming his quest for Pacific. He was unaware that Bill Hopper was already in pursuit of the same prize.

A very startled Merrill Rasmussen first learned of the sale of the Pacific shares to Petro-Canada in a telephone call from Bill Douce in Bartlesville early on the morning of Friday, November 10, 1978. A very chagrined Bob Blair learned about it later that same day after the sale had been publicly announced.

The announcement was made following the close of the stock-market by Energy Minister Alastair Gillespie at a press conference in the Hotel Toronto. Petro-Canada had paid $671 million for the 48.3 per cent Phillips interest in Pacific. The price per share was $55.50 in US funds, or $65.02 Canadian. An offer to purchase the remaining shares at the same price resulted in Petro-Canada acquiring complete ownership of Pacific by early 1979. The total cost, including brokerage commissions and other expenses, came to nearly $1.5 billion, up to then the largest corporate acquisition in Canadian history.

Pacific's assets more than doubled Petro-Canada's oil reserves, increased its natural gas reserves more than five times, and multiplied gross revenues five-fold. It made Petro-Canada the nation's seventh largest oil producer, the second largest gas producer, gave it a one-third interest in Westcoast Transmission, and a substantial interest in Westcoast Petroleum. With the acquisition of Pacific, Petro-Canada joined the ranks of the few integrated oil companies in Canada, combining refining and retail marketing with its exploration and production operations. Down came the Pacific 66 sign at 426 service stations in western Canada, and up went the new Petro-Canada maple leaf.

The purchase of Pacific was a big feather in the cap of Bill Hopper. He began his career in the oil industry as a geologist for

Imperial Oil, sitting on remote wildcats in Alberta and British Columbia, as the activities of a well-site geologist are picturesquely described. Hopper combines training in both petroleum geology and business administration with experience in both the private and public sectors. His background includes three years as senior economist with the National Energy Board, nine years as a petroleum consultant with Arthur D. Little Inc in Cambridge, Massachusetts, and three years with the Department of Energy in Ottawa, where he was first senior energy policy advisor and then Assistant Deputy Minister. He joined Petro-Canada as vice-president when the national oil company was formed on January 1, 1976, became president six months later, and was named chairman and chief executive officer in 1979.

Petro-Canada's acquisition of Pacific led the parade that saw further billions of dollars spent during the next three years by both Canadian investors and taxpayers for the purchase of foreign holdings in Canada's oil and gas industry. The movement was propelled by the federal government's National Oil Policy that aims to see the majority of the industry Canadian-owned. The controversy over whether these enormous investments will be good or bad for Canada will ultimately depend upon what the investments return, both to the investors and the nation. On that basis, at least Petro-Canada's purchase of Pacific ranks as a clear winner, acknowledged by even the staunchest critics of Petro-Canada and the government intervention that it involves. Even the author, a devoted disciple of a competitive market economy, acknowledges it. Financed entirely by bank loans, taxpayers did not contribute a cent to the $1.5 billion purchase. Revenues from the Pacific properties have repaid the loans and provided additional large revenues for further exploration and development of production. Within a year of the acquisition, the world price of oil had doubled again, and the investment looked even more astute.

THE IMPRUDENT PROMOTER

On the evening of April 8, 1980, in the ballroom of Toronto's Sheraton Hotel, a man whose age seemed to have shrunk his stature but broadened his happy grin stood up before a black-tie audience and related a long, shaggy-dog story. The occasion was the second annual induction of members into the Canadian Business Hall of Fame sponsored by Junior Achievement of Canada, and six names were to be inscribed on the honour roll. Only one of the six inducted that evening was still living, Frank McMahon.

McMahon reminisced about his days as a diamond driller and told about the time that he had been arrested for stealing a dog. McMahon was then a diamond-drilling contractor, and the black cocker spaniel was the pet of his ten-man crew. They were drilling at a remote site on Quatsino Sound, near the north end of Vancouver Island, for British Metals Corporation. The dog had been picked up by one of the drilling crew when the CPR ship he was on stopped enroute to the camp. Shortly before Christmas, McMahon and a British Metals geologist visited the camp. When they disembarked from the ship at the flag stop, so too did a member of the BC Provincial Police Force. The policeman had come to retrieve the stolen dog and arrest the culprit. Not wanting to lose a member of his drilling crew, McMahon volunteered to claim that he had stolen the dog, since he was due to return to Victoria within a few days. It was agreed he would return with the dog and the policeman.

But on its return voyage from Prince Rupert, the CPR ship sailed right past the drilling camp, and it looked as though the dog, the policeman, and McMahon were going to spend Christmas on Quatsino Sound, until McMahon chartered a fishing boat to take them out. It was a forty-foot seine boat, crewed by a captain and an engineer, and it chug-chugged along on a one-lunger, a single-cylinder gasoline engine that belched great fumes below decks. It was a stormy voyage of several days along the west coast of Vancouver Island through some of the roughest seas found anywhere.

"The captain was sick," McMahon told his audience. "The engineer was sick, and the policeman was sick. I couldn't go below with all the fumes, so I stayed on deck and tied myself to the mast. The dog and I were the only ones that weren't sick, and I thought for sure that he was going to be swept overboard."

The boat finally found refuge at the tiny fishing village of Ucluelet, where the survivors were met by the store owner, who was also the postmaster, and the justice of the peace. The policeman wanted to press charges against McMahon for the theft of the dog. McMahon just happened to have a bottle of Scotch in his bag, and he sat down at the table to discuss the matter with the store owner, the postmaster, and the justice of the peace. The two of them drank the bottle, and by that time the store owner, the postmaster, and the justice of the peace was so annoyed that he threatened to report the policeman to Victoria for such frivilous pursuit of a fine, upstanding businessman.

"Imagine!" said McMahon. "Arrested for stealing a dog."

McMahon's page in history will not record him as a *raconteur*, nor even a dog poacher. It would be an injustice if it recorded him as the businessman who bought Westcoast shares at five cents each and sold them at $20. Not because the average price that he paid for them was $4.65, but because there is more to the measure than that. History might more properly regard him as the businessman whose conviction in his vision overran standard business judgment.

McMahon had set out to make himself a millionaire, at a time when millionaires were very wealthy. It took a couple of decades, but the fortune was founded in a forty-acre lease in the middle of the Leduc field. From that he amassed wealth that was fairly large measured by the value of the dollar and the standards of the 1960s, moderate by the values of the 1970s, small by comparison with later Canadian oil fortunes created by the explosion of oil prices that started in 1973. In the hands of a more cautious investor, the McMahon fortune might well have grown enormously.

But McMahon was, or became, compelled by more than just the pursuit of wealth. He had the wildcatter's faith that the resource was there to be found, to be developed, to be put to use. Accomplishing that task, fulfilling that vision, vindicating the faith, became as important as the pursuit of wealth.

In McMahon's case, the vision was the task of developing and supplying the natural gas resources of northern British Columbia. If wealth was all that mattered, he would have been better off, after his success at Leduc and Redwater, to have dropped the idea of building what was for so long a barely profitable pipeline. There was much more profit to be made in oil than in natural gas, especially a gas pipeline.

At the very least, if wealth was all that had mattered, McMahon would have taken advantage of an offer in 1949 to join forces with Faison Dixon to build a shorter, more profitable pipeline to the West Coast from Pincher Creek. He chose, instead, to stick with the less profitable idea of developing the more distant resources in northern British Columbia.

291

If the pursuit of wealth had been the only drive, the Westcoast pipeline would not have been built in 1957; the Western Pacific Products and Crude Oil pipeline would not have been built in 1961; the Pacific Northern line to Prince Rupert would not have been built in 1968. There were safer and more profitable ways to invest money. No one else was prepared to undertake any of these projects, except McMahon and those he found to back him.

In the hands of businessmen with less vision and daring, most of British Columbia would be without the greater convenience and lower cost of natural gas, there would be smaller government revenues, and fewer jobs in the province.

The wildcatter's faith was vindicated.

Acknowledgements

This book comes equipped with the customary Bibliography appended to it, but it lists only some of the sources of information.

Additional important sources were the corporate files of Pacific Petroleums and Westcoast Transmission which were made available to me, including the minute books, correspondence files, reports, company publications, news releases, and the like. Although these files are not listed in the Bibliography, wherever they have been drawn upon they have been clearly referred to in the text.

Similar corporate files are lacking for some of the early ventures with which Frank McMahon was associated. I am indebted, however, to the BC Registrar of Companies for registration statements, prospectuses, reports, and other materials on the file related to International Pipe Lines Limited and Columbia Oils Limited.

Included in the archival material from the Pacific Petroleums files, now in the custody of Petro-Canada, was a large accumulation of newspaper and magazine clippings that provided interesting and helpful material. Newspaper and periodical indices were also searched for additional articles. Of the several hundred articles consulted, only the more relevant and interesting are listed in the Bibliography.

Two weekly financial newspapers, published in Calgary and Vancouver, provided a wealth of historical material, often very colourful. The *Western Oil Examiner* (which began publication in 1926 as *The Alberta Oil Examiner* before changing its name a year later) was carefully perused for the period 1926 to 1947 at the Glenbow-Alberta Institute library in Calgary. The weekly

Vancouver newspaper, *Financial News*, was perused for the period 1932 to 1944 at the BC Legislative Library in Victoria.

The corporate files and the materials listed in the Bibliography still do no comprise all the sources of information. They provided a skeleton for the corporate history of Pacific and Westcoast. To add meat to the bones of this skeleton, I relied on interviews with a number of people, who were generous in making their time available to me, and whose help has been invaluable.

In alphabetical order, those who granted me interviews (in some cases, several interviews) were: John Anderson, Vancouver; Jean Angus, Calgary; John Ballem, Calgary; Pat Bowsher, Calgary; Mrs Millie Dannhauer, Penticton; Gordon Davis, Calgary; Daniel Ekman, Vancouver; John Getgood, Oklahoma; Kelly Gibson, Calgary; Ned Gilbert, Calgary; Jack Gorman, Calgary; Bill Graburn, Calgary; Charles Hetherington, Calgary; John Houchin, Bartlesville; Bill Hyndman, Vancouver; Peter Kutney, Calgary; Don Lamont, North Vancouver; Cliff Lane, Kimberley; Mrs Sonya Martin, Vancouver; W.F. Martin, Bartlesville; D.P. McDonald, QC, Calgary; Frank McMahon, Acapulco; Bill McMahon, Calgary; Grennie Musser, Kimberley; Mrs Isobel Moore, Palm Springs; Al McIntosh, Calgary; Douglas Owen, Vancouver; Ed Phillips, Vancouver; James Rhodes, Surrey; W.A. Roberts, Bartlesville; Mrs Edna Stahl, Vancouver; Robert Stewart, Seattle; Len Youell, Calgary.

Special appreciation should be expressed to those whose extraordinary efforts in assisting me have made this book possible.

Frank McMahon was unstinting with this time and help during repeated interviews in Vancouver, Calgary, Acapulco, and Palm Desert, California. He was helpful in every possible way.

Kelly Gibson generously gave me the use of his office in Calgary in which to work during a five-month period in early 1981 and was also most generous in the time he made available to me.

Dolores Jordan, Kelly Gibson's secretary, performed herculean labours on my behalf to transcribe the recorded interviews, type out the mountains of research notes that I accumulated, and other chores.

D.P. McDonald provided me with a massive number of source materials, including transcripts of most of the regulatory hearings involving Westcoast Transmission, government reports and other documents, and a number of corporate files. He, too, made his time freely available to me, and his unpublished manuscript, "The Westcoast Story," was an important source of information.

Len Youell of Petro-Canada provided invaluable service, digging up materials, information, photographs, and checking facts. Other Petro-Canada staff members who were always very helpful were librarian Mary Ann Meadows, Jayne Milne, Anne Fitzpatrick, and Marg Graham. At Westcoast, librarian Mrs Beatrice Yakimchuk, and Bill Ryan and Valerie Ward in the public relations department were similarly most helpful, while special acknowledgement must be paid to Frank McMahon's long-time secretary, Mrs Edna Stahl, as well as Mrs Terri Bone.

The assistance of William Howe of Ottawa in providing authorization for me to peruse the C.D. Howe papers in the Public Archives of Canada is gratefully acknowledged.

Splendid assistance was also received from Douglas Cass of the Glenbow-Alberta Institute in Calgary; Terry Eastwood of the BC Archives, Eldon Frost of the Public Archives of Canada, the staffs of these organizations, and the BC Legislative Library in Victoria.

Frank Barraclough was of great help to me in obtaining information related to Kimberley, BC.

Finally, I must acknowledge the assistance of Frank McMahon, Ed Phillips, Kelly Gibson, D.P. McDonald, Len Youell, Pat Bowsher, and Doug Owen, in checking a draft of the manuscript for factual accuracy. If they failed in their efforts to keep me from the errors of my ways, the fault is entirely mine.

Bibliography

BOOKS

Bothwell, Robert, and William Kilbourn. *C.D. Howe, A Biography*. Toronto: McClelland and Stewart, 1979.

de Mille, George. *Oil in Canada West, The Early Years*. Calgary: de Mille, 1970.

Foster, Peter. *The Blue-Eyed Sheiks*. Toronto: Collins Publishers, 1979.

Gray, Earle. *The Great Canadian Oil Patch*. Toronto: Maclean-Hunter Limited, 1970.

_____. *Super Pipe*. Toronto: Griffin House, 1979.

Hewins, Ralph. *The Richest American, J. Paul Getty*. New York: E.P. Dutton and Company, 1960.

Kilbourn, William. *Pipeline: Trans-Canada and the Great Pipeline Debate, a History of Business and Politics*. Toronto: Clarke, Irwin & Company Limited, 1970.

Kimberley Senior Citizens History Book Committee. *Mountain Treasures: The History of Kimberley*. Kimberley, BC, 1979.

Lobsenz, Norman M. *The Boots Adams Story*. Bartlesville, Oklahoma: Phillips Petroleum Company, 1965.

Martin, Robin. *The Rush For Spoils: The Company Province*, 1871-1933. Toronto: McClelland and Stewart, 1972.

Ormsby, Margaret A. *British Columbia, A History*. Toronto: Macmillan of Canada, 1958.

Sherman, Paddy. *Bennett*. Toronto: McClelland and Stewart, 1966.

Smith, Philip. *The Treasure Seekers: The Men Who Built Home Oil*. Toronto: Macmillan of Canada, 1978.

Spassoff, Dimiter A. *My Fabulous Life*. Boynton Beach, Florida: Star Publishing Company, 1979.

Taylor, G.W. *Mining: The History of Mining in British Columbia*. Vancouver: Hancock House Publishers, 1978.

Thomson, Dale C. *Louis St Laurent: Canadian*. Toronto: Macmillan of Canada, 1967.

ARTICLES

Aitken, Hugh G.J. "The Midwest Case: Canadian Gas and the Federal Power Commission." *Canadian Journal of Economics and Political Science* (May 1959).

Business Week, "El Paso Gas Pushes New Frontier." (January 26, 1957).

_____. "El Paso Merger Heads for the Hills." (May 29, 1971).

_____. "How to Win a $160 Million Pipeline." (August 31, 1954).

_____. "Pipelines Feel the Whip."

296

(Three US gas utilities indicted on anti-trust charges related to Canadian gas import plans.) (May 10, 1958).

_____. "Race Grows to Tap Canada's Huge Gas Reserves for US." (October 11, 1958).

Byrne, Harlan. "Pacific Northwest Pipeline Seeks to Tap Major Natural Gas Sector." *Wall Street Journal* (August 18, 1952).

Calgary Herald. "Alberta Rejects Gas Export." (January 25, 1951).

_____. "Alberta Warned Sell Gas Now or Forget It." (July 15, 1950).

_____. "Backers of Big Development Plan Announced." (The Bear Oil project.) (November 18, 1948).

_____. "Dinning Commission Reports to Legislature." (March 9, 1949).

_____. "Gulf Protests Gas Export Plan." (April 7, 1952).

_____. "Pacific Aircraft Crashes." (November 7, 1949).

_____. "Plan to Pipe Gas to Coast Being Studied." (July 15, 1947).

_____. "$750,000 Distillery to Be Built Here." (August 13, 1947).

_____. "Survey Unfavorable to Canadian Gas Route." (April 27, 1953).

Carnegie, R.K. "End of Gas Line Filibuster." *Lethbridge Herald* (May 23, 1950).

Clark, Leslie M. "Fort St John sets Pace for Peace River Gas Fields." *Oil and Gas Journal* (August 19, 1957).

Daily Oil Bulletin, "Atlantic No. 3 Ends Wild Career." (September 10, 1948).

_____. "Atlantic Oil Acquires Leduc Lease for $200,000." (September 5, 1947).

_____. Calgary. "Princess Oil Strike Sparks Lease Play." (October 13, 1944).

_____. "Sun Oil Acquired CPR Lease From Calgary Syndicate." (January 2, 1945).

_____. "Westcoast and Northwest Groups Apply to Conservation Board for Gas Export Permits." (October 24, 1949).

Edmonton Journal. Reports on debate in Alberta Legislature on government proposal to approve gas export. (April 9 and 10, 1952).

Financial News, Vancouver. Numerous articles on Columbia Oils Ltd and drilling in Flathead Valley. 1930 – September 11; 1932 – July 14; 1933 – January 26, March 31, May 26, June 2, June 23, July 21, August 11, September 15, October 13; 1935 – February 8, February 15, November 29; 1936 – April 24, June 12, September 11; 1937 – August 13, September 24, November 26, December 10; 1938 – March 25; 1942 – June 19.

_____. Text of statement by BC Premier John Hart on negotiations with Ottawa concerning petroleum exploration in the Peace River area. (June 4, 1943).

Financial Post, Toronto. "Kearney Heads BTC as Canada Set to Go It Alone on Pipelines." (October 20, 1951).

Gray, Earle. "The Untold Frank McMahon Story." *Oilweek* (June 22, 1970).

Hetherington, Charles R. "Westcoast's Big-Inch Gas Line – First for Canada." and "5 Trillion Cubic Feet of Gas Ready for Westcoast." *Oil and Gas Journal.* (August 19, 1957).

Hume, George S. "Petroleum Self-Sufficiency Is in Sight." *Western Business and Industry* (November, 1947).

_____. "The Utilization of Natural Gas in Canada." *Engineering Journal* (September, 1951).

_____. "Oil seepages in the Sage Creek area, BC" *Bulletin of Canadian Petroleum Geology* (August, 1964).

Hungry Horse News, Columbia Falls, Montana. "Early Oil Exploration in the Flathead." (August 31, 1951).

Jamieson, Robert. "New Challenge

for Oilman Frank McMahon." *Executive* (August, 1960).

Nicholson, Gordon B. "Directional Hole Tames Canadian Wild Well." (Atlantic Number Three.) *World Oil* (October, 1948).

Oilweek. "FPC Decision Stirs Energy Relations." (August 21, 1967).

———. "Gas Line to Fort Nelson May Be Delayed." (May 8, 1961).

———. "Impasse on Westcoast Gas Export Price Resolved." (February 26, 1968).

———. "Pacific to Squeeze Liquids from Trans-Canada's Gas Stream." (June 11, 1962).

Osborne, John A. "A Brawling, Bawling Industry." *Life* (March 10, 1952).

Imperial Oil Review. "The Conquest of Atlantic No. 3." (January, 1949).

Kirkpatrick, Guy H. "History and Development of Flathead Valley Oil Field." *British Columbia Miner* (June, 1930).

Lincoln, Freeman. "Frank McMahon's Pipe Dream." *Fortune* (January, 1958).

Pattullo, Thomas Dufferin. "BC Premier Describes Early Work in Area Where Drilling is Planned for Coming Spring Season." *Western Oil Examiner* (January 28, 1940).

Ralph, Henry D. "Biggest Deal in Gas History." *Oil and Gas Journal* (December 20, 1954).

Rowland, Les. "Canada's Westcoast Gas to USA." *World Petroleum* (February, 1958).

Saturday Night, Toronto. "Petroleum Policy of BC Government." (May 5, 1940).

Slipper, Stanley E. "Alberta's Natural Gas Industry." *The Alberta Oil Examiner* (December 31, 1926).

Swift, Thomas P. "Bitter Fight Promised at Hearings on Bid to Supply Gas to Northwest." *New York Times* (January 25, 1953).

Time. "Battle for New England." (December 8, 1952).

Tower, Whitney. "The Man Takes Charge of His Horse." *Sports Illustrated* (June 2, 1969).

———. "Revenge Was Sweet." *Sports Illustrated* (June 16, 1969).

Vancouver Province. "BC Offers Peace River Oil to Ottawa." (April 2, 1942).

———. "House Debates Bill Giving Government Full Control of Oil Industry." (May 9, 1940).

———. "New Deal on Gas Warms Westcoast." (November 16, 1973).

———. "Oil Companies Halt BC Gas Deliveries, Government Passes Legislation." (April 26, 1940).

———. "Pipeline Chief Flies to Ottawa." (June 25, 1954).

———. "US Utilities Feud over Canadian Gas." (June 19, 1953).

Vancouver Sun. "BC Given Choice." (June 22, 1954).

———. "BC Oil Stocks Boom on Peace River Find." (November 2, 1951).

———. "BC Receives First Pipeline Gas." (November 1, 1950).

———. "Barrett Confirms Gas Stock Purchase." (January 18, 1974).

———. "Canadians Misled in Gas Price Deal." (October 12, 1957).

———. "Drilling to Resume in Flathead District." (September 27, 1931).

———. "Mr Howe Swears at Press Reporters." (May 9, 1950).

Victoria Colonist. "BC Legislation to Lift Oil Reserve." (March 29, 1947).

———. "Reserve Lifted on Coal and Petroleum Leases." (April 20, 1932).

Western Oil Examiner (Originally *The Alberta Oil Examiner*). "BC Oil Fields Have Improved Outlook." (January 11, 1930).

———. "Claims Glacier is Producing After Shooting. Testing Output of Sage Creek's Discovery Well." (July 16, 1927).

———. "Columbia Shareholders Hold Meeting in Vancouver." (January 22, 1938).

———. "Crow's Nest Glacier Flowing By Heads Following Big Shot." (September 4, 1929).

———. "Faith in Sage Creek for

Quarter Century." (June 25, 1927). _____. Full page advertisement offering 500,000 treasury shares of London Pacific Exploration Co Ltd for public sale. Lists company officers, directors, properties, and capitalization. (May 11, 1935). _____. "New Regulations for Oil and Gas Development." (April 11, 1944).

_____. "Ralph Arnold Keen on Sage Creek Field." (January 29, 1927). _____. "Sage Creek Dome Comes into Play." (May 11, 1935). _____. "Talk of Forming Flathead-Sage Creek Syndicate." (June 27, 1942). Williams, M.Y. "Oil in North-Eastern British Columbia." *The Miner*, Vancouver (August, 1942).

PROCEEDINGS AND REPORTS OF GOVERNMENTAL BODIES

Alberta:
Natural Gas Commission (Robert J. Dinning, Chairman). Proceedings and report, 1949.
Petroleum and Natural Gas Conservation Board, Calgary. Transcripts of hearings on natural gas export applications, 1949-1952.
Reports: January 20, 1951 and March 29, 1952.
British Columbia:
Department of Mines. "Report of the Minister of Mines," for the years 1901, 1913, 1915, 1929, 1930, 1932, 1933.
Energy Commission (James Rhodes, Chairman). Transcript of hearings on natural gas industry, 1973. "Report on Matters Concerning The Natural Gas Industry In British Columbia," September, 1973.
Canada:
Board of Transport Commissioners, Ottawa. "Transcript of Hearings on Application by Westcoast Transmission for Pipeline Construction Permit," 1949-1955.
Parliament, House of Commons, debates, Hansard. 1942 – May 20; 1949 – April 5, 6, 8, 27, 28, 29, 30, October 21, 28, November 1, 8, 15, 17, 21, 22; 1950 – February 28,

March 7, 14, 17, 21, 24, May 1, 2, 5, 9, 15; 1953 – March 13, April 15; 1954 – June 19, 22; 1955 – February 25; 1956 – February 15, 16, 20, 21, 24, March 12, 15, 28, April 9, 11, 13, 17, 24, May 1, 2, 3, 4, 7, 8, 9, 10, 11, 14, 15, 16, 17, 18, 21, 22, 23, 24, 28, 29, 30, 31, June 1, 4, 5, 12, 22; 1957 – February 25.
Parliament, House of Commons. Standing committee on railways, canals, and telegraph lines. Minutes of proceedings and evidence on Bill No. 7, an act to incorporate the Alberta Natural Gas Company, April 26, 27, and 28, 1950.
Parliament, Senate. Official report of debates, October 4, 1949.
Royal Commission on Energy (Henry Borden, QC, Chairman). Transcript of hearings, 1958. Interim report, October, 1958.
United States:
Federal Power Commission, Washington, DC. Transcript of hearings on applications of Northwest Natural Gas Company, Pacific Northwest Pipeline Corporation, Westcoast Transmission Inc, et al, 1952-1955. Opinion No. 271, June 18, 1954. Opinion No. 289, November 25, 1955.

UNPUBLISHED DOCUMENTS

Howe, Clarence Decatur. "Private Papers." Public Archives of Canada, Ottawa. Volumes 23 to 24.
McDonald, D.P., Calgary. "The Westcoast Story."
Smith, Sydney J. (Member of the BC Legislative Assembly for Kamloops).

"Private Paper, 1950." Archives of British Columbia, Victoria.
Walker, John Fortune (BC Deputy Minister of Mines). "Private Papers, 1941-1945." Archives of British Columbia, Victoria.

Index

301

303

304

Taylor, A.J.T., 38, 40
Taylor, Martin, 276
Tennessee Gas Transmission, 126, 142-147, 155, 186, 189, 191-198, 200-201, 205-209
Texaco, 248
Texas Eastern Gas Transmission, 143-144
Thompson, Owen C., 18, 31-33
Thomson, Dale, 199
Tidewater Associated Oil Company, 96, 108
Tolmie, Simon Fraser, 37, 39, 64
Tosh, W.T., 96, 232
Trane Company of Canada, 267
Trans-Canada Airlines, 104
Trans-Canada Pipe Lines, 117, 125, 139, 146, 148-152, 182-184, 187-207, 209, 225, 238, 244-245
Transcontinental Pipe Line, 127
Trans-Mountain Oil Pipe Line Company, 115, 165, 254-255, 258
Trans-Northern Pipe Line Company, 109
Trans-Northwest Gas Inc, 147, 155, 158-172, 174-175, 178
Trans-Prairie Pipelines, 255-256
Trumbull, J.T., 40
Tucker, Ed, 145, 186, 267
Turner, Lloyd, 208
Turner Valley Oil Field, 44-46, 51-52, 58, 60, 73, 82
Turner Valley Royalties Ltd, 46
Twaits, W.O., 257
Tye, Bill, 244, 284

Union Gas Company, 140, 185
United Mine Workers of America, 148
United States,
    Army Engineering Corps, 70
    Department of the Interior, 150-151
    Department of State, 153
    Securities Exchange Commission, 219
    Federal Power Commission, 117, 126, 140, 144, 146-161, 165-175, 179-181, 184-190, 194, 196, 198, 208-209
United States Steel Corporation, 209
University of Calgary, 234
University of Waterloo, 185
Uphill, Tom, 42

Van Nest, Gary, 280
Vancouver, 35, 38, 44, 80, 229

Walker, Cliff, 238

Walker, John F., 66-69, 71, 73
Wallace, James, 17
Wallbridge, D.S., 32-33
Wartime Oils Limited, 74-75
Washington Public Service Commission, 148
Waste, H.F., 209, 220
Watt, G.E., 68
West Turner Petroleums, 47-57
Westcoast Petroleum, 259, 288
Westcoast Transmission, 43, 109, 113, 115-118, 123-134, 136-140, 142, 145-160, 165-168, 173-182, 208-229, 247-253, 258-282, 288
Western Canada College, 17
Western Natural Gas Company, 243, 249, 250
Western Pacific Products & Crude Oil Pipelines, 258-259, 292
Western Pipe Lines, 109, 113-114, 117, 121, 125, 142, 145-148, 155, 182-184, 186-189, 196
Westmount Stock Farms, 164
White, George, 105-106
Whiteford, William K., 191
Whittall, Norman R., 49-52, 56-59, 62, 68-69, 73-77, 80, 89, 93-94, 97-98, 103, 162-163, 179, 198, 213, 218, 264
Whittelsey, Charles S., 105-106, 115-116, 145, 177
Whiteworth University, 17
Wilkinson, Robert, 39, 42, 47, 49, 51
Williams Brothers, 209, 264
Williams, Dick, 177
Williamson, Allan, 114, 183, 186
Wilton, Glenn, 127
Winch, Harold, 224
Wisener and Partners, 280
Wismer, Gordon, 112, 116
Wood Gundy Limited, 114, 183, 210, 213
Wood, Jerry, 52-53, 56, 98
Wright, Clarence, 94, 96, 98, 106, 176-178, 240
Wrong, Hume, 153-154

X-L Refineries Limited, 215-216

Yellowhead Pass, 122, 130-132
Yorkshire & Canadian Trust Company, 33
Youell, Len, 106, 219, 273